CALLED TO THE CHILDBIRTH PROFESSION:

OPPORTUNITIES FOR DOULAS, BIRTH EDUCATORS AND YOU

CALLED TO THE CHILDBIRTH PROFESSION:

OPPORTUNITIES FOR DOULAS, BIRTH EDUCATORS AND YOU

Donyale Abe

Library of Congress Control Number: 2011944997
ISBN-10: 0615578128
ISBN-13: 978-0-615-57812-5

Dreams2Life Publishing
4200 E. Commerce Way Suite 2423
Sacramento, CA 95834
(916) 525-7596
childbirthprofessionals@gmail.com
http://thechildbirthprofession.com

Discount prices available for purchasing large quantities. Contact the publisher.

Printed in the United States of America

Cover and Book Design by Professional Publications

In memory of my grandmother, Clara

A strong, talented woman

And for my girls, becoming women

I love you, heart, soul, and strength

Mommy ♥

CALLED TO THE CHILDBIRTH PROFESSION

CONTENTS

QUICK REFERENCE CHART TO PROFESSIONAL ROLES

Use this chart as a guide to the professional roles outlined in this book. Check off your favorites.

FAV	PAGE	A-Z CHILDBIRTH PROFESSIONAL ROLES
❑	58	Aromatherapist
❑	63	Baby Fair Planner
❑	66	Baby Planner
❑	69	Baby Sign Language Instructor
❑	72	Baby Yoga Instructor
❑	75	Belly Casting Artist *
❑	80	Birth Activist
❑	86	Birth Artist
❑	90	Birth Center
❑	96	Birth Dance Instructor
❑	98	Birth Doula *
❑	108	Blessingway Facilitator
❑	111	Blogger *
❑	119	Board Member *

* This role includes the self-written story of a Childbirth Professional.

BEGINNING THOUGHTS

This is the book I wish was written when I was a young girl, and wish I had access to this information as I began my career as a Childbirth Educator. The opportunities available and the various ways I would grow as a Childbirth Professional were not known to me at that time. So it is with pleasure that I share the many career possibilities awaiting both brand new and experienced professionals.

According to the *U.S. Census Bureau, International Data Base*, around the world approximately 367,642 babies are born each day, about 255 babies per minute or 4.3 babies per second.

People are always having babies.

Therefore, you are very likely always going to be employed, or be able to start a business as a Childbirth Professional. We might be able to say, this is a recession-proof career.

A NOTE

Please know that the included resources and websites were handpicked because of the quality of information, inspiration, and wisdom they share.

Take the time to explore these resources, contact them, visit their websites and you will glean the knowledge you are searching for.

In many of the resources, you will discover successful career and business models to emulate.

This compilation is my wholehearted effort to encourage you along your Career Journey...

THE CHILDBIRTH PROFESSIONAL

Throughout this book, the career descriptor *Childbirth Professional* will be capitalized in most of its usage. The reason for capitalization is to stress the importance of the term, and also to place it into official use as a descriptor of the work done by many individuals. The professional roles described within this book will also be capitalized for emphasis.

Childbirth Professionals are defined as individuals that provide services and care to:

- Pregnant women and their families

- Families who are adopting children

- Families using fertility services

- Families that decide not to continue pregnancies

- Families who experience stillbirth, miscarriage, or unexpected loss

- Women who serve as surrogates and families that use surrogacy

Childbirth Professionals assist women through their reproductive lives, before puberty, during fertility and infertility, and beyond menopause. Childbirth Professionals don't usually provide medical care unless they are additionally trained as Midwives, nurses, or doctors.

Childbirth Professionals may take on many roles providing a range of services for families such as:

- Educators teaching childbirth and infant care classes

- Doulas providing physical and emotional support during labor and birth

- Baby Planners helping navigate the many decisions and tasks related to having a baby i.e. getting the nursery prepared

- Prenatal Yoga Instructors teaching breathing, stretching, and meditation techniques

The list above is just the beginning of the opportunities that exist in the profession of childbirth.

This book will explore and describe the wide-ranging field of Childbirth Professionals. It is an occupation that people seem to find in the middle of another career.

It is not a well-known field; however, it is a career that impassions those that find it. For many it is if they have received their **calling**. The reward and fulfillment received from empowering families during one of life's most transformative events, the birth of a child, is immeasurable.

My intention is to focus a spotlight upon the Childbirth Professional. I hope that children will dream of teaching childbirth classes and of assisting new mothers to breastfeed their babies. So many are unaware that the Childbirth Profession exists and they can choose it as a life long career.

Hence, the need for this book:

- To increase awareness about the opportunities that exist in this incredible field

- To explain the different aspects and roles that individuals can attain in the profession

- To assist others in considering and creating a career plan within the field

- To provide guidance and advice from a successful, experienced and seasoned professional

I didn't have much guidance when I started, and I believe my journey to become a Childbirth Professional would have come quicker and been easier with direction and inspiration.

If only someone could tell you what steps to take. If only they could see your potential, believe in your abilities, and boost your confidence.

In this life, you need someone to give you a map, point out the way, and encourage you along your journey.

Let this book be your map.

There is so much to discover in the Childbirth Profession.

I believe you will go far and accomplish much, because you are called and capable.

I share with you the wisdom I have gained so far...

A CAREER?

I didn't know this was a career – a Childbirth Educator.

I came upon this field quite by chance, although there is the theory that nothing is chance. Amazing things take place in one's life when preparation and opportunity meet.

What I know is that from your youth you are aware of your highest skill set...meaning the skills you love to use and are most proficient at. They can be called your talents. These are the skills you are passionate about and when you use these skills, you are happiest. You are yourself without any effort.

Observe a child or think back upon your own childhood and you will find that it is where our interests and passions are true and pure. Children know what they like and do not like undisputedly. However, so often they are corrected, guided or misguided to strive for *real* occupations to appropriately focus their interests. Yet isn't passion difficult to squelch? Within every adult is the child who is a painter, ballerina, singer, astronaut, superhero, president...

Since I was a small girl about six years old, I just loved babies. I remember just looking at them and asking the new mothers in church if I could hold their babies. Surprisingly they would let me.

Babies love me, most of them, and I am able to make them smile and calm them if they are upset. Most importantly, I can get them to sleep.

I can't get enough of their new smell and those small fingers and toes. I can hold a new baby all day long.

As a girl, if you had a small baby then I was your sitter.

I dreamed of one day having babies of my own, but never did I dream how this could connect to a career since I did not want to be a nanny.

As I grew older, I discovered that I had the ability to write and speak well. Also, I loved working with computers. I enjoyed using these skills so I thought I would become a computer programmer, until realizing how much math was required for a computer science degree. I was good in math, but it wasn't my passion.

I also thought about becoming a broadcast journalist since I was good at researching, fact-finding, writing and speaking; it would be a perfect fit for my skill set. As I entered college, I had my mind focused on becoming a broadcast journalist.

After graduating UC Berkeley, I got my break into that field working at channel 13, a TV station in Sacramento, as a production assistant. I learned right away, that it is a tough field. I've had many jobs, but none that stressful. It was not the actual work that stressed me, it was my coworkers.

For the first time I experienced a work environment where people yelled and humiliated each other. That was not for me, it involved too much drama and disrespect for earning minimum wage. And the hours 3 pm to 12 am, because of my low seniority, were terrible. I quit.

I learned a great lesson in quitting – something else will come your way.

Don't be afraid to walk away if it's not working for you. If you hold on too tight – not only are you miserable which affects everything in your life – your relationships and self esteem, but most importantly there is no space for new opportunities. You're blocking them.

The very next day after I quit the phone rang and I was offered a job at an insurance company doing research, writing, and providing customer service.

It was the recession, it was a job, not my dream, but I did get to use some of my higher skills.

After three years, I knew it was time to leave. I had been moonlighting starting my own business as a career consultant. I charged clients to write their resumes, prepare them for interviews, and give career advice.

I now wanted to grow my business, so I decided to find a part-time job in order to have an additional source of income.

I ended up getting a job in customer service at Kaiser Permanente an HMO. It was perfect. I was able to use the morning to work as a career consultant, and during the evenings, 3 pm to 7 pm I worked at Kaiser answering questions about health insurance. The only downside was I had to commute a 45-minute drive from Sacramento to Stockton.

It was during this time that I was able to witness my first birth.

One day at a church event, I met a new participant that was pregnant. We chatted and I learned that her husband lived out of the country and would not be present when she went into labor. Somehow, I ended up offering to support her through her pregnancy.

We went to childbirth classes, practiced breathing and prepared for the big day.

When the day arrived, this is the truth; I slept through her first phone call, but woke up upon the second and made it to the hospital in time to offer comfort. I saw how amazing the process is for a new baby to enter the world.

In that moment my life was transformed.

I loved helping her through childbirth. Unbeknownst to me, I had become a Doula.

After that birth, anyone in my church group that was having a baby requested my support. I also volunteered at my local Birthing Project, a nonprofit group in Sacramento that matched mentors with teen moms to prepare and support them through birth.

I loved everything that I was doing just being present at births, but I was clueless that this could be a job – a career. I did not know that people pay you for this support.

I continued to build my career consultant business, and started taking classes at the local university to obtain a certificate in career development. Still working for Kaiser, I looked for openings within the company to transfer to Sacramento and cut down my commute time.

After three years working in customer service, I transferred to Kaiser's South Sacramento Health Education department where I scheduled appointments for all the childbirth education classes.

In this position, I also made sure that all the Childbirth Educators had the supplies that were needed to teach and their classrooms were set up properly.

Six months later, my manager suggested that I would be a great Childbirth Educator. I had not considered the possibility before. However, once I gave it some thought I knew she was right. I was being called! It was like a bell sounded in my mind and spirit. How did I not know about this career choice before?

It fit me so well. I loved babies and the birth process. Talking and explaining things to others was something I really liked doing. This career would combine my passions and skills.

Yes. It would be perfect.

I was planning to start a family soon and knew I wanted to be home as much as possible with my future children. This would be a great fit since most of the hours would be on the weekends and in the evenings. I could take care of my kids in the day, rotating care with their father during evenings and weekends.

I told my manager that I would like to pursue getting trained as a Childbirth Educator. I quit taking the classes to obtain my career development certificate. Although I was close to completing it and I had been working on building my consulting business, but once I discovered the opportunity to become a Childbirth Educator, I just knew it was right.

The energy experienced helping people find a job is different from helping people bring a new life into the world.

Pregnant families are happy! The thought of working with happy people was an amazing thrill. Though now I have been a Childbirth Educator for years, it just never gets old. I feel like Oprah, because people are always happy to see me and they look forward to meeting me, and taking my classes.

Not many people get to say they help *happy* people for a living. Life ebbs and flows. I am privileged to help people during an opportune moment in their lives that transforms them in so many ways.

I completed my Childbirth Educator certification within nine months. That was in 1999, it has been my calling and profession ever since.

My higher skill set is continuously being used. When I began teaching, no one had heard of PowerPoint. I was the first at my hospital to use it as a teaching tool, before that we used posters, and transparencies. I also know how to design websites, and write and create website content. So my love for computers and that particular skill has been useful as a tool to teach in different ways and communicate with families. It is affirming to my soul to be using skills from my girlhood.

If only someone told me when I was a girl you are on the right track, my journey might have been quicker. Now that I have found my life's work, the feeling is indescribable. I feel complete. I know my purpose. I was created to help families through childbirth. All my higher skills are being used for my dream career. If I knew this was a career as a girl I would have chosen it.

Now I know with certainty to use my time on this planet focused on the things that I am *so* good at.

I just imagine the power of this knowledge for a very young girl. My wish is for each individual to have this knowledge, to be affirmed in their calling, and in their purpose, becoming all they're meant to be.

AFTERTHOUGHT

In writing this book, I have come to realize that I am making use of my career consultant skills. This book is just a part of my work to guide individuals into an amazing career.

Interesting how you make use of all your higher skills, without even trying.

THIS FIELD IS A GIFT

The work you do as a Childbirth Professional supporting women and families is indescribably fulfilling. Please keep this a secret, but I would do the work for free, because I love the connection that is created when you help people through such an amazing time in their lives – birth and creating families. I am glad that I get paid, but if by chance or circumstance I don't, the work itself is payment.

In fact, there have been times that I have forgotten that I work. Believe it or not, I often forget, because I enjoy every aspect of what I do so much. The word "work" just doesn't really fit. I consider this type of work a gift, because you change lives. You touch people in so many ways that you may never see or know. That's a beautiful gift.

For example, I very often have pregnant women attend my childbirth classes and bring their mothers. After class, the mothers, not the pregnant women, come up to chat with me, and what has surprised me, they have said how thankful they are to learn about their bodies and the birth process from my class. This has been repeated to me many times. It moves me that a grandmother-to-be, after having had her own children and living her life, now in her golden years makes an inner connection to her body and how it works. They have commented that they wish they had this knowledge when they gave birth to their children. They thank me saying they are glad their daughters will have the chance to have a different birth experience.

These grandmothers just look so joyful when they thank me. I wish I could bottle the powerful feeling they radiate.

The pure and raw emotion you witness is gift. I find people so honest and trusting when it concerns building their families. It renews you.

The fathers that I have taught and supported are especially endearing. The expecting moms are a complete range of all things, and will challenge your skills, and melt your heart.

I don't think I can really describe in words the impact and influence you have upon the lives of those you serve as a Childbirth Professional. Birth is a lasting memory. If you ask anyone about the birth of their child, they can describe all the details no matter how long ago. So you become a part of their personal history.

You receive so much from the work you do as a Childbirth Professional. When you assist a mother to nurse her child, help create a belly cast, give a massage, lead a yoga class, catch a baby, blog about the latest birth research – you serve a purpose. That's the gift.

CAN I MAKE A LIVING?

Yes, you can make a living as a Childbirth Professional. This is a real profession, a real career, and a real business opportunity.

Does it all sound too good to be true? That's because it is, too good! And it's all absolutely true.

A college degree is not required. Medical training is not required. Both may be helpful, but not necessary. However, I recommend that you pursue a college degree, if possible in Childbirth Health Care Studies.

I have been able to make a living as a Childbirth Professional and I know that you can do the same. There are no promises that you will get rich, but you should be able to pay your bills. You can work for a government office, a hospital, a birthing center, or for a school to name a few options.

You can also start your own business or work as an independent contractor providing services. Research your options.

You can do both be employed and have a business at the same time. That was my choice, I was employed as a Childbirth Educator first, and then I added teaching classes in my home.

MY ADVICE

If you want to have a long, successful, thriving career as a Childbirth Professional, be open to many possibilities. That may mean working for 2-3 hospitals at a time. It could also mean adding a related skill you had not considered, such as Website Manager to increase your income.

The success of your career is determined by you.

WHERE DO I START?

The journey to becoming a Childbirth Professional involves two basic tasks:

1. **D**ecide upon a professional role to focus.

2. **O**btain training for the role you selected.

These steps can be summarized as D-O. **DO** these steps to move your career ahead.

DECIDE UPON A ROLE

This book details 66 different Childbirth Professional roles. Read about them and learn as much as you can. Then create a list of the roles that interest you most. Take the time to research the related websites. Once you've done your research and understand what each role requires, narrow your list down to one role that you can pursue with the time you have in your life right now.

OBTAIN TRAINING

Discover what type of training or certification is required for the role you select. The required training and education varies. Find out if you have to attend classes, read books, take an exam, or serve as an apprentice. Certification means completing the requirements and training to achieve a proficient skill level, in order to be recognized as certified by an organization to practice your role.

Once you understand what is needed for your selected role, then start your training program, complete the requirements, and become certified. Certification is not always necessary. Some individuals have enough experience to practice without obtaining certification or training by an organization, and some roles in the Childbirth Profession are too new to have a developed training or certification program.

Will I be successful?

You have everything to gain by pursuing any of the Childbirth Professional roles. The knowledge and skills you will gain are priceless. What you will learn will build your career, your business, your future. No one can take away from you the things that you learn.

I often talk with people that are hesitant...they want to know will this be worth it. The question they want answered is...

Will I be successful?

My answer is you will get a return on your investment. The cost of being certified is nominal if you compare it to working for six months to one year in the role you have been trained.

In 1999 I spent about $1000 to become certified as a Childbirth Educator. Once certified my manager promoted me and I was able to earn back my $1000 and more since I am still currently working as a Childbirth Educator.

I went on to be trained as a Breastfeeding Educator and Prenatal Yoga Instructor and was able to take on more responsibilities, teach more classes, and increase my income.

I love the Childbirth Profession because it is full of many related options for individuals to pursue and grow in their careers. You might be a Doula for five years, and then move on to teaching as a Childbirth Educator in order to have a set schedule. Later, you might add the role of helping women as a Lactation Consultant.

This is a career where people easily remain for 25 years or more, because they can continue to grow and gain new skills.

I'VE BEEN IN THIS FIELD AWHILE, WHAT'S NEXT?

If you have been in this field awhile, congratulations! How has your journey been? What lessons have you learned?

Before you consider what is next take the time to think about what your career journey has been like so far.

Think about all the mothers, fathers, and children, whose lives you have touched. Do you have certain memories that have stayed in your mind?

Reflecting on your past career journey can give you clarity on where you should focus next.

I encourage you to pursue a new role in the Childbirth Profession. In seeking a new role, you can revive your skills, and learn additional ones. A different role can connect you to a new network of professionals, bringing you a wealth of opportunities.

The following are suggestions for an experienced Childbirth Professional to do next:

- Pursue a new role in the Childbirth Profession

- Mentor an individual just beginning in the field

- Start or expand your business in the field

- Serve on the board of a childbirth organization

- Train other professionals to do your job

- Write a blog or article about childbirth issues

- Attend a conference or workshop for Childbirth Professionals

In this field, professionals have the ability to make a difference, to inspire, to transform, and change the lives of others. As a Childbirth Professional, you always should be at your best, be vibrant and fresh, because you personally have the opportunity to influence those you serve.

BLUEPRINT FOR CHILDBIRTH HEALTH CARE STUDIES

Individuals that are in the Childbirth Profession typically pursue training and certification for multiple roles. It is common for those in the field to be certified in these roles simultaneously. For example, an individual may be actively practicing as a Childbirth Educator, Breastfeeding Instructor, Birth Doula, Postpartum Doula, and a Perinatal Fitness Instructor. Many individuals have between three to six different certifications completed, and they have college degrees.

What is fabulous about this field is the culture of always learning, and there is much to learn. Those with multiple certifications are able to build a diverse skill bank to practice from, ensuring a thriving career and weathering challenging economic times.

However, the need to obtain multiple certifications can be costly, time consuming, and sometimes inefficient, as many of the programs cover the same core knowledge often even using the same textbooks.

I believe that a formal program of study should be offered that would lead to a college degree in Childbirth Health Care Studies. The program can be offered as either an associate's, bachelor's, or master's level degree.

This program would allow individuals to enter the Childbirth Profession upon graduation having obtained both a college degree and the practical professional skills usually only received through the certification process.

The path to enter the Childbirth Profession now does not usually make use of the time individuals have spent pursuing college degrees. Some program models are evolving that allow an individual to earn a degree related to Lactation Consulting or Midwifery, however more opportunities to earn degrees in this field are essential.

I wish that I had the opportunity to earn a degree in Childbirth Health Care Studies when I was attending college. If I knew Childbirth Health Care Studies was available, then I would have pursued it, because it is my life's work now. I obtained my childbirth health care knowledge and skills years later, after receiving my BA.

Consider the possibilities of entering the profession straight from college. It would be revolutionary.

The idea of Childbirth Health Care Studies is to develop the next generation of Childbirth Professionals that are equipped to be leaders in Childbirth Health Care policy, research, and service. We need individuals that have the comprehension and ability to build organizations and businesses to care for women, children, and families across the globe.

CHILDBIRTH HEALTH CARE STUDIES

Mission Statement

Giving students a foundation in evidence-based research, history, and the politics of Childbirth Health Care so graduates are prepared to enter the field, provide service and pursue advanced studies.

Program Overview

The Childbirth Health Care Studies program prepares students to provide evidence-based, family-centered, childbirth services and care. The curriculum core is designed to develop critical awareness of historical, cultural, political, and socio-economic childbirth health care practices.

Students are able to:

- Obtain skills needed for their career as a Childbirth Professional in diverse roles and settings

- Experience service learning opportunities and internships

- Gain preparation needed for advanced learning in a certificate program, allied health program, and/or graduate school

Learning Goals

Childbirth Studies

- Understand the emotional, physical, and spiritual process of pregnancy, labor, birth, and postpartum within a historical, social, and political context

- Recognize and analyze the medical and cultural history of childbirth health care practices

- Examine the intrinsic significance and transformative experience of childbirth and the impact it has upon women, children, families and society

- Explore and define ethical obligations of childbirth health care professionals

- Understand evidence-based childbirth health care practice and the issues pertaining to implementing evidence-based care

- Learn how Childbirth Professionals provide care and services directly to the community through advocacy, policymaking, employment, and as independent practitioners

Interdisciplinary

- Integrate and apply other fields of study

- Understand the value of expanding, crossing and bridging disciplines

Critical Thinking Skills

Analysis

- Identify and evaluate arguments

- Summarize ideas

- Develop substantiated, defined, concise arguments

Logic

- Follow a logical argument and recognize flawed reasoning

Abstract thought

- Deconstruct broad concepts to the most relevant points

- Introduce general ideas for a purpose or to clarify and bring awareness to issues

Argumentation

- Present relevant evidence or proof to support claims raised or to support a stance using rhetorical approaches

Research Skills

Problem solving

- Identify historical and contemporary issues relating to childbirth health care practices

- Analyze historical and contemporary changes in childbirth health care practices

- Contemplate the future, direction and needs of childbirth health care and how to effectively contribute

Research

- Design a research agenda

- Develop research projects using primary and secondary sources

- Collect information using advanced database search abilities, bibliographic reference materials, archival documents, videos, images, and sound resources

- Utilize various modes of research such as empirical, theoretical, and literature

Communication Skills

Written

- Create written or electronic documents that are understandable, informative, and persuasive

Verbal

- Discuss views and thoughts in small and large groups

- Speak publicly and present information, research, and anecdotes

New Technology

- Learn about current communication technologies
- Create and deliver presentations using software programs like PowerPoint
- Use the internet, social media, and other new technologies to distribute information, research, and facts

Learning Experience/Internship

Childbirth Health Care Studies majors are required to complete learning experiences in two or more Childbirth Professional roles. The learning experience allows students to gain skills and insight into the Childbirth Health Care field.

CHILDBIRTH HEALTH CARE STUDIES (CHCS) COURSES

World History of Childbirth Health Care Practices

Economics and Business Practices of Childbirth Health Care

Reproductive Justice

Core Knowledge of Pregnancy, Birth, and Postpartum

Infant Care, Mothering and Cultural Practices

Lactation Principles

Mood Disorders in the Perinatal Period

Advocacy, Policy, and Research: The Dilemma of Evidence-based Care

Teaching Skills and Group Facilitation

Business Skills and Planning for Childbirth Professionals

The Significance of Pregnancy, Birth, and Parenting Stories

Health Promotion, Communication, and Education

Doula Fundamentals

Childbirth Health, Fitness, and Nutrition

Fertility and Reproductive Health

The Male Experience of Childbirth

Introduction to Midwifery

Childbirth Professional Elective Seminars

Learning Experience

Course Descriptions

World History of Childbirth Health Care Practices

Explore anthropological health care practices for giving birth throughout human history and across continents. Compare and contrast contemporary childbirth health care practices and advancements with centuries old practices and the resulting affects upon mothers, babies, and families.

Economics and Business Practices of Childbirth Health Care

Learn how the Childbirth Health Care business has evolved. Understand the economic dynamic of the Childbirth Health Care industry. Explore how care protocols are designed. Assess the financial gains and losses of specific health care practices.

Reproductive Justice

Study the core principles and the history of reproductive justice. Examine how socioeconomic and political issues affect the reproductive health of women. Understand the implications of race, religion, culture, ethnicity, nationality, and sexuality as they influence reproductive health. Explore ways to change society and institutions to bring about reproductive justice.

Core Knowledge of Pregnancy, Birth, and Postpartum

Understand the process of childbirth, from conception to postpartum. Learn about the physical and emotional changes that women experience. Become familiar with how the parent-child relationship begins in the womb. Explore pain management and relaxation techniques. Learn all the options and choices available to women and the decisions they must consider through pregnancy and birth.

Infant Care, Mothering, and Cultural Practices

Gain an understanding of infant care practices from birth through early childhood. Learn about the transformative process into motherhood. Explore and compare the differences cultures have in caring for infants. Discuss the fourth trimester and attachment parenting.

Lactation Principles

Learn about breast anatomy, the breastfeeding process, and how the body produces milk. Discuss the history of breastfeeding and various cultural views. Comprehend proper breastfeeding techniques and management. Know about the weaning process and the evolutionary history of weaning. Become knowledgeable about breastfeeding issues and challenges.

Mood Disorders in the Perinatal Period

Learn about perinatal mood disorders. Understand and differentiate between prenatal depression, postpartum depression, anxiety, panic, bipolar disorder, and psychosis. Comprehend prenatal and postpartum risk factors. Develop psychosocial skills, self-help support and treatment plans. Know the appropriate psychotherapy techniques. Discuss psychopharmacology as it relates to pregnancy and postpartum treatment.

Advocacy, Policy, and Research: The Dilemma of Evidence-based Care

Engage in developing methodology to implement evidence-based Childbirth Health Care practices. Understand the history and challenge of advocacy in the field of childbirth. Become knowledgeable about mother-friendly, baby-friendly, family-centered, evidence-based, and informed consent philosophies. Learn to conduct research that can effectively create and influence Childbirth Health Care policies.

Teaching Skills and Group Facilitation

Learn how to present information effectively to a group. Understand the process of group development. Become familiar with a diverse set of teaching strategies. Know how to engage and manage diverse and multiple size groups.

Business Skills and Planning for Childbirth Professionals

Obtain the knowledge to start a business, a practice or become a consultant as a Childbirth Professional. Learn to write a mission statement and business plan. Become familiar with legal guidelines and business structure. Develop a strategic marketing plan. Understand basic financial management.

The Significance of Pregnancy, Birth, and Parenting Stories

Understand the value of sharing birth stories. Explore the role stories play in shaping cultural mores and lore about the childbirth experience. Examine how stories can instill confidence or fear. Gather, research, and analyze a range of pregnancy and childbirth experiences.

Health Promotion, Communication, and Education

Learn strategies to effectively disseminate health information. Understand how to design and implement health curriculum that works across various demographic groups. Integrate social networking and new media tools into health promotion.

Doula Fundamentals

Study the historical and cultural role of Doulas during childbirth. Be knowledgeable about the work a Doula performs from conception through postpartum. Learn about various comfort and non-pharmacological techniques. Know how to start a Doula business. Understand how to develop and implement a community or hospital based doula program.

Childbirth Health, Fitness, and Nutrition

Understand how nutritional and lifestyle factors effect fertility, pregnancy, and postpartum outcomes. Learn about fitness activities that are safe and beneficial for childbearing women. Develop strategies to promote healthy lifestyle choices.

Fertility and Reproductive Health

Understand the reproductive process and how to preserve life-long reproductive health. Learn holistic and traditional methods to facilitate and manage fertility. Differentiate political and societal implications of reproductive health policies. Develop strategies to implement evidence-based reproductive health care management.

The Male Experience of Childbirth

Learn how men transform through the childbirth experience. Explore and compare gender role variations. Conduct needs assessment and develop strategies to create health programs that effectively support men through the childbirth experience into fatherhood.

Introduction to Midwifery

Explore the world history of midwifery care. Understand the diverse training and educational paths that lead to a professional career in midwifery. Learn basic midwifery concepts.

Childbirth Professional Elective Seminars

Learn practical skills from experienced Childbirth Professionals. Seminars cover various career and entrepreneurial roles in the field of Childbirth Health Care.

Students must complete a minimum of two elective seminars.
- Prenatal and Postpartum Yoga Training Workshop
- Infant Massage Workshop
- Birth Dance Instructor
- Midwifery Intensive Workshop
- Aromatherapy for Pregnancy and Labor
- Placenta Encapsulation Workshop
- Henna Design
- Belly Casting

Learning Experience/Internship

It is required that students complete a minimum of two learning experiences, in which they have the opportunity to integrate their knowledge with practical skill and gain an experiential understanding of the Childbirth Health Care field.

The learning experience should involve providing care to women during fertility, pregnancy, childbirth, or postpartum.

Learning Experience Examples

These are examples that would meet the criteria of a learning experience. Students may select any relevant experience.

- Birth Doula
- Blessingway Facilitator
- Breastfeeding Counselor
- Childbirth Educator
- Infant Massage Instructor
- Prenatal Yoga Instructor
- Postpartum Doula

CHILDBIRTH PROFESSIONALS TO KNOW

This chapter provides summaries of Childbirth Professionals to know and learn about. They have contributed to the profession in a variety of ways. In them, you will find lessons to guide you along your personal career journey. Use the summaries you will read as a starting point to seek out more information regarding these professionals. You can read their books, watch their movies, Google their websites, and find them on Facebook.

These individuals provide historical background and allow us to understand the childbirth movement and how we arrived at modern day birth practices.

I find these professionals to be ordinary individuals who have done extraordinary things in their work to support pregnant women and their families. Some of them unintentionally became Childbirth Professionals through random circumstances, and some knew from a young age they had been called to this field. In their lives, I believe you will find parallels to your own lives. In their work, I know you will find inspiration.

They made a difference.

You too are called to make a difference.

The Childbirth Profession is in need of a new generation of individuals whose work inspires and brings change.

Suzanne Arms	Sheila Kitzinger
Elizabeth Bing	Ricki Lake
Robert A. Bradley, MD	Dr. Fernand Lamaze

Sarah Buckley, MD	Dr. Frederick Leboyer
Peter Chamberlen	James McKenna
Maude Callen	Heidi Murkoff
Mary Francis Hill Coley	Dr. Michel Odent
Robbie Davis-Floyd	Ivan Petrovich Pavlov
Dr. Grantly Dick-Read	Tracey Wilson Peters
Ina May Gaskin	Celeste Phillips
Doris Haire	Dr. William Sears
Barbara Harper	Penny Simkin
Majorie Karmel	Miss Margaret Smith
Marshall Klaus, MD	

SUZANNE ARMS

She is the author of *Immaculate Deception* a book that sparked and helped fuel the birth movement of the 1970's.

Arms, a founding board member for the Coalition for Improving Maternity Services (CIMS), has worked at the grassroots level for decades to implement change in the care of women and babies during the birth experience. Suzanne Arms is a filmmaker who produced *Giving Birth* and *Five Women, Five Births*. These films provide information to help women understand their choices and make informed decisions. Arms believes in the birth process and the far-reaching power a holistic birth experience can provide to women. She helped found The Birth Place, one of the first independent birth centers in the United States. The Birth Place was also a pregnancy resource center where one of the first Doula training programs began. Suzanne Arms is also a well-known photographer. Her photos have been used in childbirth books.

ELISABETH BING

She is the mother of *Lamaze* classes, and a pioneer of the birth movement.

Elisabeth Bing is author of the book, *Six Practical Lessons for an Easier Birth*. Trained as a physical therapist, her career in birth began by helping women during postpartum move and exercise. This led to opportune events for Bing to learn about natural childbirth methods compared to the medical methods used at the time. It was in the early 1950's that she decided to focus on teaching childbirth education classes, and she built her career teaching *Prepared Childbirth* classes to families at Mt. Sinai hospital in New York, and also in her apartment. Elisabeth Bing developed classes that would prepare women for childbirth beginning with concepts from Dr. Grantly Dick-Read and later incorporating breathing techniques from Dr. Fernand Lamaze. Elisabeth Bing was a founder of the organization, Lamaze International, originally named ASPO, the American Society for Psychoprophylaxis in Obstetrics.

ROBERT A. BRADLEY MD

He created the *Bradley Method* of natural childbirth.

Dr. Robert A. Bradley wrote the book *Husband-Coached Childbirth* and was an early advocate for fathers to be present at the birth of their children. Dr. Bradley believed in the ability of women to give birth successfully without medication. He was raised on a farm and witnessed animals giving birth. He thought the same techniques used by animals could be applied to women giving birth. He developed a class to teach women instinctual techniques to use during labor, avoiding medications. His techniques are used successfully during labor and birth by women who take *Bradley* classes.

SARAH BUCKLEY, MD

She is a writer, doctor, and birth advocate providing empowering information for pregnant women to become completely knowledgeable about childbirth.

Dr. Sarah Buckley is an inspiring writer who presents the facts in a manner that compels her readers to dig deeper and understand more about the subjects she discusses. She wrote the book *Gentle Birth, Gentle Mothering*, and has written numerous articles and book contributions. She has had four homebirths and draws from her own personal experiences as well as her medical training and background to advise women and Childbirth Professionals.

PETER CHAMBERLEN

He invented the forceps in 1588, which revolutionized childbirth health care and midwifery practices.

Forceps were initially used to remove infants that had died during the birth process. Later, they advanced into a useful tool to assist difficult and complicated labors. At the time, in the 1600's, female Midwives in England were banned from using instruments during a birth. So there was a need for male doctors or barber surgeons as they were called, to attend difficult births and use their instruments. Before Peter Chamberlen, male doctors rarely had a role in childbirth health care. The invention of forceps gave men an authoritarian role in the previously female only world of childbirth as men came to *rescue* women from difficult births. The Chamberlen family kept the forceps design and technical use top secret for over 100 years.

MAUDE CALLEN

She was a Midwife and nurse featured in a twelve-page Life magazine photographic essay in 1951, by famed photojournalist W. Eugene Smith.

Maude Callen had a generous spirit and served the community of Pineville, South Carolina, with her heart and soul. She delivered babies, trained Midwives, and attended to the sick and elderly providing health care to a rural population in the segregated South that otherwise would have had none. She worked and provided care to her community for over 60 years.

MARY FRANCIS HILL COLEY

She was a Georgia Midwife featured in the 1952 documentary film, *All My Babies* by filmmaker George Stoney.

This documentary of Coley's work as a Midwife was originally created as an instructional training film for the Georgia Health Department. The film shows the harsh living conditions of the rural segregated South and how skilled Midwives made an incredible difference in the lives of the families they served. Mary Francis Hill Coley had no formal education. She received midwifery training by serving as an apprentice under Alabaman Midwife, Onnie Lee Logan. The film *All My Babies*, was selected by the Library of Congress in 2002, for placement on the National Film Registry for its' cultural, historic, and artistic value.

ROBBIE DAVIS-FLOYD

She is a medical anthropologist specializing in reproductive anthropology.

Robbie Davis-Floyd is author of the book *Birth as an American Rite of Passage*, first published in 1994. She is a professor, researcher, and writer whose work has been invaluable to the ongoing discourse of childbirth health care practices.

DR. GRANTLY DICK-READ

He is author of the book *Childbirth Without Fear*, first published in 1942. His book introduced the ideal that giving birth could be pain free.

Dr. Dick-Read taught key principles about natural childbirth and its valuable benefits for mothers and babies. A well-known concept that he taught which is still being taught today, is the Fear-Tension-Pain Syndrome. As an obstetrician, he introduced concepts that went against modern childbirth care practices, such as encouraging women to be educated about the process of childbirth, believing that an informed woman in labor would have less fear, which would decrease her labor pain. He also taught about the value of hypnosis as a coping technique for laboring women.

INA MAY GASKIN

She is an unorthodox leader among Midwives having learned her skills through practice, rather than beginning with formal midwifery training.

Ina May Gaskin wrote the book *Spiritual Midwifery*, which has become a classic in the childbirth community. She is the founder of the Farm Midwifery Center located in Summertown, Tennessee. Ina May Gaskin is also known for the obstetrical procedure the Gaskin Maneuver used to manage shoulder dystocia during labor by having the mother change into the hands and knees position.

DORIS HAIRE

She wrote *The Cultural Warping of Childbirth*, a booklet published in 1972 by the International Childbirth Education Association.

This booklet analyzed worldwide birthing practices compared with the medical interventions and unscientific practices used in the United States. *The Cultural Warping of Childbirth* struck a chord among women and doctors helping facilitate changes in childbirth care practices. Doris Haire has been both a passionate and committed advocate, giving testimony at congressional hearings regarding obstetrical procedures that are not evidence-based.

BARBARA HARPER

She is known around the globe for the promotion and education of waterbirth.

Barbara Harper is the founder of Waterbirth International, and the author of *Gentle Birth Choices*. Many women have experienced the joys of waterbirth due to her work. Birthing centers and hospitals use her research and training workshops to implement waterbirth options for women at their facilities.

MAJORIE KARMEL

She is one of the first women to take a Lamaze class.

Majorie Karmel was your average woman preparing for the birth of her child. She discovered that knowledge is power. After reading the book *Childbirth Without Fear*, by Grantly Dick-Read, she was moved to find the resources to have an unmedicated birth, which included the support of her husband. Her birth story is remarkable, for the early 1950's. Unlike women of her time who knew nothing about childbirth, and even feared childbirth, she wanted to participate and be aware through birth, not in a haze from the effects of medication. While living in Paris, France, Majorie Karmel chose Dr. Fernand Lamaze to be her obstetrician, having learned that he would support women desiring to give birth without medication. She went on to have a successful natural birth and wrote the book *Thank You, Dr. Lamaze*. Her book inspired American women and they sought to learn the Lamaze techniques. Elisabeth Bing having read Marjorie's book contacted her, they met and a partnership was formed. Together they became part of the founders of the Lamaze organization in 1960, originally named the American Society for Psychoprophylaxis in Obstetrics (APSO). This organization became part of the birth movement training Childbirth Educators and teaching Lamaze techniques. They taught natural childbirth classes that facilitated changes such as the presence of fathers at birth, breastfeeding, babies rooming-in, and unmedicated birth.

MARSHALL KLAUS, MD

He is a leader in neonatology and coauthor of the book *Your Amazing Newborn.*

His groundbreaking research paved the way for medical professionals to understand the necessity for parents to bond with their babies at birth. Dr. Klaus' studies about premature infants helped change hospital policies allowing parents to have 24-hour access to their babies who were in special care or neonatal intensive care nurseries. He is a founding member of the organization DONA, which provides training for Doulas, and he advocates women having continuous support during childbirth. He also co-wrote *The Doula Book.*

SHEILA KITZINGER

She is a social anthropologist specializing in all subjects related to childbirth.

Sheila Kitzinger is the author of over twenty books and is a fierce Birth Advocate. The books she writes are rich in historical and cultural detail. She provides counseling to mothers through the

Birth Crisis Network, a hotline in Britain. Sheila Kitzinger teaches Midwives and is an honorary professor at Thames Valley University.

RICKI LAKE

She is a talk show host turned Birth Activist, and produced the much talked about film *The Business of Being Born*.

Ricki Lake had a transformative and empowering birth experience of her second child, whom she delivered at home with the assistance of a Midwife. That experience impacted her so much that she decided to become a Birth Advocate working to help women become knowledgeable about their choices during pregnancy and birth, and to also have access to birthing options.

DR. FERNAND LAMAZE

He is credited with being the creator of the Lamaze Method, breathing techniques that decrease pain for women in labor.

Dr. Fernand Lamaze learned of the techniques while visiting the Soviet Union. He witnessed them being used by laboring women who delivered their babies without anesthesia, relaxed and pain free; he was converted. Dr. Lamaze brought the method, which had been created from the theories of Ivan Petrovich Pavlov and called psychoprophylaxis, back to France in 1951. He wrote about the techniques in his book *Painless Childbirth: The Lamaze Method*. Dr. Lamaze, also organized classes and trained his entire hospital to assist women in labor with the techniques.

DR. FREDERICK LEBOYER

He is the father of gentle birth, writing the book *Birth Without Violence*.

In his book, Dr. Frederick Leboyer makes the point that an infant has rights and needs that are often overlooked during birth. His suggestion that babies should remain with their mothers at birth was ludicrous for the times. He encouraged what was called the Leboyer Bath, in which the newborn is placed in a warm bath immediately following birth to help facilitate the infant's adjustment to life outside the womb.

JAMES McKENNA

He is a leading researcher and expert regarding mother and baby sleep patterns.

Professor James McKenna has conducted studies at the University of Notre Dame Mother-Baby Behavioral Sleep Lab. He has published his work, which he presents internationally addressing questions professionals and parents have about infant sleep safety and co-sleeping. He wrote the book *Sleeping With Your Baby*.

HEIDI MURKOFF

The name of her book *What to Expect When You're Expecting* precedes her name as an author.

Heidi Murkoff decided to write her book when she was expecting her first child and could not find a book that comforted her own fears. The book she wrote has become known as the "Pregnancy Bible," and is the top selling book purchased by moms-to-be in the United States and around the world. It has been published in 30 languages.

DR. MICHEL ODENT

He is a pioneer in the field of Primal Health Research.

Dr. Michel Odent wrote the book *Primal Health* and created the Primal Health Research database available on the internet at http://www.primalhealthresearch.com. The primal period is from conception through the first year of an individual's life and it has affects upon long-term health. His work explores the human capacity to love and how it is shaped during the primal period. He has written numerous articles, and has given talks addressing the importance of the cocktail of love hormones that are released during birth, and their affect upon mother and child. Dr. Odent is also well known for supporting waterbirth beginning in the 1970's at the Pithiviers Hospital in France.

IVAN PETROVICH PAVLOV

He is known for his experiments using dogs to create a conditioned reflex.

The theories of Ivan Petrovich Pavlov were adopted for use upon pregnant women to decrease labor pain. This method was used widely by obstetricians in the Soviet Union during the 1950's. Dr. Fernand Lamaze having traveled to the Soviet Union learned of Pavlov's methods, which combined teaching the mother what to expect during birth, and teaching her breathing and relaxation techniques. Dr. Lamaze brought the method back to France and as time passed, it became known as the Lamaze Method.

TRACEY WILSON PETERS

She is the founder and CEO of CAPPA, Childbirth and Postpartum Professionals Association.

Tracey Wilson Peters is a passionate and dedicated advocate for childbearing families. The CAPPA organization she leads began in the United States in 1998 and has spread internationally to provide training and education to Childbirth Professionals and families. Tracey Wilson Peters began CAPPA with a dream, which has become a core message of the organization to imagine a different world for birthing women. A world in which women receive all they need for birth. They are informed, equipped, confident, and trust the birth process.

CELESTE PHILLIPS

She is a pioneer, leader, and expert regarding family-centered maternity care.

Celeste Phillips is an inspiring speaker and author, writing the book *Family-Centered Maternity Care*. She has worked as consultant with numerous hospitals to help them implement family-centered maternity care units. The work led by Celeste Phillips to allow families to be present during a woman's labor and allow babies to room-in with mothers has revolutionized the birth experience for modern day families. As a result, mother-child bonding has improved and breastfeeding rates have increased.

DR. WILLIAM SEARS

He is a beloved pediatrician, parenting expert, and the author of over 30 parenting-related books.

Dr. William Sears is an advocate for attachment parenting and writes about the experience of attachment parenting with his wife Martha Sears in *The Baby Book*. He is well known for answering the many questions that parents have. He and his wife, who is a nurse, have raised eight children. Dr. Sears has taken on many controversial issues such as vaccinations, long-term breastfeeding, and cosleeping, providing parents with evidence-based information so they can make informed decisions.

PENNY SIMKIN

She is a pioneer and mother of the Doula movement founding the Doula certification organization, DONA.

Penny Simkin began teaching childbirth education and providing labor support in 1968. She has written many books, among them *Pregnancy, Childbirth, and the Newborn, The Labor Progress Handbook,* and *When Survivors Give Birth.* Penny Simkin is a busy speaker, traveling around the world teaching and training Childbirth Professionals. She is passionate about making sure women are not only supported during birth, but that they also receive care that leaves a positive memory of birth. She has taught Childbirth Professionals for many years through the Seattle Midwifery School, which is now The Simkin Center for Allied Birth Vocations at Bastyr University, from which she received an honorary Doctorate degree.

MISS MARGARET SMITH

She was an Alabama Midwife and her work is documented in the book *Listen to Me Good: The Life Story of an Alabama Midwife.* Miss Margaret Smith provided midwifery services in the Deep South during the time of segregation in the United States. Without her services many families would not have had access to health care. She traveled through fields and waded through water to deliver babies. Her life as a Midwife began at age 5, when she was left with a laboring family member while the expecting father went out to get the Midwife. Upon their return, they found she had caught the baby. Miss Margaret Smith's life has been documented in a film entitled, *Miss Margaret.* She was famous for her wisdom and giving the highest level of care to her families. She expertly delivered twins, breeched, and premature babies.

CONCEPTS TO KNOW

In this chapter, you will find six core concepts to become familiar with as a Childbirth Professional. The concepts are relatively new. Some of them have been introduced by a grassroots effort to improve birth outcomes such as mother-infant bonding and breastfeeding.

Explore the history and origin of these concepts. In them, you will discover Childbirth Professionals that had a vision, and they worked as a team to change the status quo.

These changes are evident today. One example, perhaps your father or your grandfather was not allowed to witness the birth of his child, but today all family members are allowed to be present to witness birth in hospitals. Childbirth Professionals working with families brought about this change. Imagine the possibilities.

CORE CONCEPTS

The Baby-Friendly Hospital Initiative (BFHI)

Evidence-based Maternity Care

Family-Centered Maternity Care

Informed Consent

Mother-Friendly Childbirth

Reproductive Justice

THE BABY-FRIENDLY HOSPITAL INITIATIVE (BFHI)

The Baby-Friendly Hospital Initiative began as a global program in 1991, it was a collaborative effort by the World Health Organization (WHO) and the United Nations Children's Fund (UNICEF) to increase breastfeeding rates and recognize hospitals and birthing centers that have care practices leading to successful breastfeeding.

The Baby-Friendly Hospital Initiative lists the following Ten Steps to Successful Breastfeeding in the United States:

1. Have a written breastfeeding policy that is routinely communicated to all health care staff.

2. Train all health care staff in skills necessary to implement this policy.

3. Inform all pregnant women about the benefits and management of breastfeeding.

4. Help mothers initiate breastfeeding within one hour of birth.

5. Show mothers how to breastfeed and maintain lactation, even if they are separated from their infants.

6. Give newborn infants no food or drink other than breastmilk, unless *medically* indicated.

7. Practice "rooming in"-- allow mothers and infants to remain together 24 hours a day.

8. Encourage breastfeeding on demand.

9. Give no pacifiers or artificial nipples to breastfeeding infants.

10. Foster the establishment of breastfeeding support groups and refer mothers to them on discharge from the hospital or clinic.

RESOURCES

An online course, the Ten Steps to Successful Breastfeeding is offered by Jones & Bartlett Learning at http://tensteps.jbpub.com

A booklet by the World Health Organization, *Evidence for the ten steps to successful breastfeeding* is downloadable at the following link: http://tiny.cc/tensteps

EVIDENCE-BASED MATERNITY CARE

Evidence-based maternity care applies proven and current research to maternity care practice.

Evidence-based care is recommended as the standard for treatment and the use of procedures in maternity health care.

RESOURCES

A report titled, *Evidence-Based Maternity Care: What It Is and What It Can Achieve*, by Carol Sakala and Maureen Corry can be found at:

http://tiny.cc/evidencematernity

FAMILY-CENTERED MATERNITY CARE

Family-Centered Maternity Care is a philosophy that considers the physical, social, psychological, spiritual and economic needs of a family throughout the birth experience. Families are self-defined and their diversity respected. Families are an integral part in the decision making of health care treatment and procedures. Incorporating the family unit into the process of maternity care with minimal separation is a vital component of this philosophy.

INFORMED CONSENT

Informed consent means that a patient understands the treatment being offered by their health care provider, and knows the benefits as well as the risks, and is able to refuse or accept the suggested treatment.

RESOURCES

Childbirth Connection has detailed information at this link:

http://tiny.cc/informedconsent

MOTHER-FRIENDLY CHILDBIRTH

Mother-Friendly Childbirth is a term coined by the Coalition for Improving Maternity Services (CIMS), a nonprofit group founded in 1997 and made up of individuals and organizations that promote the well-being of mothers, babies, and families. CIMS worked with a collaborative group of professional organizations to write the Mother Friendly Childbirth Initiative (MFCI), which is the first consensus document to recommend evidence-based maternity care practices in the United States.

The Ten Steps of Mother Friendly Care are:

1. Offer all birthing mothers unrestricted access to birth companions, labor support, and professional midwifery care.

2. Provide accurate, descriptive, statistical information about birth care practices.

3. Provide culturally competent care.

4. Provide the birthing woman with freedom of movement to walk, move, and assume positions of her choice.

5. Have clearly defined policies and procedures for collaboration, consultation, and links to community resources.

6. Do not routinely employ practices and procedures unsupported by scientific evidence.

7. Educate staff in nondrug methods of pain relief and do not promote use of analgesic or anesthetic drugs.

8. Encourage all mothers and families to touch, hold, breastfeed, and care for their babies.

9. Discourage nonreligious circumcision of the newborn.

10. Strive to achieve the WHO/UNICEF Ten Steps of the Baby-Friendly Hospital Initiative to promote successful breastfeeding.

Appendix: Birth can safely take place at home and in birthing centers.

A downloadable copy can be found at the following link: http://tiny.cc/motherfriendly

REPRODUCTIVE JUSTICE

Reproductive Justice addresses the social, economic, and political issues that are related to reproductive health. Reproductive Justice calls for equality while acknowledging that inequality prevents access to reproductive health care. Reproductive Justice emphasizes that women have the right grounded in basic human rights to decide to have children, or not to have children, and to parent their children in a safe and healthy environment.

SELECTING A TRAINING ORGANIZATION

There are multiple training organizations for many of the Childbirth Professional roles listed in this book. How do you select the right organization? You want to invest your time, money, and energy into a program that will be beneficial. Think about the following factors as you decide.

Consider the organization's reputation.

You should be able to easily find positive information about the organization.

Who knows about the organization?

Ask people in the childbirth field if they have heard of the organization and find out their opinions.

What are your professional objectives? Will you be employed or work for yourself?

Not all organizations are acceptable to employers that might hire you. Check with your potential employer to find out if they would accept your certification from this organization. If you intend to be self-employed then this might not be an issue for you.

Is this a global organization?

You may not always live in the same place. You want to have training and certification that will be accepted wherever you live, even if it is in a different country.

Is the curriculum comprehensive?

Find out what the program teaches. You want to receive proper training, increasing your knowledge and gaining new skills.

What is the process of training and certification?

Find out the steps you must take to complete your certification or training. Is the process confusing or easy to understand? How long will the process take? Consider if this is something, which you can realistically finish or will the process be tedious. You don't want to start the program, get discouraged, and quit. What type of support is offered to help you see your training through to completion?

Is the training and certification process credible?

Investigate how certification is awarded. Is a test offered? You want to make sure that the certification is challenging and upholding a high level of knowledge and skill. The certification should have some prestige and value, not be a piece of paper that can be paid for.

Does the organization have a professional journal or published books available to members?

Well-established organizations have materials available to help their members grow and learn. Find out if the organization has published articles or books, and if they have a journal, newsletter, or magazine available to their members or to the public.

What is the philosophy?

Find out the beliefs and philosophy of the organization. Make sure that you agree with the organization.

Talk to the staff.

Call the office of the organization. Talk to the staff and ask them any questions you may have. A conversation will give you an idea if you should align with this organization or not.

Email the organization.

Send the organization an email to ask any questions you may have. This will give you an idea if they are responsive and helpful.

Will this organization benefit you?

Consider what benefits you will receive by training with this organization, or becoming a member. Will it help your career? Will you be able to build up your professional network? Will you be properly trained and be able to get a job or start a business? Will you gain access to beneficial resources?

A TO Z CHILDBIRTH

PROFESSIONAL ROLES

This chapter introduces 66 roles practiced by Childbirth Professionals. In my research for this chapter, I learned that the Childbirth Profession is vast and diverse. If you have an interest in the subject of childbirth then a related role exists to match your skills and abilities.

Each role contains the following information:

- A brief explanation of the role

- Search words to seek out more information

- Ideas on how to get started in that role

- Resources to start your journey such as books, organizations, schools, and business examples

The resources that are included will depend upon the type of role and also, the length of years that a role has existed, as some newer roles have less information available.

This chapter is meant as a guide to start you off. I encourage you to do your own additional research and exploration in the field of childbirth.

When I began writing, I did not expect to find as many different roles as I discovered within this field. I found quite a few I never knew about. I am excited to share them with you, because in learning about these roles, I am certain you will hear your calling.

AROMATHERAPIST

Aromatherapists provide blends of essential oils to help comfort women and assist them in coping with the challenges of pregnancy, labor, birth, and postpartum. The science and art of aromatherapy uses the aromatic essence of natural plants to promote physical, mental, and spiritual health producing balanced energy and a healthy state of well-being. Aromatherapists provide holistic care for women through childbirth and they are trained to know which essential oils are safe.

Search words: aromatherapy school, aromatherapy childbirth, aromatherapy pregnancy, aromatherapy association, aromatherapy childbirth training, aromatherapy workshop

GETTING STARTED

Read books about the practice of aromatherapy, and its specific use for the childbirth experience. Enroll in a school or take an online certification program for training as an Aromatherapist, with classes that focus on the use of aromatherapy for pregnant women. Join an association for Aromatherapists. Ask a practicing Aromatherapist that cares for pregnant women to serve as your mentor.

BOOKS

Clinical Aromatherapy for Pregnancy and Childbirth, by Denise Tiran

ORGANIZATIONS

International Federation of Professional Aromatherapists

The International Federation of Professional Aromatherapists (IFPA) is a professional aromatherapy practitioner organization. The IFPA believes in the principles and philosophies of holistic health care and the promotion of well-being for the individual.

International Federation of Professional Aromatherapists
82 Ashby Road
Hinckley
Leicestershire
LE10 1SN
United Kingdom
http://ifparoma.org
email: admin@ifparoma.org
phone: 01455 637987

Aromatherapy Registration Council

The Aromatherapy Registration Council (ARC) endorses the concept of voluntary, periodic registration by examination for all individuals practicing aromatherapy. Registration focuses specifically on the individual and provides formal recognition of a basic level of knowledge in the field of aromatherapy.

Aromatherapy Registration Council
http://aromatherapycouncil.org
email: contact@aromatherapycouncil.org

National Association for Holistic Aromatherapy

The National Association for Holistic Aromatherapy is an educational organization dedicated to enhancing public awareness of the benefits of true aromatherapy.

National Association for Holistic Aromatherapy
PO BOX 1868
Banner Elk, NC 28604 USA
http://www.naha.org
email: info@naha.org
phone: 828-898-6161

Alliance of International Aromatherapists

The Alliance of International Aromatherapists (AIA) is an independent, international member-based organization providing education, using scientific research and traditional information to promote the responsible use of aromatherapy.
Alliance of International Aromatherapists
Suite 323
9956 W. Remington Place - Unit A10
Littleton, CO 80128 USA
http://www.alliance-aromatherapists.org
email: info@alliance-aromatherapists.org
phone: 303-531-6377

EDUCATION PROGRAMS

American College of Healthcare Sciences

The American College of Healthcare Sciences (ACHS) provides holistic health education worldwide through accredited online programs.

American College of Healthcare Sciences
5940 SW Hood Avenue
Portland, OR 97239 USA
https://www.achs.edu
phone: 800-487-8839

Institute of Traditional Herbal Medicine and Aromatherapy

The Institute of Traditional Herbal Medicine and Aromatherapy (ITHMA) offers an Aromatherapy and Massage in Pregnancy course designed for Aromatherapists who seek to enhance their practical skills and knowledge in the therapeutic care of pregnant clients.

Institute of Traditional Herbal Medicine and Aromatherapy
11 Denman Road
London SE15 5NS
United Kingdom
http://www.aromatherapy-studies.com/pregnancy.html
email: info@aromatherapy-studies.com

Birth Arts International

Birth Arts International offers the Aromatherapy for Doula Practice Course – This advanced learning module, covers extensive aromatherapy practice and care for pregnancy, labor and postpartum care.

Birth Arts International
501 Lindsey St
Reidsville, NC 27320 USA
http://birtharts.com/aroma.htm
email: demetria@birtharts.com
phone: 866-303-4372

Life Cycles Center

Life Cycles Center offers a workshop that introduces the use of essential oils during pregnancy and birth.

Life Cycles Center
289 Summer Street
Buffalo, NY 14222 USA
http://www.lifecyclescenter.org
email: info@LifeCyclesCenter.org
phone: 716-464-5040

From the Seed

From the Seed offers a two-day interactive course to develop your skills and knowledge of aromatherapy for pregnancy.

From the Seed
http://www.fromtheseed.co.uk/cpd-training
email: jo@fromtheseed.co.uk
phone: 07970 773030

BABY FAIR PLANNER

A Baby Fair is an event held on one day inviting women who are pregnant and their families to learn about resources, products, and services in the community that would benefit them during and after pregnancy. The event usually hosts various prenatal health and parenting classes.

The Baby Fair Planner manages the event, arranging meeting space, advertising and inviting speakers. They recruit sponsors, exhibitors, and vendors. If the Baby Fair is connected to an organization then the planner will often have access to a group of volunteers to help manage the event.

Search words: baby fair, birth fair, babies fair, event planner certificate, meeting planner certificate

GETTING STARTED

There are no specific Baby Fair Planner associations or organizations, however individuals can pursue a certificate as a Meeting Planner or Event Planner.

EXAMPLE SCHOOL PROGRAMS

George Washington University

Event Management Certificate

George Washington University offers event management classes to meet the training needs of the emerging field of meeting and event planning professionals.

http://www.gwu-aqe.org

San Francisco State University

Event and Meeting Planning Certificate

The SF State Extended Learning Event and Meeting Planning Certificate has been developed to acquaint students with the common components of managing and planning well-executed meetings and events; including selection of appropriate sites, pre-event publicity and marketing, audio-visual aids, budgeting, negotiation, and contracts.

http://www.cel.sfsu.edu/eventplanning

EXAMPLE BABY FAIRS

San Francisco Birth and Baby Fair

The Birth and Baby Fair showcases local businesses, resources, and independent designers with the aim to educate and expose new and expecting parents to unique products and services.

http://www.birthandbabyfair.com

Your Natural Baby Fair

Your Natural Baby Fair partners with local businesses to reinvent the traditional baby fair by focusing awareness on natural and holistic support.

http://www.yournaturalbabyfair.com

It's a Baby & Family Expo

It's a Baby & Family Expo brings together the newest products and services to raise a happy, healthy baby in a safe, clean world.

http://www.itsababyexpo.com

The Baby and Toddler Show

The Baby and Toddler Show features products, advice, entertainment and information about pregnancy, infants and toddlers.

http://www.babyandtoddlershow.com.au

The BabyTime Show

The BabyTime Show provides a comfortable and inspiring environment for expecting parents, grandparents and caregivers to discover products and information related to babies and young children.

http://www.babytimeshows.ca

BABY PLANNER

Baby Planners help expecting or adopting families complete the necessary tasks to prepare for their babies. They are a resource and guide helping to alleviate the worry and stress of organizing for a new baby. They have a list of trusted contacts and can recommend a Doula, Nanny, Midwife or hospital.

New parents feel more confident when they have an experienced planner helping them understand which baby products are essential and which are not. Baby Planners can help with creating the nursery and arranging the baby shower. They offer expertise and professional support.

Search words: baby planner, baby planner training, baby planner workshop, baby planner certificate, baby planner business

GETTING STARTED

There are international organizations that offer training, certification, and support for Baby Planners. To begin you can enroll in a training course, or simply read a book and go for it. Try contacting experienced Baby Planners by phone or email to ask questions. Set up informational interviews with them to learn more about the services they provide. Use the internet to research and discover what established Baby Planners are doing. Implement some of their business practices.

BOOKS

The Baby Planner Profession: What You Need to Know by Mary Oscategui

The Baby Planner's Business Plan by April Beach and Elizabeth McFadden

Your Future as a Baby Planner (e-book)
http://www.babyplannerbook.com

ORGANIZATIONS

International Maternity Institute

The International Maternity Institute provides training programs, products and services for Childbirth Professionals.

International Maternity Institute
http://www.babyplannerinstitute.com
email: certification@iabpp.com

International Baby Planner Association

The International Baby Planner Association (IBPA) supports consultants in the baby planning industry.

International Baby Planner Association
http://internationalbabyplanners.com
email: becomeababyplanner@gmail.com

EXAMPLES OF BABY PLANNERS

The Baby Planners, LLC

The Baby Planners is a baby and maternity concierge and consulting service.

The Baby Planners, LLC
3940 Laurel Canyon Boulevard #308
Studio City, CA 91604 USA
http://www.thebabyplanners.com
email: ellieandmelissa@thebabyplanners.com

It's a Belly

It's a Belly Baby Planners guide parents through the process of preparing for their babies.

It's a Belly
http://www.itsabelly.com
email: info@itsabelly.com

Baby Sign Language Instructor

Baby Sign Language Instructors teach classes to parents and family members to encourage preverbal communication with babies and very young children. A background in sign language is helpful but not required.

Search words: baby sign language, baby signs teacher, baby sign language instructor, baby sign classes, baby sign language franchise, baby preverbal communication

Getting Started

To teach Baby Sign Language, partner with an established instructor and learn about their practice. You can also purchase a popular Baby Sign Language franchise, and receive training, marketing and support to launch your business. Another option is to take an online training class or learn from a Baby Sign Language DVD program. Also, take sign language classes in your community.

Organizations

Baby Signs

Baby Signs is a program that encourages infant-parent communication through natural baby sign language using simple signs.

Baby Signs
859 Cotting Court, Suite C
Vacaville, CA 95688 USA
https://www.babysigns.com
email: talk@babysigns.com
phone: 707-469-7406

Tiny Talk

Tiny Talk provides baby sign language classes for mums and dads in the United Kingdom, Ireland, New Zealand, and Australia. They train teachers and offer franchise opportunities.

TinyTalk
Unit 3 The Dairy
Tilehouse Farm Offices
East Shalford Lane
Guildford GU4 8AE
United Kingdom
http://www.tinytalk.co.uk
email: sandrine-admin@tinytalk.co.uk
phone: 01483 301 444

Sign2Me

Sign2Me provides a training program to certify instructors to teach baby sign language classes using ASL (American Sign Language).

Sign2Me
12125 Harbour Reach Drive
Suite D
Mukilteo, WA 98275 USA
http://sign2me.com
phone: 877-744-6263

Kindersigns

Kindersigns teaches baby sign language so parents can communicate effectively with their babies, and they offer a variety of business opportunities for those interested in becoming teachers.

Kindersigns
http://www.kindersigns.com
phone: 877-249-9666

Example Baby Sign Businesses

Hop to Signaroo

Hop to Signaroo offers baby signing classes for hearing families in Seattle.

Hop to Signaroo
P.O. Box 30604
Seattle, WA 98113 USA
http://www.hoptosignaroo.com
email: nancy@hoptosignaroo.com
phone: 206-789-7446

Visually Speaking

Visually Speaking instructors teach Sign Language to children and their families. All Visually Speaking instructors are fluent in ASL (American Sign Language), with a minimum of two-years ASL education and extensive knowledge in Deaf Culture.

Visually Speaking
http://visuallyspeaking.info
email: info@visuallyspeaking.info
phone: 206-282-7571

BABY YOGA INSTRUCTOR

Baby Yoga Instructors teach yoga classes that include parents and their new babies. The classes help nurture the parenting bond. They also provide a safe and supportive community for new parents. Teachers have a background in yoga and they are professionally trained.

Search words: baby yoga instructor, baby yoga class, baby yoga training, baby yoga certificate, baby yoga workshop

GETTING STARTED

To become a Baby Yoga Instructor you should be experienced in the basics of yoga and it is recommended that you attend a Baby Yoga teacher training. You should find someone in your community already teaching baby yoga classes and observe them teaching. Ask the instructor if they would be willing to serve as your mentor.

BOOKS

Yoga Mom, Buddha Baby by Jyothi Larson

Baby Om: Yoga for Mothers and Babies by Laura Staton and Sarah Perron

Itsy Bitsy Yoga by Helen Garabedian

ORGANIZATIONS

Baby Om

Baby Om offers a teacher training for yoga teachers and health care professionals with an active yoga practice. Learn how to teach mother and baby yoga classes in your community.

Baby Om
250 Riverside Drive #25
New York, NY 10025 USA
http://www.babyom.com
email: info@babyom.com

Itsy Bitsy Yoga International

Itsy Bitsy Yoga is a development-based yoga program for babies, toddlers, and preschool-aged children. This unique program includes over 150 yoga poses, songs, and developmental activities created by Helen Garabedian.

Itsy Bitsy Yoga International
P.O. Box 282
Sudbury, MA 01776 USA
http://www.itsybitsyyoga.com
email: office@itsybitsyyoga.com
phone: 978-310-7000

Birthlight

Birthlight is a friendly charity, focusing on a holistic approach to pregnancy, birth and babyhood through yoga and breathing methods.

Birthlight
PO Box 148
Cambridge
CB4 2GB
United Kingdom
http://birthlight.com
phone: 01223 362288

Jyothi Larson

Jyothi Larson is the author of *Yoga Mom, Buddha Baby*, and she offers teacher training workshops.

Jyothi Larson
http://www.easefulbodyyoga.com
email: info@easefulbodyyoga.com

BELLY CASTING ARTIST

Belly Casting Artists assist women in decorating their pregnant bellies to celebrate and honor their birth experience and transition into motherhood. A belly cast is created by placing strips of plaster upon the pregnant body to create a three-dimensional art sculpture of pregnancy. Many families hang them upon their walls as keepsakes of each child born.

Search words: belly casting, belly cast, belly casting artist, belly casting service, belly casting party, belly casting kit

GETTING STARTED

Find a Belly Casting Artist in your community to observe and ask questions about the process. Purchase supplies or kits for casting and begin practicing on pregnant women.

୨୦ଓଃ

Career Journey ...

Belly Casting Artist, Roxane O'Brien

How did you get started as a Belly Casting Artist?

During my eighth month of pregnancy, I had my partner help me make a casting of my "Baby Belly". I wanted to capture the amazing transformation of my body during a momentous time in my life.

As an Artist and Mother-to-be, I began wondering how I could stay home with my first-born and still continue to work?

When friends and family came to visit and viewed my Baby Belly Casting hanging on our wall, they asked me who did it? I told them we had. This is when through word of mouth; people started asking me to do castings for them as well.

The finished product was rewarding to see and I realized the gift I'd given my child and myself and felt the same might be true for other women too. It could be something other women have always wanted to do for themselves, just like I did.

How amazing it is to look at oneself AFTER the baby is born.

Baby Belly Casting was born!

Why do you do this work? What do you enjoy?

I do this work because as an Artist, my work is my life. Everything I experience is expressed through the creations I make.

I enjoy most of all, seeing the expression on a Mothers face (and Dad's too) when we peel the casting off her body and she truly gets to see herself.

It's like seeing yourself for the first time "through the forest of your own trees."

How do you like running a business? What business advice can you share?

I love running my own business! It has allowed me to stay home with my children (2 & 6 years old) and still be the creative person I am. I can make my own schedule and share something I feel is important for women to do 'for themselves' at a time when the focus is so much on the 'baby'.

Business Advice? Do something you love. Make a good business plan. Keep your overhead low so your pricing doesn't have to be high. Don't over-extend yourself physically, financially and emotionally (especially if you are doing it all by staying at home with children).

What type of training or education did you receive?

I am professionally trained from the Ontario College of Art. I have always been an Artist (even as a child) and always knew I would live my life expressing myself this way.

I have also been a practicing professional Artist for the last 19 years in film, TV, commercial, theatre, retail visual display and art education for children, adults and seniors.

Do you have any "aha" moments or insights to share about your work?

After beginning doing Baby Belly Castings for others, I realized I had the opportunity to bring women "out of the attics" and "out from under flowery muumuus!" That we needed to love and embrace our beautiful pregnant bodies and give ourselves the freedom to enjoy the miracle of life we were creating. Making a baby is more than making a baby. It is a freedom from pre-conceived ideas of body image and a time to truly enjoy being exactly who we are and being present in the moment.

What advice can you give to anyone that wishes to become a Belly Casting Artist?

Seek out mentorship from practicing body casting artists or take formal classes. Casting and mold making are fine arts. Ask yourself if you are a 'people person'. This business is very intimate, and is an experience that is forever treasured by those you work with. It is not your generic 'retail business'. It is a relationship.

∞⃝

EXAMPLE BELLY CASTING ARTISTS

Mama's Belly

Mama's Belly creates bronze heirloom bowls from the cast of a pregnant woman's belly that are musical and ring with a beautiful tone.

Mama's Belly
4985 S. Galapago Street
Englewood, CO 80110 USA
http://www.mamasbelly.com
email: info@mamasbelly.com
phone: 303-765-2320

Belly Art

Belly Art is an Australian owned company creating innovative keepsake products that uniquely capture treasured moments in time.

Belly Art
700 Inkerman Road
North Caulfield
Melbourne
Vic 3161 Australia
http://www.bellyart.com.au
email: info@bellyart.com.au
phone: 03 9509 4060

Ottawa Belly Casts

Ottawa Belly Casts offers a unique way to preserve the amazing changes pregnant bodies achieve in growing babies.

Ottawa Belly Casts
http://www.ottawabellycasts.com
email: julie@mncs.ca
phone: 613-646-9912

Baby Belly Casting

Baby Belly Casting focuses on helping families create a visually memorable experience from a special time in their lives.

Baby Belly Casting
http://www.roxie.ca
email: rox@roxie.ca
phone: 416-535-9243

Proud Body

Proud Body sells art products and belly casting materials that are easy-to-use to capture and remember pregnancy.

http://www.proudbody.com

BIRTH ACTIVIST (ALSO SEE NON PROFIT FOUNDER)

No training or certification is required to be a Birth Activist. Many Childbirth Professionals can consider themselves activists just by simply being educated and informed about evidence-based maternity care practices. Birth Activists share and promote evidence-based information within their communities, to pregnant families, to health care workers, and to government entities.

Search words: birth activist, birth activism, childbirth activist, childbirth grassroots, childbirth advocacy, childbirth advocate, homebirth

GETTING STARTED

To become a Birth Activist you can join an organization that supports evidence-based maternity care. Some Birth Activists write, podcast, blog, or tweet about the current research, discussions, and opinions surrounding childbirth. You can lobby your political representatives or insurance companies. Speak with your local hospital or health care workers about changing maternity care practices that are not evidence-based. Sharing birth stories, donating money, volunteering time, and speaking out against the status quo are all ways to be a Birth Activist.

ORGANIZATIONS

BOLD

BOLD is a global movement to make maternity care mother-friendly.

BOLD
PO Box 42292
Washington, DC 20015 USA
http://boldaction.org

BirthNetwork National

BirthNetwork National promotes the awareness and availability of mother-friendly maternity care, and is leading a grassroots movement based on the belief that birth can profoundly affect physical, mental and spiritual well-being.

BirthNetwork National
P.O. Box 2370
Birmingham, MI 48012 USA
http://www.birthnetwork.org/birthactivist_info.htm
email: info@birthnetwork.org
phone: 888-452-4784

International Cesarean Awareness Network

International Cesarean Awareness Network (ICAN) works to improve maternal-child health and prevent unnecessary cesareans through education, providing support for cesarean recovery, and promoting Vaginal Birth After Cesarean (VBAC).

International Cesarean Awareness Network
Post Office Box 98
Savage, MN 55378 USA
http://www.ican-online.org
email: email@ican-online.org

The Birth Survey

The Birth Survey is an effort to bring transparency to maternity care. It is an ongoing online consumer survey, which asks women to provide feedback about their birth experience.

The Birth Survey
http://thebirthsurvey.org
email: info@thebirthsurvey.com

Homebirth Australia

Homebirth is a group of consumers and Midwives committed to ensuring the survival of homebirth as a birth option for Australian women, with the overall aim of public funded homebirth across the country.

Homebirth Australia
ABN 57 416 702 216
PO BOX 103
Macquarie Fields NSW 2564
Australia
http://www.homebirthaustralia.org
phone: 0414 812 144

Childbirth Connection

Childbirth Connection promotes safe, effective and satisfying evidence-based maternity care and is a voice for the needs and interests of childbearing families.

Childbirth Connection
260 Madison, 8th Floor
New York, NY 10016
http://childbirthconnection.org
phone: 212-777-5000

Choices in Childbirth

Choices in Childbirth helps women make informed decisions about where, how and with whom to birth. They work to ensure that women have access to the full range of birth options. They strive to ensure that the birth of each child is treated with the reverence that it deserves.

Choices in Childbirth
441 Lexington Ave, 19th Floor
New York, NY 10017 USA
http://www.choicesinchildbirth.org
email: info@choicesinchildbirth.org
phone: 212-983-4122

Our Bodies, Ourselves

Our Bodies, Ourselves is an organization that works to provide information about health, sexuality and reproduction from a feminist and consumer perspective.

Our Bodies, Ourselves
http://www.ourbodiesourselves.org
email: office@bwhbc.org

Citizens for Midwifery

Citizens for Midwifery strives to see that the Midwives Model of Care is available to all childbearing women and universally recognized as the best kind of care for pregnancy and birth.

Citizens for Midwifery
P.O. Box 82227
Athens, GA 30608 USA
http://cfmidwifery.org/Advocacy
email: info@cfmidwifery.org
phone: 888-236-4880

Coalition for Improving Maternity Services

The Coalition for Improving Maternity Services (CIMS) is a coalition of individuals and national organizations with concern for the care and well-being of mothers, babies, and families. They strive to promote a wellness model of maternity care that will improve birth outcomes and reduce health care costs.

Coalition for Improving Maternity Services
P.O. Box 33590
Raleigh, NC 27607 USA
http://motherfriendly.org
email: info@motherfriendly.org
phone: 866-424-3635

Home Birth Consensus Summit

Home Birth Consensus Summit is a national meeting of stakeholders and leaders working together to make homebirth more accessible within the greater context of maternity care in the United States.

http://www.homebirthsummit.org
email: info@homebirthsummit.org

Trust Birth

Trust Birth is an all-volunteer advocacy and support group. They believe that women are born to trust birth; but have been taught not to. The Trust Birth organization exists for the sole purpose of telling the truth about birth.

Trust Birth
http://www.trustbirth.com
email: trainingdirector@trustbirth.com

Trust Birth Conference
http://www.trustbirthconference.com

National Advocates for Pregnant Women

National Advocates for Pregnant Women (NAPW) work to secure the human and civil rights, health and welfare of all women, focusing particularly on pregnant and parenting women, and those who are most vulnerable - low income women, women of color, and women with addictions.

National Advocates for Pregnant Women
15 West 36th Street Suite 901
New York, NY 10018 USA
http://advocatesforpregnantwomen.org
email: info@advocatesforpregnantwomen.org
phone: 212-255-9252

EXAMPLE BIRTH ACTIVIST BLOGS

SQUAT Birth Journal

SQUAT is a quarterly magazine and an online blog written by individuals that support healthy and empowering birthing practices.

http://squatbirthjournal.blogspot.com

Birth Activist

A blog written by multiple bloggers that strive to bring awareness to stories, activities, causes and anything that requires action to help moms, babies and families have safe and satisfying births.

http://www.birthactivist.com

Gloria Lemay Birth Blog

Childbirth Activist Gloria Lemay shares her perspective.

http://www.glorialemay.com/blog

BIRTH ARTIST

Birth Artists create all forms of art that reflect fertility, pregnancy, giving birth, and mothering. Birth is a common experience shared by all cultures and is visible in traditional and contemporary art forms, and well documented throughout human history.

Search words: childbirth artist, birth art, birth sculpture, mother birth pottery, childbirth painting, birth painting

GETTING STARTED

If you have a background in art then use whatever art form you are passionate about and incorporate your knowledge, experience, and emotion about birth. No formal training is required. You might consider taking art classes in your community and use childbirth as your theme for the art you create.

EXAMPLE BIRTH ARTISTS

Janet Ashford

Janet Ashford collects examples of childbirth as it's depicted in art and medical illustrations, from pre-history to the present.

http://www.jashford.com/jashford.com/Childbirth.html
email: jashford@jashford.com

Belly As Art

Belly As Art uses the pregnant belly as the art canvas. They create lasting memories of pregnancy through art and photography, offering unique belly painting and henna designs.

Belly As Art
http://www.bellyasart.com
email: contact@BellyAsArt.com
phone: 845-729-2685

Mother Art

Mother Art is owned and created by Susan Kirk in reverence for the mystery of life, celebrating motherhood in all its stages. Her work honors a woman's experience in childbirth.

Mother Art
P.O. Box 1491
Chico, CA 95927 USA
http://www.mother-art.com
phone: 530-896-1325

La Belle Dame

La Belle Dame offers handcrafted jewelry to celebrate and honor women through their reproductive lives in sterling silver, gemstones, and crystal by designer Kimberly McIntyre-de Montbrun.

La Belle Dame
2476 TransCanada Highway
Flat River, PEI
C0A 1B0
Canada
http://www.labelledame.com
email: orders@labelledame.com
phone: 902-659-2667

Daniel Edwards Exhibit

Artist Daniel Edwards exhibits a controversial birth art statue depicting Britney Spears on a bearskin rug while giving birth to her firstborn child.

Daniel Edwards Exhibit
c/o Capla Kesting Fine Art
121 Roebling Street
Brooklyn, NY 11211 USA
http://tiny.cc/birthonknees
phone: 917-650-3760

The Mandala Journey

The Mandala Journey shows Amy Swagman's birth art. She has found the mandala to be a perfect way to express birth art, as a circle, the shape of pregnancy itself. The circle represents feminine energy and endless perfection.

http://themandalajourney.com

The Art of Birth

The Art of Birth offers parents, families and communities the materials and guidance to create art as they participate in the ultimate creative process, birth.

The Art of Birth
http://artofbirth.org
email: artofbirth@gmail.com
phone: 303-532-6660

Birth Work

Birth Work is a blog where a photographer shares her interpretation of birth. She has posted photographic and video artworks reappropriating the subjective experience of childbirth for the birthing woman.

http://claireharbottlebirthwork.blogspot.com

Birth Art Cafe

The Birth Art Cafe is a new concept in enriching the experience of preparing for childbirth and motherhood by exploring the motherhood journey and connecting with one's own inner wisdom through meditation and making art.

Birth Art Cafe
http://www.facebook.com/BirthArtCafe
email: info@womantomother.co.uk
phone: 01923 260050

Fyrestorm Creations

Fyrestorm Creations provides unique jewelry representing the experience of pregnancy, birth, birth trauma, mothering, and nursing.

Fyrestorm Creations
http://www.fyrestormcreations.com/id37.html
email: Fyrestormcreations@yahoo.com

BIRTH CENTER

Birth Centers also called Free-Standing Birth Centers provide midwifery care and are a place where families can have their babies in a home-like environment. Currently, there are approximately 110 Birth Centers in the United States. A great need exists for more centers to be opened.

Search words: birth center, birthing center, birth house, free standing birth center, birth center agency, birthing center license

GETTING STARTED

Visit a Birth Center near you. Learn how they began and see how their facility operates. Contact organizations that support Birth Centers or midwifery services to receive advice and assistance. Research what support government agencies provide to promote Birth Centers in your community. Also, contact your local health care licensing board to see if there are any requirements to open a Birth Center.

RESOURCES

American Association of Birth Centers

The American Association of Birth Centers (AABC) is the nation's most comprehensive resource on Birth Centers. AABC is committed to the promotion of the rights of healthy women and their families, in all communities, to birth their children in an environment, which is safe, sensitive and economical with minimal intervention.

American Association of Birth Centers
3123 Gottschall Road
Perkiomenville, PA 18074
http://www.birthcenters.org
phone: 215-234-8068

Birth Center by Design

Birth Center by Design is committed to empower and enable both aspiring and existing birth centers—as well as home birth practices—to grow and expand their businesses. They work to support Midwives in the manifestation of their unique vision, contributing to the larger vision for gentle birth.

Birth Center by Design
149 N. Main Street #207
Lakeport, CA 95453
http://birthcenterbydesign.com
email: info@birthcenterbydesign.com
phone: 888-512-4412

Wyoming Birthing Center Licensure Information

They Wyoming Department of Health offers state licensing for services provided by Birthing Centers.

Wyoming Birthing Center Licensure Information
400 Qwest Bldg, 6101 Yellowstone Rd
Cheyenne WY 82002 USA
http://tiny.cc/wybirthcenter
email: wdh-ohls@health.wyo.gov
phone: 307-777-7123

EXAMPLE BIRTHING CENTERS

The Birth Place

The Birth Place is a unique full service facility providing midwifery and health care for women. They strive to create a supportive experience for women in a relaxed and professional environment.

The Birth Place
213 South Dillard Street, Suite 340
Winter Garden, FL 34787 USA
http://thebirthplace.org
phone: 407-656-6938

Mamatoto Resource & Birth Centre

Mamatoto is committed to establishing a community-based, accessible, equitable, and innovative childbirth centre. They offer family-centered, individualized care to the healthy woman and her family.

Mamatoto Resource & Birth Centre
32 - 34 Clifford Street
Belmont
Trinidad & Tobago
West Indies
http://www.mamatoto.net
email: info@mamatoto.net
phone: 868-621-2368

The Birthing Inn

The Birthing Inn is a Free-Standing Childbirth Center, a place where women can find resources regarding their birth options, and deliver their babies in the safety and comfort of a peaceful home-like setting.

The Birthing Inn
6002 N. Westgate Blvd. Suite 120
Tacoma, WA 98406 USA
http://www.thebirthinginn.com
email: info@thebirthinginn.com
phone: 253-761-8939

Connecticut Childbirth & Women's Center

Connecticut Childbirth & Women's Center is the only free-standing facility of its kind in Connecticut. They are located across from the Danbury Hospital in Connecticut, and provide women with the best of both worlds - expert care by certified nurse-midwives, while emergency care is nearby.

Connecticut Childbirth & Women's Center
94 Locust Avenue
Danbury, CT 06810 USA
http://www.ctbirthcenter.com
email: info@ctbirthcenter.com
phone: 203-748-6000

Bumi Sehat Foundation International

Bumi Sehat is a non-profit, village-based organization that runs two by-donation community health centers in Bali and Aceh, Indonesia. They provide over 17,000 health consultations for both children and adults each year. Midwifery services ensure gentle birth is at the heart of Bumi Sehat and their clinics welcome approximately 600 new babies into the world every year.

Bumi Sehat Foundation International
Yayasan Bumi Sehat Bali
Banjar Nyuh Kuning
Ubud, Bali, Indonesia 80571
http://www.bumisehatbali.org
email: info@bumisehatinternational.org
phone: 0361 970002

Mountain Midwifery Center

Mountain Midwifery Center provides a full range of midwifery services for clients in the Denver Metro Area. For birth, the center provides prenatal care, natural birth, water birth in Aqua Doula tubs, nutritional counseling and more.

Mountain Midwifery Center
3555 S. Clarkson St. Suite 300
Englewood, CO 80113 USA
http://www.mountainmidwifery.com
email: questions@mountainmidwifery.com
phone: 303-788-0600

Aqua Birth House

At Aqua Birth House, they believe each woman is able to choose her own natural birthing style with her own strength. The Midwives of Aqua Birth House are there to help those who wish to have a natural birth. At the Birth House, there is no cold delivery table. They do not force any particular birthing position or breathing method. Every labor should be different like every individual's life is unique and special.

Aqua Birth House
http://www.aqua-birthhouse.com
email: info@aqua-birthhouse.com

Mejiro Birth House

At Mejiro Birth House, they support "active birth". They tell expecting mothers, "You will feel what you want, what your baby wants. You are the person to decide what kind of atmosphere you want when you give birth." Women are told, "The staff at Mejiro Birth House will wait quietly by your side."

Mejiro Birth House
http://www.birthhouse.com
email: info@birthhouse.com

Madison Birth Center

Madison Birth Center is a Free-Standing Birth Center providing holistic women's health, pregnancy, birth, and after birth care. Their patients can choose to give birth at the center or in their own homes.

Madison Birth Center
6720 Frank Lloyd Wright, Suite 103
Middleton, WI 53562 USA
http://www.madisonbirthcenter.com
phone: 608-821-0123

BIRTH DANCE INSTRUCTOR

Birth Dance Instructors teach classes that lead pregnant women through dance movements that help them connect to their bodies and their babies. The classes teach pregnant women safe exercises they can do throughout their pregnancy, and it helps them prepare for labor and birth.

Search words: birth dance class, childbirth dance class, pregnancy dance, belly dance for birth, dancing for birth

GETTING STARTED

A background in dance is not usually required. Sign up for a teacher training workshop or correspondence course through one of the organizations that certify Birth Dance Instructors. Purchase a DVD about Birth Dance. Attend a Birth Dance class in your community and ask the instructor for advice on how to get started.

ORGANIZATIONS

Dancing for Birth

Dancing for Birth prenatal and postpartum dance classes incorporate dance moves from around the world that best prepare women to give birth. Birth can be like a marathon, and Dancing for Birth classes prepare women for the challenge.

Dancing for Birth
http://www.dancingforbirth.com
email: Info@DancingForBirth.com
phone: 866-643-4824

Belly Dance for Birth

Belly Dance for Birth is a safe and effective dance expression that supports women throughout pregnancy and labor providing a natural birthing technique that encourages active birth.

Belly Dance for Birth
http://www.bellydanceforbirth.com

Dancing Thru Pregnancy

The Dancing Thru Pregnancy program relieves discomforts, reduces the risk of some disorders of pregnancy, provides stamina and movement skills for birth while reducing the need for interventions, and speeds recovery.

Dancing Thru Pregnancy
Box 3083 Stony Creek
Branford, CT 06405 USA
http://dancingthrupregnancy.com
email: director@dancingthrupregnancy.com
phone: 203-481-2200

BIRTH DOULA

Birth Doulas support women and their families through pregnancy and the childbirth experience. The word Doula is an ancient Greek word that means woman servant. Doulas offer emotional and physical support to women when they are in labor, such as massages and kind words. They also serve as the mother's advocate. A Doula does not deliver babies or provide medical services.

Search words: birth doula, doula, labor doula, labor partner, birth assistant, doula training, doula association

GETTING STARTED

Learn about the requirements to become a Doula by going to the certification organization's websites. Enroll in a Doula program and start working on the certification requirements. Contact Doulas in your local community and ask them any questions you have. Read the *Birth Partner* by Penny Simkin.

ᏁᏣ

Career Journey ...

Doula, Allie Sakowicz, CD (DONA)

How did you get started as a Doula at such a young age?

I became a Doula when I was 15, in 2009. I've always been interested in medicine, and have possessed a particular love for Ob/Gyn since I was nine. Knowing that it would be a long time until I entered medical school, I thought that becoming a Doula would give me a chance to study the field that I was passionate about at a young age. I've always been fascinated by childbirth, and having the chance to be involved in it as a teenager is a huge honor and responsibility.

Why do you do this work? What do you enjoy?

To me, there's absolutely nothing like the feeling I get when I witness a new life come into the world. It's truly an indescribable feeling, and it's something that I'm looking forward to experiencing the rest of my life. I love being able to work in a field that I am passionate about, and having the opportunity to help my peers at the same time. It is a privilege to work with these young mothers, and many of them are also very inspirational to me. They are facing the challenges of being a teen, and they do it while raising a child.

I provide all of my services to teen mothers free of charge, so I don't really run a business. I think that this work is so important that any mom who wants a Doula should have one, and I refuse to let lack of finances stop them from having someone by their side as they give birth.

What type of training or education did you receive?

I began the process when I was fourteen. Earning certification through DONA International involves completing a reading list, attending a 3-day workshop, writing several essays, and providing support to 3-7 women and receiving evaluations from the mom, her nurse, and her care provider, among other things. It's not an easy process, especially because I was completing it while being a full-time high school student!

Do you have any "aha" moments or insights to share about your work?

Every patient I work with is very special to me, and I learn something from each and every one. I remember working with a young mother last summer who had just graduated high school and was pregnant with her second child. She was an honor student and was planning on attending college in the fall. It was just amazing to me that she was doing so well in school while raising children, as that's not something I can even imagine. I've met so many amazing people during my time as a Doula, and I could really tell stories for hours!

What advice can you give to anyone that wishes to become a Teen Doula?

It's a long road and can be very challenging at times, but if you have a passion for birth and helping others, then it's all worth it. The best advice I can give is not to get discouraged or frustrated during the learning process. It takes time to become educated on how to best serve teen moms, and the more you learn, the better Doula you will be.

Anything else you would like to share?

Being a Doula is something that I'm extremely passionate about, as I enjoy working with teen mothers who may not otherwise have anyone to be by their side during their pregnancy and birth. I'm given the chance to not only serve those in my community, but also learn more about this field that I love so much. I hope that someday the combination of the physical and emotional support techniques that I have learned as a Doula will combine with my future medical knowledge in order to make me a skilled obstetrician.

૪૦(જ

BIRTH DOULA CERTIFICATION ORGANIZATIONS

Doula C.A.R.E.

Doula C.A.R.E. is a Canadian association committed to providing emotional and physical support for women during the childbirth process. They work to foster a positive and informed birth experience.

Doula C.A.R.E.
Maple Grove Village
P.O. Box #61058
Oakville, Ontario L6J 6X0
http://www.doulacare.ca
email: info@doulacare.ca
phone: 905-842-3385

International Childbirth Education Association

The International Childbirth Education Association (ICEA) is a professional organization supporting educators and other health care providers who believe in freedom to make decisions based on knowledge of alternatives in family-centered maternity and newborn care.

International Childbirth Education Association
1500 Sunday Drive, Suite 102
Raleigh, NC 27607 USA
http://www.icea.org
email: info@icea.org
phone: 919-863-9487

DONA International

DONA international is a professional organization of that strives to provide high quality training for Doulas and establish quality standards for the birth and postpartum care provided to pregnant women and their families. DONA promotes continuing education for Doulas and provides a strong network between Doulas, families and the medical community.

DONA International
1582 S. Parker Rd, Suite 201
Denver, CO 80231 USA
http://www.dona.org
email: dona@dona.org
phone: 888-788-3662

Nova Scotia Doula Association

The Nova Scotia Doula Association (NSDA) cultivates the growth of individual Doulas and the collective profession, thereby increasing the quality of prenatal, birth and postpartum support given to women and their families in Nova Scotia.

NSDA Nova Scotia Doula Association
http://nsdoulas.ca
email: info@nsdoulas.ca

Doula Consultancy

The objective of Doula Consultancy Services is to provide high quality training for Doula, nanny and au pair care. They are a social enterprise company that uses their profits for the public good. They believe women who are socially disadvantaged should have access to Doula care.

Doula Consultancy
145 - 157 St John's Street
London, EC1V 4PY
United Kingdom
http://doulatraining.org.uk
email: doula.consultancy.services@gmail.com
phone: 0844 2510 374

European Doula Network

European Doula Network (EDN) is a network of Doulas across Europe that support and learn from each other and exchange ideas.

European Doula Network
http://www.european-doula-network.org
email: info@european-doula-network.org

Childbirth and Postpartum Professional Association

Childbirth and Postpartum Professional Association (CAPPA) offers comprehensive, evidence-based education, certification, professional membership and training to Childbirth Educators, Lactation Educators, Birth Doulas, Antepartum Doulas and Postpartum Doulas worldwide.

Childbirth and Postpartum Professional Association
PO Box 2406
Buford, GA 30515 USA
http://www.cappa.net
email: info@cappa.net
phone: 770-932-7281

Doula UK

Doula UK supports Doulas by offering guidance and support with preparation courses and ongoing study days. Doula UK also provides information about Doulas to parents, the media, and health professionals.

Doula UK
1 Rockfield Business Park
Old Station Drive
Leckhampton, Cheltenham
Glos, GL53 0AN United Kingdom
http://doula.org.uk
email: membership@doula.org.uk
phone: 0871 4333103

The Doula Council

The Doula Council is a voluntary self-regulation organization for certified Doulas and student Doulas in the UK. The Doula Council is the voice of Doulas in the UK.

The Doula Council
http://www.doulas.org.uk
email: doulacouncil@gmail.com

Dolphin Doula

Dolphin Doula offers a unique Doula training program and certification for those seeking careers as Childbirth Professionals. The training teaches hypnosis techniques for pregnant women and couples to use prior to birth, during birth, and also covers labor support skills.

Dolphin Doula
http://www.dolphinyoga.com
email: training@dolphindoula.com

Birth Arts International

Birth Arts International trains dynamic wise women Doulas, Postpartum Doulas, Childbirth Educators, Midwife Assistants, and Breastfeeding Educators, in their flexible education programs.

Birth Arts International
501 Lindsey St
Reidsville, NC 27320 USA
http://www.birtharts.com
email: demetria@birtharts.com
phone: 866-303-4372

Birthing From Within

The Birthing From Within Doula program is different. Many programs focus primarily on techniques to care for the parents in labor and postpartum. The Birthing From Within program begins training with the focus upon the Doulas views and core beliefs.

Birthing From Within
PO Box 60259
Santa Barbara, CA 93160 USA
http://www.birthingfromwithin.com
email: contact@birthingfromwithin.com
phone: 805-964-6611

Birth Works

BirthWorks embodies the philosophy of developing a woman's self-confidence, trust, and faith in her innate ability to give birth. BirthWorks trains Childbirth Educators and Doulas who in turn provide evidence-based, current information to birthing families through a unique experiential approach that is based upon human values.

Birth Works
P.O. Box 2045
Medford, NJ 08055 USA
http://www.birthworks.org
email: 888-862-4784
phone: info@birthworks.org

Childbirth International

Childbirth International provides a unique approach to training and certification for Childbirth Professionals. The Childbirth International programs have all been designed specifically for home-based learning, with different learning styles in mind.

Childbirth International
http://www.childbirthinternational.com

MaternityWise

MaternityWise was founded with the belief that every woman and her family deserve the benefits of positive community with informative, encouraging support during the childbearing years.

MaternityWise
8503 NW Military Hwy, Suite 105-11
San Antonio, TX 78231 USA
http://www.maternitywise.com
email: trainings@maternitywise.com
phone: 952-457-6506

Madriella Doula Program

Madriella offers an online Doula training course, which covers birth physiology, how to write a birth plan, how to present birth options, providing emotional support, and providing postpartum care.

Madriella Doula Program
P.O. Box 3181
Merced, CA 95344 USA
http://www.madriella.com
phone: 209-777-6305

Aviva Institute

Aviva Institute provides comprehensive and accessible education for Midwives and health care providers, based in their own communities, providing the highest standards of academic excellence, which encompasses a holistic model of integrating mind, body, heart and spirit.

Aviva Institute
1660 South Highway 100 Suite 500
St. Louis Park, MN 55416 USA
https://avivainstitute.org
email: nikkiguerton.aviva@gmail.com
phone: 800-951-4110

Doula Ireland

Doula Ireland offers Doula training workshops and services.

Doula Ireland
http://www.doulaireland.com
email: TracyDonegan@DoulaIreland.com
phone: 087 057 2500

Optimum Birth

Optimum Birth is an online Doula training course that individuals can take at their pace.

http://www.optimumbirth.com.au/index.html

BLESSINGWAY FACILITATOR

Blessingway Facilitators help plan and lead ceremonies that can involve music, singing, storytelling, pampering, rituals, and communal creativity that honors expecting mothers. The Blessingway ceremonies connect the mother to a circle of women and family members that nurture and support her throughout the birth experience.

Search words: blessingway, blessing way, blessingway facilitator, blessing way facilitation, blessingway ceremonies, blessing way ceremonies

GETTING STARTED

To become a Blessingway Facilitator there are no requirements or certifications needed. Observe Blessingway ceremonies from a facilitator leading them in your community. Read books about Blessingway ceremonies. Be familiar with some of the rituals offered during the ceremonies such as belly casting and henna belly painting. Use the internet to research Blessingway ceremonies and find out what services facilitators are offering.

BOOKS

Pride & Joy: African-American Baby Celebrations by Janice Robinson

Mother Rising by Yana Cortlund, Barb Lucke, and Donna Miller Watelet

Blessingways: A Guide to Mother-Centered Baby Showers by Shari Maser

Mother Blessings: Honoring Women Becoming Mothers by Anna Stewart

RESOURCES

The Canadian Women's Health Network

Article describing a Blessingway ceremony

http://www.cwhn.ca/node/39613

EXAMPLES

The Blessing Circle

The Blessing Circle offers gifts and ideas for creating community celebrations to mark turning points and important life events.

The Blessing Circle
http://www.theblessingcircle.com
email: mail@theblessingcircle.com
phone: 0421 079 644

Easli Birth

Easili Birth provides Blessingway Facilitation, in the spirit of time-honored practices. Traditionally, Blessingway ceremonies were held as a celebration to honor and bless women as they transitioned into motherhood.

Easli Birth
100 Bull Lane
Ravenswood, WV 26164 USA
http://esalibirth.com/support/blessingways
email: info@esalibirth.com
phone: 304-273-4190

Mama Roots

Mama Roots offers Blessingway Facilitation. Mama Roots states that Blessingway ceremonies are often given to the mama as an alternative to a baby shower. A Blessingway provides the mama to be with the strength and support of her tribe of womyn as she makes the transition from maiden to mama.

Mama Roots
http://www.mamaroots.com/my_weblog/blessingways.html
email: willow@mamaroots.com

Birthing Life

Birthing Life offers Blessingway ceremonies that are individualized based upon a families' heritage and aesthetic.

Birthing Life
http://birthingforlife.com/babyblessings.html
email: info@birthingforlife.com
phone: 508-668-4247

BLOGGER

Using internet websites and online tools, Bloggers write and share their thoughts and opinions about everything. They share important research and news regarding pregnancy, childbirth, breastfeeding, mothering and so much more. Bloggers are effective at creating communities and forums where education, discussion, and debate can take place.

Search words: how to start blogging, wordpress, blogger, blogging tools, blogging tips, doula blog, pregnancy blog, free blog

GETTING STARTED

Beginning to blog is simple. Decide on a name for your blog. Sign-up for a free blog creation website, select a template for your blog, and then start typing and post a topic that interests you. Read blogs and take note of techniques that bloggers use. Attend blog conferences or take classes to learn more about blogging. Read books and articles about blogging. Join a blog community.

ℰℭ

Career Journey . . .

Blogger, Kimmelin Hull, PA, LCCE, FACCE

How did you get started as a Blogger?

In 2008, I began with my own blog, *Writing My Way Through Motherhood and Beyond*. I wrote of the indignities and joys of mostly stay-at-home motherhood after having had a career in medicine as a Physician's Assistant. In the early years of parenting (when our three children were age four and under), it seemed like those experiences—indignities and joys—often conjoined or played off each other in head-spinning perpetuity and sometimes on an hourly basis! Two years later, I began writing for Lamaze's Science & Sensibility, and became the managing editor of that blog site in November 2010.

Why do you do this work? What do you enjoy?

At this point, my blogging work is no longer about sharing personal stories, it is an extension of the work I've done for the past six years as a Lamaze Certified Childbirth Educator. I use my on-line writing, and editing/publishing of other professionals' writings, as a way to disseminate information about evidence-based maternity care to Childbirth Professionals, and to women of childbearing age, beyond my community, as Science & Sensibility is read in 129 different countries.

I particularly enjoy the interactions I have had—and continue to have—with folks all over the world who are also interested in improving the experience and safety of pregnancy, labor, delivery and the postpartum period. One great example of this is the email conversations I've had with Charlie Saunders who is the editor of Talking CENZ Magazine—a publication geared toward Childbirth Educators in New Zealand.

Ms. Saunders has re-purposed several Science & Sensibility blog posts in Talking CENZ, helping to spread the evidence-based writings of our blog site well beyond the borders of the United States. As a result of my public-facing work with Lamaze, I have been asked to write a chapter for a midwifery-geared textbook, I have delivered webinars and conference lectures on maternity care-related issues and I've been asked to be a part of this book! Web-based writing has the potential to open doors for motivated individuals who recognize—and jump on— opportunities.

How do you like running a business? What business advice can you share?

My business, Pregnancy to Parenthood, LLC ("PtoP") is set up as a childbirth education program in the small Montanan town where I live. For the first five years after establishing PtoP, I taught independent childbirth education and early parenting classes. More recently, I have operated through Pregnancy to Parenthood to write and publish a book, to work as a contract editor and writer for Lamaze International, and also to provide childbirth education video script editing work for a prominent childbirth education video production company.

I can't say enough about the importance of integrity—whether you are a one-person show or a corporation. Follow-through, honesty, and bridge building within a community are all operating policies that garner win-win results, in business relationships, in a reputation locally and on-line, and in the quality of service one provides. Also, celebrating achievements is a must—no matter how large or small. This advice was passed onto me by a childhood friend of mine—a woman business owner in the Seattle area where I grew up. Owning your own business is a different beast than working for someone else and comes with its own inherent stresses and challenges; each step in the right direction needs to be acknowledged and celebrated!

What type of training or education did you receive?

Beyond my undergraduate degree in writing, I completed my PA degree at Saint Francis University in Loretto, PA in 1999, my

Lamaze Certified Childbirth Educator training in 2005,and am currently pursuing a Masters in Public Health—Maternal & Child Health (University of Minnesota) that I expect to complete in 2013. Additionally, I have attended numerous writer's workshops and conferences to hone my writing skills.

Do you have any "aha" moments or insights to share about your work?

Follow your heart. There is an adage in the literary/writer's world that tells us to write about that which we are passionate or that which we know. Of course, sometimes folks don't follow this advice (I dearly hope Stephen King's work doesn't embody his "passion," aside from the process of writing in and of itself) but, in general, following our passion is a good way to ensure longevity in career and happiness in life. While working medically as a PA, I was miserable, and it took me nearly ten years to admit to this. Following my passion for patient education and maternal advocacy has leant a degree of satisfaction and happiness I couldn't have anticipated while still trying to force myself to "like" practicing medicine. I could be earning ten times the salary I currently am, if I was still practicing medicine. However, feeling happy and fulfilled is far more important to me than that.

What advice can you give to anyone that wishes to become a Blogger?

Find a shtick and stick with it. Blog sites that topically roam widely can be hard to follow and risk losing readership. Use a blogsite to act upon the advice I offered above. What do you love? What are you most interested in? What gets you the most fired up? Write about that. Also, interact with and learn from other bloggers. Figure out whom else is writing in the same space as you, and form some connections with those folks. Offer to write a guest post for another blogger, or ask for the same favor for your blog site. Comment on other people's blog sites. Every blogger knows that posting a piece you spent time on and receiving no (or little) response back is disheartening. Help other bloggers out by letting them know their work is being read. I would add a caution about monetizing a blog site. While I understand some folks have found a way to make this very lucrative (Dooce.com anyone?) it must be said that writing for money changes your writing, sometimes in big ways (if answering to an editorial board or single editor) or small ways (one of your advertisers doesn't like something you write and pulls their ad—and a piece of your income, along with it.) This may be neither here nor there, but it just is.

ജ

RESOURCES

Problogger

Problogger is a blog that will teach you to effectively blog. It is filled with tips and advice written by Darren Rowse who is a full-time Blogger making a living from blogging.

http://www.problogger.net

Wordpress.com

Wordpress.com is an easy to use blog tool with many helpful features.

http://wordpress.com

Blogger.com

With Blogger.com create a free blog with beautiful, customizable templates and layouts.

http://blogger.com

Blog.com

Blog.com provides a powerful publishing platform for free.

http://blog.com

Mom Bloggers Club

The Mom Bloggers Club Network is one of the largest social networks for mom bloggers. With over 17,000 members, the Mom Bloggers Club Network is a place where moms who blog converge to talk about the latest trends in blogging and to support each other in their blogging endeavors.

http://www.mombloggersclub.com

Top Mommy Blogs

Top Mommy Blogs is a rating and directory of mommy blogs.

http://www.topmommyblogs.com

BLOG EXAMPLES

Science & Sensibility

Science & Sensibility is a research blog about healthy pregnancy, birth and beyond from Lamaze International.

http://www.scienceandsensibility.org

Mother Love

A blog with current childbirth related information by Mother Love a company that creates and sells herbal products for pregnancy, birth, breastfeeding and babies.

http://motherloveblog.com

Childbirth Solutions

Childbirth Solutions compiles information about childbirth including preconception, pregnancy, birth, and postpartum. The goal of the site is to answer any question a mother-to-be may have.

http://childbirthsolutions.com

Birth Without Fear Blog

The author of Birth Without Fear started the blog to help women work through their fears and heal from traumatic experiences. She supports women to achieve empowering births.

http://birthwithoutfearblog.com

Bellies and Babies

Bellies and Babies is the diary of a mother, Childbirth Educator, Doula, and aspiring Midwife.

http://wonderfullymadebelliesandbabies.blogspot.com

Lactation Journey Blog

The author shares her perspective as she works to obtain certification as a Lactation Consultant.

http://lactationjourney.blogspot.com

Stand and Deliver

Stand and Deliver reflects on pregnancy, birth, and mothering.

http://rixarixa.blogspot.com

Radical Doula

Radical Doula connects the dots between issues that are often seen as contradictory: reproductive rights, birth activism, doula work, LGBT issues, immigrant rights, and racial justice.

http://radicaldoula.com

Homebirth: A Midwife Mutiny

The author shares her professional experiences and opinions for the purpose of encouraging others to open their eyes to what is happening in the *birth business*.

http://www.homebirth.net.au

Blacktating

Blacktating shares breastfeeding news and views from a mom of color.

http://www.blacktating.com

The Mommyhood Memos

The Mommyhood Memos offers a humorous perspective about being a mom, while at other times it offers thought-provoking parenting topics, practical every-day tips for flourishing in life with little ones, musings about the pain and joy of motherhood, and inspiration for the journey as a woman.

http://themommyhoodmemos.com

BOARD MEMBER

Board members assist in managing companies, nonprofits, and associations. They are responsible for delegating the many different tasks an organization requires to run productively and effectively, such as operations, finances, and marketing. Although service upon a board is not always paid, the opportunity to contribute, network, and gain new skills is invaluable.

Search words: apply serve board director, childbirth board member, doula board member

GETTING STARTED

Contact an organization that you are a member of or have an interest in and find out what is required to serve as a Board Member. Ask individuals that have previously served on a board for their thoughts and advice. Obtain and practice filling out forms to apply for board positions in order to become familiar with the process.

ℰℭ

Career Journey ...

Board Member, ICEA, Jeanette Schwartz

How did you get started as a Board Member for ICEA?

I became a member of the International Childbirth Education Association (ICEA) in 1987 because the philosophy of ICEA resonated with me. I fully believed in "freedom to decide based on knowledge of alternatives" for all birthing families, and my passion to work towards making this a reality for women brought me to ICEA. I volunteered to serve on the nominating committee to the board of directors for many years. Then in 2005, I took the step to apply to the Board. In 2007, I was asked to apply to the position as President and served 2008-2010.

What do you enjoy about service on a Board?

I loved the professional connections and personal friendships that develop while serving on the board. Together we made decision to strengthen programs, financial worth, and the reputation of ICEA. It is very exciting/terrifying to know the board decisions affect the membership and families we serve.

What type of training or education did you receive?

The beauty of membership on the Board of Directors is the need for a variety of background in training and education. For me, this was twenty years of nursing, working in management, being a Childbirth Educator, and a Doula. I have a Master's Degree in Nursing leadership. My first two years on the board consisted of learning the by-laws and structure of the ICEA Board of Directors. Past members of the board were also readily available to help with questions and concerns.

Do you have any "aha" moments or insights to share about working on a Board?

First, learning that anyone can serve on the board; it takes commitment and a desire to improve the organization. You don't have to have degrees or credentialing. The more diverse the board membership can be, the stronger it is. Second, many hands make light work. Serving on the board could be overwhelming, but when everyone uses their strengths to help with an issue, respect each other's ideas, and commit to finding a solution, the best decision will be implemented.

What advice can you give to anyone that wishes to become a Board Member?

Believe in the organization and its philosophy. Believe in your capability to contribute. Take the leap. The rewards far outweigh the work.

8003

EXAMPLE BOARD OPPORTUNITIES

DONA International

Opportunity: http://www.dona.org/develop/get_involved.php

DONA international is a professional organization of that strives to provide high quality training for Doulas and establish quality standards for the birth and postpartum care provided to pregnant women and their families. DONA promotes continuing education for Doulas and provides a strong network between Doulas, families and the medical community.

DONA International
1582 S. Parker Rd, Suite 201
Denver, CO 80231 USA
http://www.dona.org
email: dona@dona.org
phone: 888-788-3662

Doula Care

Opportunity: http://www.doulacare.ca/about.cfm

Doula C.A.R.E. is a Canadian association committed to providing emotional and physical support for women during the childbirth process. They work to foster a positive and informed birth experience.

Doula C.A.R.E, Incorporated
Maple Grove Village
P.O. Box #61058
Oakville, Ontario
L6J 6X0
http://www.doulacare.ca
email: info@doulacare.ca
phone: 905-842-3385

NSDA Nova Scotia Doula Association

Opportunity: http://nsdoulas.ca/about/board-directors

The NSDA cultivates the growth of individual Doulas and the collective profession, thereby increasing the quality of prenatal, birth and postpartum support given to women and their families in Nova Scotia.

NSDA Nova Scotia Doula Association
http://nsdoulas.ca
email: info@nsdoulas.ca

Coalition for Improving Maternity Services

Opportunity: http://motherfriendly.org/coalition

The Coalition for Improving Maternity Services (CIMS) is a coalition of individuals and national organizations with concern for the care and well-being of mothers, babies, and families. They strive to promote a wellness model of maternity care that will improve birth outcomes and reduce health care costs.

Coalition for Improving Maternity Services
P.O. Box 33590
Raleigh, NC 27607 USA
http://motherfriendly.org
email: info@motherfriendly.org
phone: 866-424-3635

Association of Midwifery Educators

Opportunity: http://tiny.cc/ameboard

The Association of Midwifery Educators (AME) has undertaken the mission of advancing direct-entry midwifery education through strengthening schools and supporting teachers through connection, collaboration and coordination.

Association of Midwifery Educators
24 S. High Street
Bridgton, ME, 04009 USA
http://associationofmidwiferyeducators.org
email: info@associationofmidwiferyeducators.org
phone: 207-647-5968

BirthWays

Opportunity: http://birthways.org/board

BirthWays is a comprehensive pregnancy, birth and parenting education and resource center.

BirthWays
1600 Shattuck Ave. Suite 122
Berkeley, CA 94709 USA
email: contact@birthways.org
phone: 510-869-2797

BREASTFEEDING COUNSELOR ALSO LACTATION COUNSELOR

Breastfeeding Counselors are usually woman that have successfully breastfed at least one child and offer support and guidance to other breastfeeding mothers. They are trained to provide evidence-based information and answer mother's questions. Breastfeeding Counselors increase confidence, dispel misinformation, and ease fears.

Search words: breastfeeding counselor, breastfeeding counselor training, breastfeeding peer counselor, breastfeeding counselor certification, nursing mothers counsel, nursing mothers council

GETTING STARTED

Some training is available through local government agencies and nonprofits that support and promote breastfeeding in your community; contact them. Also, read books about breastfeeding. Find an experienced counselor in your area whom you can observe and ask questions.

ORGANIZATIONS

La Leche League International

La Leche League helps mothers worldwide to breastfeed through mother-to-mother support, encouragement, information, and education, and to promote a better understanding of breastfeeding as an important element in the healthy development of the baby and mother.

La Leche League International
957 N. Plum Grove Road
Schaumburg, IL 60173 USA
http://www.lalecheleague.org/lad/talll/talll.html
phone: 800-525-3243

Childbirth International

Childbirth International (CBI) provides a unique approach to training and certification for Childbirth Professionals. The Childbirth International programs have all been designed specifically for home-based learning, with different learning styles in mind.

Childbirth International
http://www.childbirthinternational.com

Healthy Children, Center for Breastfeeding

Healthy Children, Center for Breastfeeding is the largest national provider of lactation management education for health care providers.

Healthy Children, Center for Breastfeeding
327 Quaker Meeting House Road
East Sandwich, MA 02537 USA
http://www.healthychildren.cc
email: info@healthychildren.cc
phone: 508-888-8044

BREASTFEEDING EDUCATOR ALSO LACTATION EDUCATOR

Breastfeeding Educators support mothers, answer questions, and teach classes about breastfeeding. They provide breastfeeding education to women during pregnancy, often becoming their first source of accurate information.

Search words: breastfeeding educator, breastfeeding educator certification, lactation educator, lactation educator training

GETTING STARTED

Take a class to learn the basics about breastfeeding. Attend mother and new baby groups to discover what are common concerns and questions. Ask a Breastfeeding Educator to serve as your mentor. Join a breastfeeding group or association. Read breastfeeding books.

CERTIFICATION ORGANIZATIONS & TRAINING PROGRAMS

Birth Arts International

Birth Arts International trains dynamic wise women Doulas, Postpartum Doulas, Childbirth Educators, Midwife Assistants, and Breastfeeding Educators, in their flexible education programs.

Birth Arts International
501 Lindsey St
Reidsville, NC 27320 USA
http://www.birtharts.com/beced.htm
email: demetria@birtharts.com
phone: 866-303-4372

Childbirth and Postpartum Professional Association

Childbirth and Postpartum Professional Association (CAPPA) offers comprehensive, evidence-based education, certification, professional membership and training to Childbirth Educators, Lactation Educators, Birth Doulas, Antepartum Doulas and Postpartum Doulas worldwide.

Childbirth and Postpartum Professional Association
PO Box 2406
Buford, GA 30515 USA
http://www.cappa.net
email: info@cappa.net
phone: 770-932-7281

Prepared Childbirth Educators, Inc.

Prepared Childbirth Educators, Inc. (PCE) is a national organization of nurse educators. The goal of PCE certification is to recognize excellence in the nurse's specialty role, and contribute to the nurses' professional development.

Prepared Childbirth Educators, Inc.
219 Central Avenue
Hatboro, PA 19040 USA
https://www.childbirtheducation.org
email: info@childbirtheducation.org
phone: 888-344-9972

UC San Diego Extension Lactation Education

Lactation Education at UC San Diego Extension offers students a nationally recognized university program and access to high caliber instructors and trainers.

http://www.breastfeeding-education.com

Bastyr University Department of Midwifery

The Department of Midwifery has workshops that focus on essential maternity care issues and lactation certification courses.

Bastyr University Department of Midwifery
14500 Juanita Drive NE
Kenmore, WA 98028 USA
http://www.seattlemidwifery.org
phone: 425-602-3000
email: midwifery@bastyr.edu

Australian Breastfeeding Association

Australian Breastfeeding Association is a leading source of breastfeeding information and support in Australia. They strive to support and encourage women who want to breastfeed their babies, and to raise community awareness of the importance of breastfeeding and human milk to child and maternal health.

Australian Breastfeeding Association
1818-1822 Malvern Road
Malvern East Vic 3145
Australia
http://www.breastfeeding.asn.au
phone: 03 9885 0855

BUSINESS COACH

The Business Coach helps Childbirth Professionals build a thriving practice, earn a profit, and achieve success. They give practical A to Z business advice. Business Coaches are familiar with the latest social media and new technology to assist Childbirth Professionals in marketing their services.

Search words: birth professional business, birth business coach, doula business coach

GETTING STARTED

Success attracts success. If you have a thriving birth business others will want to learn from you. Write down the strategies that you know work well. Develop a class to share your business knowledge. Create a newsletter or downloadable document with your business strategies to share with Childbirth Professionals. Offer your advice through phone calls, conference calls, and webinars as well as through services like Skype.

EXAMPLES

Inspired Birth Pro

Inspired Birth Pro helps Childbirth Professionals start and grow their businesses.

http://www.inspiredbirthpro.com

Get Birth Clients

Get Birth Clients assists confused, overwhelmed, and sometimes technically challenged business owners learn a simple system to reach new clients through the internet.

http://childbirthpro.com

The Birthing Business

They help Childbirth Professionals start-up and build their birth related business.

http://www.birthingbusiness.com

Business Owner

Most of the Childbirth Professional roles can become independent businesses. For example as a Childbirth Educator you can teach classes at a hospital as an employee, and also charge couples for classes held in your own living room. Many professionals choose to be self-employed and operate their own business; others work for a company and operate a business at the same time.

Search words: birth network, birth business, childbirth professional business

Getting Started

Decide on which Childbirth Professional role suits you best and would make a good business. Locate a similar business, contact the owner, and learn as much as you can about their experience. Create a networking group of similar professionals for advice, support, and referrals.

Examples of Businesses

See directory listings at these websites

Bloom Spokane

Bloom Spokane directory lists professional members who provide mother-friendly services to expecting women and their families. Their members support a woman's right to make informed decisions and advocate evidence-based, mother-friendly care.

http://www.bloomspokane.com/provider-directory

Central Oregon Birth Network

The Central Oregon Birth Network (COBN) is an organization committed to helping women and families have safe and fulfilling pregnancy and birth experiences while empowering them in their role as health care consumers. They promote an awareness of evidence-based care and informed decision-making through advocacy, education and support.

http://www.centraloregonbirthnetwork.org

Australian Birth and Parenting Network

The Australian Birth and Parenting Network is national body of health professionals dedicated to increasing awareness about conscious parenting. They support the parenting journey from fertility, preconception, pregnancy, birth, and parenting.

http://www.abpn.com.au

UK Birth Network

The UK Birth Network is a one-stop shop to find professionals in the local area that offer services or products relating to fertility, pregnancy, birth, babies and toddlers.

http://www.ukbirthnetwork.com

CHILDBIRTH EDUCATOR

Childbirth Educators teach classes about pregnancy, childbirth, newborn care, and related subjects to expecting women and their families. They can teach in a variety of settings such as a hospital, home, school, or community center.

Search words: childbirth educator, birth educator, childbirth educator certification, certified childbirth educator

GETTING STARTED

Contact organizations that certify Childbirth Educators and find out what they require. Childbirth Education organizations vary in their certification process and their philosophies. Consider which organizations align best with your own philosophy. Also, talk to educators in your community to inquire which organization they chose for certification, and why. If you want to be employed as a Childbirth Educator, check which organization is preferred by your future employer. If you want to work independently, find out which organizations can assist you towards that goal. It is also not uncommon for Childbirth Educators to receive certification from more than one organization.

CHILDBIRTH EDUCATOR CERTIFICATION PROGRAMS

International Childbirth Education Association

The International Childbirth Education Association (ICEA) is a professional organization supporting educators and other health care providers who believe in freedom to make decisions based on knowledge of alternatives in family-centered maternity and newborn care.

ICEA
1500 Sunday Drive, Suite 102
Raleigh, NC 27607 USA
http://www.icea.org
email: info@icea.org
phone: 919-863-9487

Mindfulness-Based Childbirth and Parenting Program

Integrating mindfulness practices such as meditation, breath awareness, and yoga with childbirth and parenting education, the Mindfulness-Based Childbirth and Parenting (MBCP) Education Program helps parents and parents-to-be cultivate life-long practices for healthy living and wise parenting.

MBCP Program
http://www.mindfulbirthing.org
email: nancy@mindfulbirthing.org

Lamaze International

Lamaze International serves as a resource for information about what to expect and what choices are available during the childbearing years. Lamaze education and practices are based on the best, most current medical evidence available.

Lamaze International
2025 M Street, NW, Suite 800
Washington, DC 20036 USA
http://www.lamaze.org
phone: 202-367-1128

Childbirth and Postpartum Professional Association

Childbirth and Postpartum Professional Association (CAPPA) offers comprehensive, evidence-based education, certification, professional membership and training to Childbirth Educators, Lactation Educators, Birth Doulas, Antepartum Doulas and Postpartum Doulas worldwide.

CAPPA
PO Box 2406
Buford, GA 30515 USA
http://www.cappa.net
email: info@cappa.net
phone: 770-932-7281

Childbirth International

Childbirth International (CBI) provides a unique approach to training and certification for Childbirth Professionals. The Childbirth International programs have all been designed specifically for home-based learning, with different learning styles in mind.

Childbirth International
http://www.childbirthinternational.com

The International Birth and Wellness Project

The Association of Labor Assistants and Childbirth Educators (ALACE) training program is offered by International Birth and Wellness Project (IBWP) and was developed by Midwives. The program is recognized for its holistic, women-centered approach. IBWP childbirth classes provide evidence-based information about the birth process and provide the tools to empower women and their partners to make informed choices throughout pregnancy and birth.

The International Birth and Wellness Project
12 Batchelder Street, Suite 2
Boston, MA 02125 USA
http://www.alace.org
email: info@ibwponline.org
phone: 877-334-4297

Prepared Childbirth Educators, Inc.

Prepared Childbirth Educators, Inc. (PCE) is a national organization of nurse educators. The goal of PCE certification is to recognize excellence in the nurse's specialty role, and contribute to the nurses' professional development.

Prepared Childbirth Educators, Inc.
219 Central Avenue
Hatboro, PA 19040 USA
https://www.childbirtheducation.org
email: info@childbirtheducation.org
phone: 888-344-9972

Academy of Certified Birth Educators

The Academy of Certified Birth Educators (ACBE) is an organization dedicated to providing education and skills for professionals who wish to become certified Childbirth Educators or trained Birth Doulas.

Academy of Certified Birth Educators
815 S. Clairborne Suite 125
Olathe, KS 66062 USA
http://www.acbe.com
phone: 913-782-5116

BirthWorks

BirthWorks embodies the philosophy of developing a woman's self-confidence, trust, and faith in her innate ability to give birth. BirthWorks trains Childbirth Educators and Doulas who in turn provide evidence-based, current information to birthing families through a unique experiential approach that is based upon human values.

BirthWorks
P.O. Box 2045
Medford, NJ 08055 USA
http://www.birthworks.org
email: 888-862-4784
phone: info@birthworks.org

Birthing From Within

Birthing From Within has a Mentor Certification program that teaches and supports professionals through self-study, retreats, workshops and more so they can be effective educators making a difference in the lives of families.

Birthing From Within
PO Box 60259
Santa Barbara, CA 93160 USA
http://www.birthingfromwithin.com
email: contact@birthingfromwithin.com
phone: 805-964-6611

Active Birth

Active Birth teaching effectively empowers women and their partners for natural birthing in a way that is practical and fun.

Active Birth Centre
25 Bickerton Road
London N19 5JT
United Kingdom
http://www.activebirthcentre.com
email: mail@activebirthcentre.com
phone: 020 7281 6760

Calmbirth

Calmbirth empowers pregnant couples with the knowledge and skills to make the birthing process as pleasurable as possible.

Calmbirth
Unit 1, 19 Lyell Street
Mittagong NSW 2575
Australia
http://calmbirth.com.au
email: pjackson@calmbirth.com.au

Bradley Method

The Bradley Method is a system of natural labor techniques in which a woman and her coach play an active part. It is a simple method of increasing self-awareness, teaching a woman how to deal with the stress of labor by tuning into her own body.

American Academy of Husband-Coached Childbirth
Bradley Method
PO Box 5224
Sherman Oaks, CA 91413 USA
http://www.bradleybirth.com
phone: 818-788-6662

HypnoBirthing

HypnoBirthing - The Mongan Method is a unique method of relaxed, natural childbirth education, enhanced by self-hypnosis techniques. The techniques allow women to use their natural instincts to bring about a safer, easier, more comfortable birth.

HypnoBirthing Institute
PO Box 810
Epsom, NH 03234 USA
http://www.hypnobirthing.com
email: hypnobirthing@hypnobirthing.com
phone: 603-798-4781

Hypnobabies

Hynobabies provides classes for parents and training workshops for professionals to teach hypnosis techniques for childbirth.

http://www.hypnobabies.com
phone: 714-952-2229

Aviva Institute

Aviva Institute provides comprehensive and accessible education for Midwives and health care providers, based in their own communities, providing the highest standards of academic excellence, which encompasses a holistic model of integrating mind, body, heart and spirit.

Aviva Institute
1660 South Highway 100 Suite 500
St. Louis Park, MN 55416 USA
https://avivainstitute.org
email: nikkiguerton.aviva@gmail.com
phone: 800-951-4110

Birth Arts International

Birth Arts International trains dynamic wise women Doulas, Postpartum Doulas, Childbirth Educators, Midwife Assistants, and Breastfeeding Educators, in their flexible education programs.

Birth Arts International
501 Lindsey St
Reidsville, NC 27320 USA
http://www.birtharts.com/beced.htm
email: demetria@birtharts.com
phone: 866-303-4372

Birthingway College of Midwifery

Birthingway College of Midwifery offers training programs for Labor Doulas, Postpartum Doulas, Childbirth Educators, Breastfeeding Educators, and Lactation Consultants.

Birthingway has developed a model of caring for women and families during the childbearing year and beyond called the Biodynamic model, in which birth is not only a natural part of human life, but also a necessary part, and one that is intimately connected with what it is to be human.

Birthingway College of Midwifery
12113 SE Foster Road
Portland, OR 97266 USA
http://birthingway.org
email: info@birthingway.edu
phone: 503-760-3131

Brio Birth

Brio Birth childbirth classes offer the perfect mix of time-honored traditions and cutting edge research to empower 21st century moms to give birth with confidence. Brio Birth is made up of a team of top Childbirth Educators and professionals.

Brio Birth
http://www.briobirth.com

Childbirth Education Association of Metropolitan New York

The Childbirth Education Association of Metropolitan New York (CEA/MNY) offers a certification program designed to prepare lay people and health care professionals to teach independent childbirth classes. Their program promotes proper nutrition, exercise, relaxation, consumer activism, family-centered maternity care and breastfeeding.

CEA/MNY
539 West 112th Street, #6C
New York, NY 10025 USA
http://www.ceamny.org
email: tcp@ceamny.org
phone: 917-740-4511

Childbirth Education Association of Orange County

The Childbirth Education Association of Orange County (CEAOC) is committed to professional and community enrichment, providing a forum for professional interaction and continuing education. They offer assistance to others within the Maternal-Child health care community.

CEAOC
PO Box 51074
Irvine, CA 92619 USA
http://www.ceaorangecounty.com
email: ceaorangecounty@yahoo.com

Great Starts

Great Starts offers a training that combines all the best techniques from a wide variety of childbirth education methods with current, evidence-based information on maternity care practices, and concrete tools for how to present the information in an engaging, memorable way.

Great Starts
2200 Rainier Avenue South
Seattle, WA 98144 USA
http://www.parenttrust.org/great-starts-workshop
email: information@parenttrust.org
phone: 206-233-0156

National Association of Childbirth Educators

The National Association of Childbirth Educators Incorporated (NACE) is an Australian organization, which supports a diverse group of professionals committed to preparing and supporting women and their families for birth and early parenting.

National Association of Childbirth Educators
P.O. Box 3211
Mentone East Victoria
Australia
http://www.nace.org.au

Federation of Antenatal Educators

The Federation of Antenatal Educators (FEDANT) is the UK Regulator for Antenatal Educators and providers of Antenatal Education in the United Kingdom. The primary reason for the existence of FEDANT is to protect the public by providing a National Register of validated professionals within the field of Antenatal Education. This provision extends to Antenatal Educators, as well as

Breastfeeding Counselors, Doulas and Complementary Practitioners.

FEDANT
Enterprise House Wales
Ty Menter
Navigation Park
Abercynon
CF45 4SN United Kingdom
http://fedant.org
email: info@fedant.org
phone: 0870 312 0428

Douglas College Perinatal Program

The Douglas College Perinatal Program is recognized as a leader in perinatal education and provides high-quality educational opportunities for those working or planning to work in the perinatal field.

Douglas College Perinatal Program
PO Box 2503
New Westminster, BC
V3L 5B2 Canada
http://www.douglascollege.ca/ce/perinatal
email: lindstromk@douglas.bc.ca
phone: 604-777-6529

Aoraki Polytechnic

Aoraki Polytechnic offers an introductory program, the only one of its kind in New Zealand, providing training to become a Childbirth Educator and to teach prenatal classes to expectant parents in a wide variety of settings.

Aoraki Polytechnic
Private Bag 902
32 Arthur Street
Timaru 7940 New Zealand
http://www.aoraki.ac.nz/programmes/health-education
email: study@aoraki.ac.nz
phone: 0800 426 725

CHRISTIAN CERTIFICATION PROGRAMS

Charis Childbirth

Charis workshops are taught from a Christian perspective, giving God the glory for His marvelous creation and how He so wonderfully created women to bear children.

Charis Childbirth
P.O. Box 6900
North Port, Fl 34290 USA
http://charischildbirth.org
email: administration@charischildbirth.org
phone: 941-441-6410

Apple Tree Christian Childbirth Program

The Apple Tree courses are scripturally and physiologically sound and they will enhance the experiences of pregnancy, birth, breastfeeding, and parenting. Educators and affiliates learn to "gently lead those who are with young" (Isaiah 40:11) into a deeper relationship with God while ministering to each one through the gifts of the Holy Spirit.

Apple Tree Family Ministries
PO Box 759
Artesia, CA 90702 USA
http://www.appletreefamily.org
email: info@appletreefamily.org
phone: 562-925-0149

Cascade Christian Childbirth Association

Cascade Christian Childbirth Association is dedicated to glorifying the Lord Jesus Christ during childbirth through supporting parents, encouraging church ministries, and equipping Christian Childbirth Professionals.

Cascade Christian Childbirth Association
PO Box 3004
Gilbert, AZ 85299 USA
http://www.christianchildbirth.org
email: christianchildbirth@yahoo.com
phone: 480-295-9438

CHILD PASSENGER SAFETY TECHNICIAN

Child Passenger Safety Technicians install car seats according to current safety standards. They also conduct safety checks to make sure that parents have installed car seats properly.

Search words: child passenger safety, car seat installation, car seat safety, car seat inspection

GETTING STARTED

Take the national training course for Child Passenger Safety Technicians. Become familiar with current child restraint laws and best practices to prevent child injuries and fatalities.

ORGANIZATIONS

National Child Passenger Safety Certification Program

The National Child Passenger Safety Board (NCPSB) was established to provide program direction and technical guidance to states, communities and organizations as a means to maintain a credible, standardized child passenger training and certification program.

http://cert.safekids.org

National Highway Traffic Safety Administration

National Highway Traffic Safety Administration carries out the highway safety and consumer programs.

http://www.nhtsa.gov

SeatCheck

SeatCheck is a national campaign to help parents properly secure their children in motor vehicles.

http://www.seatcheck.org

CHILDPROOFING CONSULTANT

Childproof Consultants assist parents in making sure their home is a safe environment for babies and small children. They conduct in home consultations to identify hazards and recommend solutions to remove them. They also sell and install safety products such as fences, childproof locks, alarms and more.

Search words: childproof service, baby proofing service, childproof consultant, baby proof home, child safe home, babyproofer

GETTING STARTED

Childproof Consultants can obtain certification through the International Association for Child Safety (IAFCS). Contact them to learn about the process and requirements for certification.

ORGANIZATIONS

The International Association for Child Safety

The International Association for Child Safety (IAFCS) is a worldwide network of child safety professionals and babyproofers.

http://www.iafcs.org
email: info@iafcs.org

Baby Proofing Directory

Baby Proofing Directory is the most comprehensive source for baby proofing professionals, pool fence installers, baby proofing product manufacturers, child safety products, and home safety advice to keep children safe.

http://www.babyproofingdirectory.com

BUSINESS EXAMPLES

Baby Solutions Childproofing Services

Baby Solutions Childproofing Services strives to help families create a safe physical environment for their children.

http://www.babyproofyourhome.com

Baby Safe Homes

Baby Safe Homes is a professional baby proofing service. They provide families with peace of mind by creating an environment for children to explore, learn and grow safely.

http://www.babysafehomes.com

Baby Proofing Pros

Babyproofing Pros started with a vision of providing San Diego families with the very best baby proofing and home safety services available. They work to safeguard and protect young children from the dangers within the home.

http://www.babyproofingpros.com

Kidproteq

Kidproteq is a professional baby proofing service that addresses the critical need for in-home child proofing, combining the best of child safety products and baby proofing installation.

http://www.kidproteq.com

Child Safety Teacher

Child Safety Teachers work in the local community to teach children and parents safety precautions to prevent falls, drowning, choking, poisoning, fires, etc. They also lead empowerment classes that give kids the skills to stand up against bullying, the knowledge to handle strangers, and awareness of internet dangers.

Search words: child safety teacher, child safety educator, child safety classes, child safety products

Getting Started

Contact organizations that promote child safety and find out what programs they offer and the training requirements to become a Child Safety Teacher. Attend and observe a child safety class. Find a Child Safety Teacher in your community to serve as your mentor.

Organizations

Kidproof

Kidproof is an international organization with branches in many countries. They are committed to providing families with critical child safety resources. Their team is continuously developing new child safety courses, parent seminars, and services that enrich and empower families and keep children safe.

Kidproof USA
17470 N. Pacesetter Way
Scottsdale, AZ 85255 USA
https://www.kidproofusa.com
email: info@kidproofusa.com
phone: 480-305-2049

Safe Kids

Safe Kids USA is a nationwide network of organizations working to prevent unintentional childhood injury, the leading cause of death and disability for children ages 1 to 14. They educate families, provide safety devices to families in need and advocate for better laws to help keep children safe, healthy and out of the emergency room.

Safe Kids Worldwide
1301 Pennsylvania Avenue N.W.
Suite 1000
Washington, DC 20004 USA
http://www.safekids.org
email: worldwide@safekids.org
phone: 202-662-0600

Home Safety Council

The Home Safety Council (HSC) is the only national nonprofit organization solely dedicated to preventing home-related injuries.

Home Safety Council
1250 Eye Street, NW
Suite 1000
Washington, DC 20005 USA
http://www.homesafetycouncil.org
email: info@homesafetycouncil.org
phone: 202-330-4900

Consumer Product Safety Commission

The Consumer Product Safety Commission (CPSC) is committed to protecting consumers and families from products that pose a fire, electrical, chemical, or mechanical hazard and can injure children.

Consumer Product Safety Commission
4330 East West Highway
Bethesda, MD 20814 USA
http://www.cpsc.gov
phone: 301-504-7923

Child Safe Canada

Child Safe Canada provides child safety education. Educators offer a wealth of valuable knowledge, compassion, and caring to students through school, private and community based programs.

Child Safe Canada
#102-6449 Crowchild Trail South West
Calgary, AB, T3E 5R7 Canada
http://www.childsafecanada.com
email: info@childsafecanada.com
phone: 403-202-5900

Health Canada

Health Canada is the federal department that helps Canadians maintain and improve their health, while respecting individual choice.

Health Canada
Address Locator 0900C2
Ottawa, Ontario
K1A 0K9 Canada
http://www.hc-sc.gc.ca/index-eng.php
email: info@hc-sc.gc.ca
phone: 613-957-2991

Kid Safe

Kidsafe is dedicated to preventing unintentional childhood injuries and reducing the resulting deaths and disabilities associated with injuries in children under the age of 15 years.

http://www.kidsafe.com.au

Kids and Traffic

Kids and Traffic works to achieve improvements in young children's safety in the short term and developing safe community attitudes towards road use in the long term by increasing awareness of the need for road safety education for children and their families.

Early Childhood Road Safety Education Program
Level 1, 3 Innovation Road
Macquarie University NSW 2109
Australia
http://www.kidsandtraffic.mq.edu.au
email: kidsandtraffic@mq.edu.au

Child Safe

Childsafe is a campaign of the Child Accident Prevention Foundation of Southern Africa (CAPFSA) and Safe Kids Worldwide. They promote optimal health and development of all children under the age of 18. Childsafe assists in reducing injuries of all severity through research, education, environmental change and recommendations for legislation.

Childsafe South Africa
6th Floor, ICH building
Red Cross Children's Hospital
Rondebosch 7701
Cape Town South Africa
http://www.childsafe.org.za
email: capfsa@pgwc.gov.za
phone: 021 685 5208

I'm Safe, Child Safety Solutions, Inc.

Child Safety Solutions, Inc. brings together the creative energy and successes of parents, child safety experts, community health educators, law enforcement, firefighters, teachers, nurses and pediatricians who are dedicated to teaching children not only how to act safely and responsibly, but to think safely and responsibly.

Child Safety Solutions, Inc.
P.O. Box 1403
Rockland, ME 04841 USA
http://www.imsafe.com
email: info@imsafe.com
phone: 877-669-7233

Juvenile Products Manufacturers Association

Juvenile Products Manufacturers Association (JPMA) is recognized as an organization dedicated to enhancing children's product safety.

Juvenile Products Manufacturers Association
15000 Commerce Parkway, Suite C
Mt. Laurel, NJ 08054 USA
http://www.jpma.org
email: jpma@jpma.org
phone: 856-638-0420

CHILD SLEEP CONSULTANTS

Child Sleep Consultants assist parents to understand and resolve sleeping issues and challenges with their children.

Search words: child sleep consultants, child sleep specialist, sleep consultant qualifications

GETTING STARTED

Research the process that current practicing Sleep Consultants have taken to enter the field. Contact a Sleep Consultant for advice and ask if they would consider mentoring you. Read books about infant sleep. Take related college courses about sleep behaviors. Use your own educational background, training, wisdom and experience caring for children to build a Sleep Consultant practice.

BOOKS

The Baby Sleep Book: The Complete Guide to a Good Night's Rest for the Whole Family by William Sears MD, Martha Sears RN, Robert Sears MD, James Sears MD

The No-Cry Sleep Solution: Gentle Ways to Help Your Baby Sleep Through the Night by Elizabeth Pantley

ഔഇ

Career Journey . . .

Child Sleep Consultant, Deborah Pedrick

How did you get started as a Child Sleep Consultant?

About 14 years ago I gained an interest in children's sleep issues mainly because my pediatrician's specialty was in children's sleep. At the time there were a few books on the subject, but no place for parents to find support and guidance when trying to find solutions to their children's sleep struggles. I started the first Sleep Forum for Children on a major parenting site named Parent Soup where 1,000's of families flocked to voice their options, suggestions, and support. Over a few years I gathered the information and organized it into a simple, easy to follow, website called Famiysleep.com. Familysleep.com now is the go to place for families to get accurate, updated information about how to establish and maintain healthy sleep habits in their children.

Why do you do this work?

Helping families get the rest they all need means a happy family. Helping families achieve this state of well-being is extremely rewarding.

How do you like running a business?

Having your own business is the ultimate job, but really loving what you do, and the outcomes of the work you do, really makes this profession a gem.

What type of training or education did you receive?

At the time when I first became interested in this subject, there were no certifications, so we were all self-taught, however now one can be certified in this field. I am currently teaching an online certification course through the International Maternity Institute.

Do you have any "aha" moments or insights to share about your work?

I would say the biggest aha moments I had, is realizing the large numbers of children and families that are critically overtired and how critical it is to get these families sleeping the way that need to.

What advice can you give to anyone that wishes to become a Child Sleep Consultant?

You have to have a passion for helping others and be a good listener. Being able to communicate with families, break down their problems, respect their parenting philosophies, and work with them to come up with solutions that they feel comfortable with, makes for a successful sleep consultant.

80CB

ORGANIZATIONS

International Maternity Institute

The International Maternity Institute provides training programs, products and services for Childbirth Professionals.

International Maternity Institute
http://www.babyplannerinstitute.com
email: certification@iabpp.com

International Association of Child Sleep Consultants

The International Association of Child Sleep Consultants (IACSC) works to bring together Sleep Consultants from around the world that share a solid foundation of knowledge, ethics, and experiences.

http://www.iacsc.com
phone: 203-559-4674

Naturally Nurturing

Naturally Nurturing is a UK-based private sleep clinic and training centre.

http://www.naturallynurturing.co.uk

Sleep Sense Program

The Sleep Sense Program believes that healthy sleep habits make for healthy children.

Sleep Sense Publishing Inc.
Suite 1151
5557 Dolphin St.
Sechelt, BC
V0N 3A0 Canada
http://www.sleepsense.net
email: dana@sleepsense.net
phone: 206-923-9489

Family Sleep

Family Sleep is a website that focuses on children's sleep issues. They have resources and information to assist parents and professionals.

Family Sleep Services
http://www.familysleep.com
email: deb@familysleep.com
phone: 203-559-4674

EXAMPLE CHILD SLEEP CONSULTANTS

Angelique Millette

Angelique Millette, parent and Family Coach, helps to nurture the innate wisdom and intuition of both parents and children by forging a unique family style that strengthens and supports the family to meet life's challenges.

Angelique Millette
2269 Chestnut Street #389
San Francisco, CA 94123 USA
http://www.angeliquemillette.com
email: info@angeliquemillette.com

Andrea Grace

Andrea Grace offers personal and tailor made approaches to babies' and children's sleep problems, which address the specific reasons for each individual's sleeplessness. Although the solutions are gentle, they are highly effective and safe even for children who have health problems or learning challenges.

http://www.andreagrace.co.uk
phone: 0208 348 6959

Helen Sands

Helen Sands has 30 years' experience working with infants and children in Australia and Canada. She is a dedicated professional, committed to assisting children to learn how to sleep well. She is located in British Columbia, Canada, but assists families all over the world.

http://www.helensands.com
phone: 604-803-0068

Kate Daymond

Kate Daymond has a wealth of knowledge and experience in helping parents and their young children resolve sleep issues.

http://www.katedaymond.co.uk
phone: 07810 440535

Cheeky Chops Consulting

Cheeky Chops Consulting work as Sleep Consultants and Parenting Coaches to make positive changes and help families with sleeping behaviors.

http://www.cheekychops.ca
email: Kim@cheekychops.ca
phone: 778-908-8206

CONFERENCE SPEAKER

Conference Speakers present research, information, and new techniques at conventions, conferences, and seminars. They both educate and inspire Childbirth Professionals. Speakers often travel to various conferences throughout the year to make presentations.

Search words: doula conference, midwifery conference, childbirth educator conference, breastfeeding conference, childbirth conference speaker abstracts, midwifery conference speaker abstracts, breastfeeding conference speaker abstracts

GETTING STARTED

Attend conferences for Childbirth Professionals to learn about the process of speaking at a conference. Seek advice from an experienced Conference Speaker. Submit a speaker abstract to make a presentation at an upcoming conference.

EXAMPLES OF CONFERENCES

Trust Birth Conference

http://www.trustbirthconference.com

DONA International

http://www.dona.org

Midwifery Today

http://www.midwiferytoday.com/conferences

CAPPA

http://www.cappa.net

REACHE Conference

http://www.reache.info

CONFERENCE SPEAKER EXAMPLES

Penny Simkin

Penny Simkin, PT, is a physical therapist who has specialized in childbirth education and labor support. She has written numerous books. Her work consists of childbirth education, birth counseling, and labor support, combined with a busy schedule of courses, conferences and workshops.

http://www.pennysimkin.com/workshop_schedule.htm

Sarah Buckley

Sarah Buckley is a physician with qualifications in obstetrics and family planning. She is the mother of four home-born children, and currently combines full-time motherhood with her work as a writer on pregnancy, birth, and parenting,

http://www.sarahbuckley.com/sarahs-schedule

Dr. Harvey Karp

Dr. Harvey Karp is a pediatrician, child development specialist and Assistant Professor of Pediatrics at the USC School of Medicine.

http://www.happiestbaby.com/dr-karps-appearances

Kittie Frantz

Kittie Frantz, RN, is internationally known for her work developing breastfeeding programs. She blends scholarship with personal experience, having breastfed her own children.

http://www.geddesproduction.com/conference-dates.php

CONSULTANT

Consultants take the success and proven practices they have in building their professional careers and use their experience and knowledge to work with organizations, companies, and businesses to help them develop and grow. Consultants help solve problems and increase work place productivity. They assist with long term planning and with implementing change.

Search words: childbirth hospital consultant, birth consultant, maternity healthcare consultant

GETTING STARTED

Identify and summarize your key professional strengths and successes. Research and investigate if a need exists for your expertise. Create a list of skills and services that you could share within your profession to encourage and facilitate industry growth. Consider what you can share to help your peers reach to the next level, to spur creativity, to inspire innovation, to bring about change.

EXAMPLE CONSULTANTS

New Birth Company

New Birth Company provides boutique consulting and managed services for Free-Standing Birth Centers. They help develop high performing Birth Centers, assist Birth Centers to meet state and national accreditation requirements and optimize performance for long-term sustainability.

New Birth Company
http://www.newbirthcompany.com/opportunities
email: info@newbirthcompany.com
phone: 913-735-4888

Phillips+Fenwick, Inc.

Phillips+Fenwick has professional skills and experience in planning, developing and managing state-of-the-art, consumer-responsive maternity and women's programs in hospitals.

Phillips+Fenwick
631 Park Way
Santa Cruz, CA 95065 USA
http://www.pandf.com
email: celesterph@aol.com
phone: 831-426-1961

Birth Center by Design

Birth Center by Design brings together four women entrepreneurs with over 50 years of combined expertise. Specializing in development, management and marketing, Birth Center by Design helps professionals start, grow or expand their practice.

Birth Center by Design
149 N. Main Street #207
Lakeport, CA 95453 USA
http://birthcenterbydesign.com
email: info@birthcenterbydesign.com
phone: 888-512-4412

Center for the Childbearing Year Doula Programs

Patty Brennan, Director of Center for the Childbearing Year LLC, has been an advocate for childbearing families for over 28 years. She is a grant-writing consultant and Doula program development specialist.

Center for the Childbearing Year
722 Brooks St.
Ann Arbor, MI 48103 USA
http://center4cby.com/doula-programs.html
email: patty@center4cby.com
phone: 734-663-1523

CONTINUING EDUCATION PROVIDER

Continuing Education Providers offer classes, seminars, webinars, workshops, conferences, self-paced classes, and e-Learning for continuing education units or contact hours. The courses they provide are usually approved by a government licensing board or professional association. For example, a state nurses licensing board or Doula association can approve an *"Advanced Labor Support"* class to earn 8 contact hours. Childbirth Professionals that are certified by an organization are usually required to continue to attend courses to keep their skills current. Continuing Education Providers charge registration fees for the courses and give learning opportunities to professionals, providing a valuable service.

Search words: continuing education provider, state licensing continuing education, nurses licensing board, approved contact hour provider, continuing education health care

GETTING STARTED

Contact government agencies or professional associations and find out the process to become an approved Continuing Education Provider. Create courses that meet the criteria of continuing education for Childbirth Professionals as set forth by government agencies or professional associations.

EXAMPLES

CE Broker

CE Broker is the official continuing education system for the Florida Department of Health and the District of Columbia Board of Nursing.

CE Broker
9550 Regency Square Blvd
Suite 1000
Jacksonville, FL 32225 USA
https://www.cebroker.com
email: helpdesk@cebroker.com
phone: 877-434-6323

Western Schools

Western Schools is a leader in healthcare continuing education, offering in-depth, peer-reviewed courses for nursing and behavioral health professionals.

Western Schools
P.O. Box 1930
Brockton, MA 02303
https://www.westernschools.com
email: customerservice@westernschools.com
phone: 800-953-8731

International Childbirth Education Association

International Childbirth Education Association (ICEA) contact hours are approved for traditional face-to-face learning situations and are reviewed based on program content and faculty qualifications. Organizations related to childbirth education can apply for contact hours for face-to-face instruction programs.

http://www.icea.org/content/icea-contact-hours

ICEA
1500 Sunday Drive, Suite 102
Raleigh, NC 27607 USA
http://www.icea.org
email: info@icea.org
phone: 919-863-9487

DONA International

DONA international is a professional organization of that strives to provide high quality training for Doulas and establish quality standards for the birth and postpartum care provided to pregnant women and their families. DONA promotes continuing education for Doulas and provides a strong network between Doulas, families and the medical community.

http://www.dona.org/develop/continuing_ed.php
DONA International
1582 S. Parker Rd, Suite 201
Denver, CO 80231 USA
http://www.dona.org
email: dona@dona.org
phone: 888-788-3662

Eco-Consultant also Greenproofing Consultant

Eco-Consultants evaluate homes, businesses, and organizations to find and recommend steps that can be implemented to save energy, water, and other natural resources, while at the same time protecting the environment and reducing toxicity in the built environment.

Search words: eco-consultant, eco-consultant training, green consultant, eco-friendly, eco-consultant families, eco-consultant service, green proofing

Getting Started

Take a training program that offers certification as an Eco-Consultant or Greenproofing consultant. Contact an Eco-Consultant business owner and ask for an informational meeting to learn about the industry. Research and become familiar with eco-friendly products, companies and practices.

Organizations

International Maternity Institute

The International Maternity Institute Greenproofer certification program is comprehensive and provides practical experience to prepare new and expecting parents for toxic free living and gives individuals the opportunity to work as eco-consultants and earn a solid income.

International Maternity Institute
http://www.babyplannerinstitute.com
email: certification@iabpp.com

Eco Institution

Eco Institution trains Eco-Consultants, who conduct comprehensive surveys in order to identify energy and water saving opportunities and they make recommendations to implement them. The goal is saving the homeowner or business owner money as well as benefiting the environment. It is a process that the Eco Institution encapsulates in the phrase: "Saving Green by Living Green."

Eco Institution
700 West E St Suite #101
San Diego, CA 92101 USA
http://www.ecoinstitution.com
email: info@ecoinstitution.com

EcoEducation Center

The EcoEducation Center is committed to providing education and advocacy for green practices in every community.

http://www.greenconsultanttraining.com
email: office@ecoeducationcenter.com
phone: 330-766-6524

Green Irene

Green Irene provides the training, tools and infrastructure to start an Eco-Consultant business. They provide the infrastructure to run a consulting business such as an e-commerce enabled website and marketing tools.

http://www.greenirene.com/Articles.asp?ID=255
email: ecoconsultant@greenirene.com

Eco-officiency

Eco-officiency provides business advisors who customize and implement sustainability plans that improve a business's environmental footprint.

http://www.eco-officiency.com/resources_eco-consultants.html
email: greenme@eco-officiency.com
phone: 303-517-5300

Ecofirms.org

EcoFirms.org is committed to connect all eco-friendly companies and organizations in the world and provide information about green products and services.

http://www.ecofirms.org

Simcoe Consulting

Simcoe Consulting has a revolutionary training program to help individuals launch an eco-consulting business.

http://www.jimsimcoe.com/services/training-programs
email: jim@jimsimcoe.com
phone: 760-271-7128

EDITOR

An Editor oversees content to produce either an electronic or print magazine, journal, or book. Editors have the ability to set the tone and message of a publication. Decisions made by an Editor can influence readers.

Search words: childbirth journal editor, pregnancy magazine, midwife journal editor, childbirth magazine editor

GETTING STARTED

A great way to begin is by writing an article, story, or essay and submitting it to a magazine or journal that you like. If your writing is not strong, then enroll in a writing class. Take the time to think about what messages you want to get across to an audience. Look for openings in current magazines or journals to serve as an Editor. Start your own magazine or journal in print or electronically.

EXAMPLES

Birthing Magazine

Birthing Magazine is published quarterly and is the source for relevant, current information about pregnancy, birth and parenting alternatives in Alberta, Canada.

Birthing Magazine
c/o Arbour Birth Center
1616 - 20A Street N.W.
Calgary, Alberta, T2N 2L5
Canada
http://www.birthingmagazine.ca
email: admin@birthingmagazine.ca
phone: 403-237-8839

Midwives

Midwives is the official magazine of the Royal College of Midwives, and is published eight times each year.

The Magazine of the Royal College of Midwives
15 Mansfield St,
London, W1G 9NH United Kingdom
http://www.rcm.org.uk/midwives/news
phone: 20 7312 3535

SQUAT Birth Journal

SQUAT is a quarterly publication that is put together by a just a few people who dedicate their time to create a magazine to support healthy and empowering birthing practices.

http://squatbirthjournal.blogspot.com
email: squattingbirth@gmail.com

International Journal of Childbirth Education

This is a peer-reviewed journal and accepts submissions from practitioners, prenatal educators, researchers, and scholars.

http://www.icea.org/content/guide-authors
email: editor@icea.org

Kindred

The Kindred community serves as a gathering place for families to explore and share their experiences of writing a new story of childhood, motherhood, fatherhood and the ever changing and evolving adventure of being fully human.

Kindred
P.O. Box 3653
Williamsburg, VA 23187 USA
http://www.kindredcommunity.com
email: info@familiesforconsciousliving.org
phone: 757-566-7224

Journal of Perinatal Education

The *Journal of Perinatal Education* (JPE) is a peer-reviewed journal specifically for Childbirth Educators. JPE advances the knowledge of aspiring and seasoned educators through evidence-based articles.

http://www.ncbi.nlm.nih.gov/pmc/journals/359

FERTILITY AWARENESS TEACHER ALSO NATURAL FAMILY PLANNING TEACHER

Fertility Awareness Teachers provide a holistic approach to birth control educating women about alternative methods that are noninvasive, do not use synthetic hormones, artificial devices, or require surgery. They help women become more knowledgeable about their bodies and their reproductive and sexual health.

Search words: fertility awareness teacher, fertility awareness educator, fertility awareness, alternative birth control class, natural family planning, natural family planning teacher training

GETTING STARTED

Read and learn about fertility awareness and natural family planning philosophy and techniques. If possible, start using some of the methods yourself. Contact fertility awareness and natural family planning organizations to learn about their training requirements. Take a training workshop or online class. Find a practitioner to serve as your mentor.

ఴಂఆ

Career Journey ...

Natural Fertility Educator, Robyn Fausett

How did you get started as a Natural Fertility Educator?

I got started as an experienced Registered General Nurse, specialized in fertility and having worked in Assisted Conception Units in London and New Zealand, I am very aware of the high tech treatments available to couples and women seeking assisted reproductive care. I also discovered that many women have little to no knowledge of their reproductive systems and how to utilize this knowledge for fertility (whether to avoid or enhance conception).

This knowledge can save time, worry and costly investigations in the quest of getting pregnant; it alerts women very quickly to potential fertility issues and provides a level of empowerment to those taught. They are able to recognize what their body is telling them.

In terms of using the method for contraception, it allows women and their partners to have choices and work as a partnership in taking responsibility. It is a greener option for the body and the environment, is non-invasive with no side effects all whilst being as effective as the mini-pill (at least 98% effective).

I was inspired to train as a Natural Fertility Educator. Once qualified I initially saw clients in their own home before finding clinic space in a couple of strategic areas of Auckland. In addition to business hours, I generally offer a before and after work service a couple of times a week, as it is great to be able to see women and their partners together.

Why do you do this work? What do you enjoy?

I really enjoy teaching and contributing to couples' feeling empowered to make informed choices about their health and lifestyle. It is always fantastic to hear from a couple that they are pregnant and just as rewarding hearing from clients that they have learnt something new that contributes to their lifestyle. The positive response from clients makes this profession a pleasure.

I also teach PreConception care, which has an ongoing positive effect on the next generation. In addition, I teach Positive Puberty and Fertility Awareness at schools which is incredibly rewarding. In my opinion, the earlier education can begin, if taught at an age appropriate level, the better.

How do you like running a business? What business advice can you share?

Running my own business has its positives and negatives for me. On the positive side, it allows me autonomy, flexibility and choices around the hours that I work. It also gives me space to think outside the square and expand services, and so forth. However, the constant promotion of services can be time consuming and overwhelming in the beginning. In the initial set up of a business, there are expenses and apprehension as to whether the business will be sustainable. It has taken me a while to decide how and where to advertise.

My advice is: realize that it takes time to build a business, and speculate to accumulate, but sensibly! Offer a few free 'talks' to GPs and organizations to get the word out.

Also, it is well worth understanding the legal and financial aspects of having your own company. Have a business plan and do your research.

What type of training or education did you receive?

I trained for about eight months, part-time at about five hours each week, (it can take up to a year) which involved some distance learning, many assessed assignments, two full weeks in college, delivering an informative 'talk' to a group and two supervised/recorded clients (four sessions).

The criteria for entry does not rely on a medical background such as nursing. Each application is screened individually and on its own merits, some Fertility Educators are Naturopaths, etc. Upon qualifying, in New Zealand, educators then work through their own business, building their own client base whilst being accredited to Natural Fertility New Zealand (NFNZ), and abiding by NFNZ's framework, which includes an amount of study each year (continuing medical education), a yearly conference, and regular auditing.

Do you have any "aha" moments or insights to share about your work?

Being able to listen and establish trust is incredibly important. On many occasions a woman (and her partner) express that they have never felt really 'heard' before. There can be myths and fears that need explaining. Also, the subject can be very personal and 'embarrassing' for some individuals, so creating a confidential and safe environment is key.

What advice can you give to anyone that wishes to become a Natural Fertility Educator?

Go do it! If you have an interest and a background in the health of women and/or fertility, invest in good training, and also, in an organization who will continue to offer further education, business planning, and support.

ℰℭℜ

ORGANIZATIONS

American Academy of FertilityCare Professionals

The American Academy of FertilityCare Professionals works to foster, advance, and promote the Creighton Model FertilityCare System through service, education, leadership, and research.

American Academy of FertilityCare Professionals
11700 Studt Ave., Suite C
St. Louis, MO 63141 USA
http://www.aafcp.org
phone: 402-489-3733

Natural Fertility New Zealand

Natural Fertility New Zealand (NFNZ) is a national organization of trained and continuously up-dated Fertility Educators who have undergone an extensive training program in natural fertility management. Fertility Educators provide education on fertility awareness and teach natural fertility management to individuals, couples, and health professionals.

Natural Fertility New Zealand
P O Box 10-617
The Terrace
Wellington 6143
New Zealand
http://www.naturalfertility.co.nz
email: info@naturalfertility.co.nz

Fertility Awareness Network

The Fertility Awareness Network (FAN) is an educational coalition of teachers of Fertility Awareness Method (FAM). They promote the knowledge and practice of FAM and Natural Family Planning (NFP) among the public.

http://www.fertaware.com/professionals.html#top
email: admin@fertaware.com
phone: 212-475-4490

The Garden of Fertility

The Garden of Fertility provides information and training for Fertility Awareness Teachers and teachers of Natural Family Planning.

The Garden of Fertility
P.O. Box 6574
Santa Fe, NM 87502 USA
http://www.gardenoffertility.com/teaching.shtml
email: katiesinger@gardenoffertility.com

Justisse Healthworks for Women

Justisse Holistic Reproductive Health Practitioners (HRHPs) are highly trained in areas including reproductive anatomy, fertility awareness, sexuality, birth control, fertility and counseling. Perhaps, most importantly, they are guided by an ethic that respects a woman's ultimate right to make her own reproductive and life choices.

Justisse Healthworks for Women
10145 - 81 Ave
Edmonton, AB
Canada T6E 1W9
http://www.justisse.ca
email: info@justisse.ca
phone: 780-420-0877

HypnoBirthing Fertility Consultant

The HypnoBirthing Fertility Consultant certification program trains consultants to help families understand their options when choosing medically assisted conception or alternative methods. Consultants learn about the causes of infertility and how stress can affect the hormonal balance of the body, interfering with conception.

HypnoBirthing Institute
PO Box 810
Epsom, NH 03234
http://www.hypnobirthing.com/fertilityconsultant.htm
email: hypnobirthing@hypnobirthing.com
phone: 603-798-4781

Natural Family Planning International

Natural Family Planning International works to promote and teach chastity and natural family planning.

NFP International
P. O. Box 11216
Cincinnati, OH 45211 USA
http://www.nfpandmore.org
email: nfpandmore@nfpandmore.org

Billings Ovulation Method Association

The Billings Ovulation Method is a simple yet scientific method of Natural Family Planning.

Billings Ovulation Method Association
PO Box 2135 St
Cloud, MN 56302 USA
http://www.boma-usa.org
email: boma-usa@msn.com
phone: 651-699-8139

Couple to Couple League International

The Couple to Couple League (CCL) is a volunteer organization dedicated to promoting and teaching fertility awareness and natural family planning to married and engaged couples.

Couple to Couple League International
P.O. Box 111184
Cincinnati, OH 45211 USA
http://ccli.org
phone: 513-471-2000

Institute for Natural Family Planning

The Marquette University College of Nursing Institute for Natural Family Planning (INFP) works to provide professional education, research and service in Natural Family Planning (NFP).

Marquette University College of Nursing
Institute for Natural Family Planning
P.O. Box 1881
Milwaukee, WI 53201 USA
http://nfp.marquette.edu/about.php
email: mary.schneider@mu.edu
phone: 414-288-3854

FILMMAKER

Filmmakers show us childbirth from an educational, historical or reality based perspective. Many documentaries are being created that reflect medical policies and practices that are not evidence-based and negatively affect new families. Some Filmmakers specialize in one area of childbirth such as breastfeeding or prenatal yoga exercises; these films are made as instructional and informational DVDs.

Search words: birth films, birth film festival, childbirth film festival, childbirth documentary, midwife film, natural birth film

GETTING STARTED

Watch films or DVDs about the childbirth experience and related subjects. Contact Filmmakers to learn about their process and motivation. Take film or video production classes. Earn a certificate or degree as a Filmmaker. Complete an internship with Filmmakers who specialize in childbirth films. Make a film about childbirth and enter it in a Birth Film Festival.

ℰℭ

Career Journey ...

Filmmaker, Toni Harman

How did you get started as a Filmmaker?

After graduating from the London Film School, I worked full-time as a Producer/ Director making documentaries and factual entertainment programs. Fast-forward a few years and I set up my own independent production company with my partner Alex

Wakeford so that we could make our own short films, documentaries and feature film projects. After having a child four years ago, recently we've focused on making films about birth. Right now, our passion project is a cross-media film project about the politics of birth ONE WORLD BIRTH.

Why do you do this work? What do you enjoy?

I love making films. Many Midwives, Doulas and Birth Educators say they have a calling for birth. For me, I had a calling for film! I love thinking of an idea, then grabbing the camera and going out filming. Then coming back to our edit suite and crafting the story together - hours will go past and I won't notice, I am so involved in what I am doing. And I particularly love making films about birth. There is something magical about birth that is transformative, beautiful and wonderful. Yet the magic of birth seems to be lost for so many people - my mission is to raise awareness of that magic within the mainstream population in order to bring about change.

How do you like running a business? What business advice can you share?

I enjoy the entrepreneurial side of business. Having our own production company, I like the freedom to create new products and new films. However, the downside is that it is difficult to make money in the birth world. All the money we have raised from the sale of our previous birth films, "Doula!" and "Real Birth Stories", has gone into our current birth project, ONE WORLD BIRTH, which has made things difficult for us financially. Our long-term business objective is to have enough money to sustain ourselves; we're not in this to become rich. We want to change the world! So my advice is to think strategically - to work out where you want to be and then work backwards to where you are now!

What type of training or education did you receive?

After my University degree, I trained at the London Film School for two years. The training covered all aspects of filmmaking; from script writing, to camera, sound, editing, directing and producing, so when I graduated, I had a pretty good working knowledge of technical skills.

Do you have any "aha" moments or insights to share about your work?

Filmmaking requires creativity, technical knowledge, communication skills, and above all, it requires passion and commitment. My "aha" moment was realizing that filmmaking is actually really hard work and sometimes, when the chips are down and things aren't going right, the only thing that keeps you going is your passion and your commitment to that passion. Someone once told me that if you can walk away from making a film, don't just walk, run! And that is absolutely true. For filmmaking drains you financially, physically and emotionally and yet, if you truly believe in the importance of what you are doing, then you will keep going, and that's what I love. There is something deep inside me that drives me forward to make bigger and hopefully better films.

What advice can you give to anyone that wishes to become a Filmmaker?

With high-quality video cameras and editing equipment so affordable right now, I would suggest to anyone who wants to become a Filmmaker that they grab a camera and start making films as soon and as often as they can. The more films you make, the more mistakes you make. But also, the more you learn from those mistakes and so you never make those mistakes again! So go out, start shooting, start editing, start directing and if you need help, then don't be afraid to ask!

ഇൽരു

RESOURCES

Women in Film and Video

Women in Film and Video (WIFV) strives to advance the professional development and achievement for women working in all areas of film, television, video, multimedia and related disciplines.

Women in Film & Video
3628 12th Street, NE
Second Floor
Washington, DC 20017 USA
http://www.wifv.org
email: membership@wifv.org
phone: 202-429-9438

Center for Social Media

The Center for Social Media showcases and analyzes media for public knowledge and action—media made by, for, and with the public to address shared problems. They especially pay attention to the evolution of documentary film and video in a digital era.

Center for Social Media
3201 New Mexico Ave
NW, Suite 330
Washington, DC 20016 USA
http://www.centerforsocialmedia.org
email: socialmedia@american.edu
phone: 202-885-3107

International Documentary Association

The International Documentary Association (IDA) promotes nonfiction filmmakers, and is dedicated to increasing public awareness for the documentary genre.

International Documentary Association
1201 West 5th Street, Suite M270
Los Angeles, CA 90017 USA
http://www.documentary.org
phone: 213-534-3600

University Film Producers Association

The University Film Producers Association (UFVA) is an international organization where media production and writing meets the history, theory and criticism of the media.

http://www.ufva.org
email: ufvahome@gmail.com
phone: 866-647-8382

The Independent

The Independent has been the leading source of information for independent, grassroots, and activist media-makers, providing inspiration and information for their films and video projects, as well as creating connections to the larger independent media community.

Independent Media Publications
PO Box 391620
Cambridge, MA 02139 USA
http://www.aivf.org
email: info@independent-magazine.org
phone: 877-513-7400

CHILDBIRTH FILM EXAMPLES

One World Birth

One World Birth is a free online video resource for Childbirth Professionals, activists and parents who want to keep their finger on the pulse of birth around the globe today. The world's birth experts discuss current topics and research in short, bite-sized video clips that are based upon a theme each month.

http://www.oneworldbirth.net

Doula Film

The Doula is a documentary-style film about the work of birth and postnatal Doulas. The film intimately captures in close-up detail the practical and emotional support given to the parents by their Doula at each stage of their unique birthing journey.

http://doulafilm.com
email: info@altofilms.com

The Connected Baby

The Connected Baby explains how babies arrive already connected to other people. Science shows babies have brains already tuned into people's body rhythms, vocal tones, and movements making them much more communicative and sophisticated than they have been credited.

http://www.theconnectedbaby.org

Real Birth Stories

Real Birth Stories is a 3 DVD box set of true life stories told by first time parents.

http://realbirthstories.com

Sage Femme

Sage Femme sells and produces a wide range of childbirth films. They work to increase awareness of the benefits of natural childbirth and homebirth by sharing empowering information with women, families and the healthcare community.

http://www.sagefemme.com

Motherbaby International Film Festival

The Motherbaby International Film Festival (MIFF) is a showcase of the best and most amazing films about pregnancy, birth and babies. MIFF screens only soul nourishing, eye opening films from around the world.

http://www.sagefemme.com/miff.html

Birth Talk Productions

Birth Talk Productions produced a film that celebrates lesbian families and shares about their experience to have children from choosing a sperm donor through postpartum.

http://productions.birthtalk.com
email: ami@birthtalk.com

U & MI Filmmakers

U & MI Filmmakers produced a film about their childbirth experience, called *Birth Dialogue* The film shows the process they went through to decide to have a homebirth. They also produce other birth films.

http://www.u-mi.com (A Hebrew website translate at
http://translate.google.com)
email: info@u-mi.com

Skwatta Camp Productions

Shwatta Camp Productions follows Robin Lim a Midwife into the
trenches of her work in Bali, Indonesia.

http://www.skwattacamp.com

Dusty's Big Day Out

Dusty's Big Day Out produced by Di Diddle, a Childbirth Educator,
follows the labor and birth of baby Dusty. The film shows how
women can deal with pain and how the people around them can
provide support.

http://www.birtheducation.com.au/dvd.htm
email: di@birtheducation.com.au

Birthing Sense

Leanne Cummins, a Midwife and Childbirth Educator, assembled a
team of 26 experts from around Australia to make the Birthing
Sense DVD series, an informative prenatal and birth education class
for in home use.

http://www.birthingsense.com
email: leanne@birthingsense.com

Geddes Productions

Geddes Productions produces breastfeeding DVDs to teach families
and professionals techniques and provide current evidence-based
information.

Geddes Productions
PO BOX 41761
Los Angeles, CA 90041 USA
http://www.geddesproduction.com
email: orders@geddesproduction.com
phone: 323-344-8045

Giving Birth

The film *Giving Birth* by Suzanne Arms contrasts the medical model for birth with the biological or midwifery model. It has inspired thousands of women and men to make different choices about how to bring their baby into the world.

Suzanne Arms Presents
P.O. Box 1040
Bayfield, CO 81122 USA
http://www.suzannearms.com/OurStore/videos
email: suzanne@suzannearms.com
phone: 970-884-4005

Laboring Under An Illusion

In the film, *Laboring Under An Illusion*, anthropologist Vicki Elson explores media-generated myths about childbirth. As a Childbirth Educator for 25 years, she observes daily how our culture affects our birth experiences.

http://birth-media.com

Mother's Advocate

Mother's Advocate is dedicated to helping families have the healthiest, safest, most satisfying birth possible. They offer free video clips and print materials to educate and inform the public.

http://injoyvideos.com/mothersadvocate/videos.html

Born in the USA

Born in the USA shows three birth caregivers—an obstetrician, a nurse-midwife, and a licensed homebirth Midwife—each with dramatically different ideas about what constitutes best care for birthing women. The film shows how medical professionals that care for pregnant women see their work and what factors such as medical, legal, and cultural work to influence a woman as she gives birth.

PatchWorks Films
663 7th Avenue
San Francisco, CA 94118 USA
http://www.patchworksfilms.net/films/born_usa.html
email: info@patchworksfilms.net

The Business of Being Born

The Business of Being Born explores the role profit plays in the United States modern maternity care system.

http://www.thebusinessofbeingborn.com

Orgasmic Birth

Debra Pascali-Bonaro is producer and director of the films *Orgasmic Birth* and *Organic Birth*, two films documenting the sensual and life changing aspects of undisturbed childbirth.

http://www.orgasmicbirth.com

InJoy Videos

InJoy Videos produces and sells childbirth education DVDs for professionals to use in teaching families about pregnancy, birth, newborn care, and parenting.

InJoy Birth & Parenting Education
7107 La Vista Place
Longmont, CO 80503 USA
http://injoyvideos.com
phone: 303-447-2082

FULL SPECTRUM DOULA

A Full Spectrum Doula provides care and support to women throughout the range of the reproductive health cycle. They assist women through birth, abortion, adoption, surrogacy, and unintentional pregnancy loss. Full Spectrum Doulas work to ensure that women have positive experiences and support through all their reproductive health choices.

Search words: full spectrum doula, abortion doula, adoption doula, loss doula

GETTING STARTED

Contact a Full Spectrum Doula organization to learn about their training program. Find a Full Spectrum Doula that can give you advice and mentor you. Gain experience by volunteering as a Full Spectrum Doula at a women's health center in your area.

RESOURCES

Read this narrative, http://tiny.cc/doulastory, from Miriam Zoila Pérez about her experience as an Abortion Doula.

ORGANIZATIONS

The Doula Project

The Doula Project works to affect change on an individual and societal level by providing an advanced model of alternative reproductive health care so that women not only have a positive abortion or birth experience but also feel empowered to become advocates for their own sexual and reproductive health for the rest of their lives.

http://www.doulaproject.org

Full Spectrum Doulas

Full Spectrum Doulas is a collective of Doulas and Reproductive Justice Advocates who work throughout the Pacific Northwest to bring the Doula model of care to people across the full spectrum of pregnancy experiences, including abortion, adoption, surrogacy, miscarriage and stillbirth.

Full Spectrum Doulas
PO Box 28138
Seattle, WA 98118 USA
http://www.fullspectrumdoulas.org
email: sea@fullspectrumdoulas.org

Open Umbrella Collective

The Open Umbrella Collective believes each person's unique pregnancy experience should be respected and supported. Their work as Doulas fosters a culture that values individuals, families, and the strength found in community. As Full Spectrum Doulas, they offer support to women and families regardless of the pregnancy outcome.

Open Umbrella Collective
http://openumbrellacollective.yolasite.com
email: openumbrellacollective@gmail.com
phone: 828-738-6736

Full Spectrum Doula Network

Full Spectrum Doula Network is a networking community for Full Spectrum Doulas. They support non-mainstream views in the Doula community.

http://www.fullspectrumdoulanetwork.org

Loss Doulas International

Loss Doulas International certifies Loss Doulas who offer compassionate and informed support to women and their families.

Loss Doulas International
P.O. Box 46758
Kansas City, MO 64188 USA
http://lossdoulasinternational.com
email: info@lossdoulasinternational.com

HENNA BELLY DESIGN ARTIST

Henna Belly Design Artists pamper pregnant women and assist them in celebrating a rite of passage, becoming a mother and giving birth to a child. The artists paint beautiful designs upon pregnant bellies, feet, or hands. The tradition of using henna, a paste made from the leaves of the henna plant *lawsonia inermis*, to paint beautiful designs and bring the wearer good luck dates back over 5,000 years.

Search words: henna belly artist, henna artist training, henna pregnant belly, henna artist business, henna certification workshop

GETTING STARTED

Use the internet to search and learn as much as you can about the technique, art, and business of henna design. Locate a Henna Belly Design Artist that can train you. Take a workshop about the art of henna. Be informed about the toxic chemicals that should not be used in henna paste.

ಬಿಆ

Career Journey ...

Henna Belly Design Artist, Khadija Dawn Carryl

How did you get started as a Henna Belly Design Artist?

I am an artist at heart, and love drawing. Henna Body Art was my artistic outlet. I started doing prenatal belly art due to my love of pregnancy, and childbirth. It's a special time in a person's life, a time to adorn, embrace, and love yourself and your new baby to come.

Why do you do this work? What do you enjoy?

I do this work because I am also able to earn an income from doing what I love. I enjoy all aspects of Henna Body Art and the people I get to meet.

How do you like running a business? What business advice can you share?

I've been running Henna Sooq since 2005. As a businesswoman, I'd recommend a person develop an amazing, well organized website that can easily attract clients, and include plenty of clear, beautiful photos. You may need to get yourself a good camera or hire a professional to take photos for you of your work. Be who you are, and let that radiate onto others. People know a good person when they meet them.

What type of training or education did you receive?

With henna, there is no formal training here in North America. There are opportunities to teach others, which I do now. I did take an introduction to Henna Body Art class to learn the very basics. However, I am mostly self-taught.

Do you have any "aha" moments or insights to share about your work?

At about 3-4 years into doing Henna Body Art, I finally felt that I had gained a lot of confidence and my own style. It was my moment of satisfaction in myself as an artist.

What advice can you give to anyone that wishes to become a Henna Belly Design Artist?

I recommend they take a Henna Body Art workshop, and attend a henna conference if they're able to, as this is where a good foundation starts in Henna Body Art.

Anything else you would like to share?

I am also a mother of six, and used Midwives with all of my children. I specialize in natural hair care. We work together at Henna Sooq, our family owned business.

ဆಿಧ

ORGANIZATIONS

International Certification for Natural Henna Arts

The International Certification for Natural Henna Arts (ICNHA) is a volunteer peer assessment for Henna Artists to certify they use only natural, chemical free henna and understand the cultural, traditional uses of henna.

http://icnha.org

Riffat Henna Training

Riffat, an international Henna Artist, offers the ultimate henna training program to share her years of creative skills and knowledge. Individuals learn the secrets of the ancient art form and master the skills of applying freehand Mehndi designs and rolling their own cones.

http://www.hennatraining.co.uk
email: riffat184@hotmail.com

Henna by Holly

Holly has been instrumental in promoting and supporting the growth of henna artistry in Canada. As a formally trained graphic designer and fine artist, she has always been an advocate for self-expression through body art.

http://www.hennabyholly.com/lessons.html
email: info@hennabyholly.com

Henna Tribe

The Henna Tribe is a professional network and informational resource for individuals interested in the ancient art of henna.

http://hennatribe.org
email: info@hennatribe.org

The Henna Page

The Henna Page is an educational resource devoted to the art of henna, and also the history, tradition, technique, and science of henna.

http://www.hennapage.com

EXAMPLE HENNA BELLY ARTISTS

Henna Caravan

Henna Caravan specializes in custom henna designs inspired by the art of the African and European continents.

http://www.hennacaravan.com/pregnancy.html
email: info@hennacaravan.com
phone: 805-248-7413

Henna Sooq

Henna Sooq sells henna products, they teach workshops, and provide henna design services.

http://www.hennasooq.com/prenatal-belly-art
email: info@hennasooq.com
phone: 410-579-4543

The Original Henna Company

The Original Henna Company provides henna design services, sells products, and teaches classes.

The Original Henna Company
1130 Yale St.
Houston, TX 77008 USA
http://www.hennacompany.com
phone: 281-630-8389

Belly Beautiful

Belly Beautiful provides in-home pregnancy Henna Body Art sessions. They create unique belly designs that reflect a woman's feelings about pregnancy, birth, and motherhood.

Belly Beautiful
560 Little Lake Drive
Ann Arbor, MI 48103 USA
http://www.bellybeautifulhenna.com
email: Keleigh@BellyBeautifulHenna.com
phone: 734-218-0348

Karen Weiss

Karen Weiss is a multimedia artist working as a painter, photographer, jewelry designer and body artist. She loves doing body art and the connection it brings between people. She is grateful to make a living and support her family as a full-time artist. She encourages everyone to pursue dreams.

http://www.hennatattoosdallas.com/Prenatal.htm
email: karenweissnet@gmail.com
phone: 972-661-3092

Birthing Body

Amy at Birthing Body is an experienced professional Henna Artist. She does henna designs upon pregnant women. She advocates henna as one of the gentlest things women can put on their skin during pregnancy, and states that it is a beautiful way to celebrate the life growing inside.

http://birthingbody.org/services-i-offer/henna-belly-art
phone: 720-771-9573

Aurora Mehndi

Bridget of Aurora Mehndi is a Henna Artist that trains professionals across the country on the safe use of henna and essential oils during pregnancy.

http://www.auroramehndi.com/bellies.html
email: bridget@auroramehndi.com
phone: 847-800-8984

INFANT MASSAGE INSTRUCTOR

Infant Massage Instructors give parents the skills to massage their babies providing nurturing and increasing the parental bond. Massage has many benefits, decreasing crying and stress in babies and small children, improving sleep, digestion, and weight gain. Infant Massage Instructors offer ongoing classes to new parents building community and providing support. They assist parents and babies to grow in their relationships through massage.

Search words: infant massage instructor, infant massage certification, infant massage class

GETTING STARTED

Enroll in a training course to become an Infant Massage Instructor. Seek out an Infant Massage Instructor in your community to mentor you. Read books and watch DVDs about infant massage.

೮ಾ೧೩

Career Journey ...

Infant Massage Instructor, Sharon Melvin

How did you get started as an Infant Massage Instructor?

As a Massage Therapist, my clients were having babies and were interested in how to give their baby a massage and what the benefits could be. Then, moving to Calgary I started to teach Self Massage classes for the (then) Calgary Grace Women's Hospital. It seemed like the perfect setting to try out a talk on baby massage in their Pre and Postnatal classes. There were about six couples and their babies and the couples were very interested in baby massage. What won me over was how one little baby totally relaxed under his parent's scalp massage; it was like everyone in the room could feel his relaxation and all of us relaxed as well. After that talk, I knew I wanted to become a Certified Infant Massage Instructor. About a year later a training instructor came up from the United States and taught the course to about 10 of us, the first course of its kind in Alberta. That was in 1993 and I have been teaching infant massage ever since in all kinds of settings: hospitals, private organizations, conferences, and in homes.

Why do you do this work? What do you enjoy?

I teach infant massage because I love it. The whole area of touch and how we grow

and develop is fascinating to me, there is always new research coming out to keep up on. It is very satisfying to help a parent or caregiver, and babies come together and bond, connecting in a very beautiful way through the ancient art of baby massage.

How do you like running a business?

Running a business has a lot of challenges, but when you are inspired and love what you do, all of it can be fun, and I enjoy the freedom of when and where I teach. I very much enjoy the whole process of having a vision, (i.e. a new workshop idea), and then developing the idea, marketing it, and eventually teaching it. It can be a very creative process.

What type of training or education did you receive?

I became a Certified Massage Practitioner through Grant MacEwan College in Edmonton, then went on to become a

Holistic Health Practioner from a school in California. Then, in 1993, I became a CIMI, or Certified Infant Massage Instructor, through the International Association of Infant Massage.

Do you have any "aha" moments or insights to share about your work?

This is the kind of work you do if you have a certain connection to it, if it is your heart's calling, that is the only way it works

What advice can you give to anyone that wishes to become an Infant Massage Instructor?

It would be very helpful to find out where you could visit and experience some infant massage classes to see if it feels like something you would like to do. Infant Massage classes are often noisy and chaotic and not everyone would feel comfortable with that. You could also interview an Infant Massage Instructor to find out why they do it and what they like about it.

Anything else you would like to share?

Often, we have the idea that "experts" do a better job at something than we do. When it comes to baby massage, I always tell parents that "you are the expert" when it comes to massaging their babies. The instructor can give them the technique and the tools, but they are the ones who have the relationship, the love, and care for their child. That is a big part of infant massage, contributing to the many known and researched benefits of calming, loving, touch.

෨෬

ORGANIZATIONS

International Association of Infant Massage

The International Association of Infant Massage (IAIM) believes that by fostering and encouraging infant massage and other cultural traditions, which enhance the parent bond, and by helping create more family-centered values, we will begin to see whole generations expressing more compassion toward and responsibility for their fellow human beings.

The International Association of Infant Massage
Heidenstams Gata 9
S-422 47 Hisings Backa
Sweden
http://iaim.net

Infant Massage USA

Infant Massage USA educators are trained to empower families as the caregivers and nurturers of their children. A baby's first language is touch, and massage is a foundation to establish a strong bond and attachment.

Infant Massage USA
7481 Huntsman Blvd #635
Springfield, VA 22153 USA
http://www.infantmassageusa.org
email: general.info@infantmassageusa.org
phone: 703-455-3455

International Loving Touch Foundation

International Loving Touch Foundation offers training for professionals that work with families and parents with infants and young children in the art of infant massage.

Loving Touch Headquarters
2122 SE Division Street
Portland, Oregon 97292 USA
http://www.lovingtouch.com
email: info@lovingtouch.com
phone: 503-253-8482

Liddle Kidz

Liddle Kidz Foundation is committed to furthering the development of touch therapy services for vulnerable and underserved populations internationally. They strive to address the critical tactile needs of underserved children by working directly with their families and healthcare providers in pediatric hospitals, hospices, and orphanages to provide comprehensive nurturing services, consultation, education, and program development.

http://www.liddlekidz.com
email: info@liddlekidz.com
phone: 818-209-1918

Baby's First Massage

Baby's First Massage is committed to helping new parents everywhere learn how to massage their babies as soon after birth as possible.

http://www.babysfirstmassage.com
email: teresa@babysfirstmassage.com

The Heart Touch Project

The Heart Touch Project is an organization dedicated to the training of individuals to bring compassionate and healing touch to those that are homebound or hospitalized.

The Heart Touch Project
3400 Airport Avenue, Suite 42
Santa Monica, CA 90405 USA
http://www.hearttouch.org
phone: 310-391-2558

International Institute of Infant Massage

The International Institute of Infant Massage provides workshops designed to train instructors to teach infant touch and massage to parents and caregivers.

International Institute of Infant Massage
605 Bledsoe Rd NW
Albuquerque, NM 87107 USA
http://infantmassageinstitute.com
email: info@infantmassage.com
phone: 505-341-9381

Healthy Family Living

Healthy Family Living (HFL) Certified Instructors of Infant Massage (CIIM), enjoy teaching and empowering families to express nurturing parenting practices using interactive massage skills with their children. HFL's program and teaching are inclusive of principles that support emotional attunement and bonding.

Healthy Family Living
Kalena Babeshoff
153 Theodor Lane
Sonoma, CA 95476 USA
http://www.healthyfamily.org/pub/htdocs/imt
email: info@healthyfamily.org
phone: 707-996-3545

INFANT MUSIC TEACHER

Infant Music Teachers provide classes for babies, young children, and parents to build a lifelong musical foundation. Teachers believe that all children have musical abilities and benefit from early childhood musical play and discovery. Through movement and music, children are taught to sing in tune and keep an accurate beat.

Search words: infant music teacher, infant music classes, baby music classes, child music classes

GETTING STARTED

Some musical ability and skill are required to teach music classes. Attending a teacher training workshop is a good place to learn the basics of teaching music to young children and parents. Find infant music classes in your community to observe; ask the instructor if they would be willing to serve as your mentor.

℘℘

Career Journey ...

Kindermusik Educator, Sunny Kira, M.A.

How did you get started as a Kindermusik Educator?

I first heard about Kindermusik through my sister who is a piano teacher. At the time, I was a full time elementary school teacher and was busy teaching children their 3 R's. One day my sister asked me to come observe her Kindermusik class of preschoolers. I immediately fell in love with the program and her class! That's when I decided I wanted to do this myself. I left the public school system five years ago to become a licensed Kindermusik educator and never looked back.

Why do you do this work? What do you enjoy?

I love the connections that are made through the Kindermusik program, whether it's a parent to child connection; child-to-child; or parent-to-parent. We create an incredible community through music, and every day I am affirmed of the power music has on the human soul. On a more educational perspective, children come away from the program able to make wonderful connections in the realm of musical, social, emotional, cognitive, physical and linguistic learning. And it's just fun!

How do you like running a business? What business advice can you share?

I love the multitasking aspect of running your own business. There's never a dull moment as there's always something to be done. It's a constant work in progress but the best part is seeing your business grow, develop and transform on a daily basis.

My advice to others would be to just be persistent and determined! Believe in what you do and work hard to offer the best service that you can. I always consider it a privilege to be able to work with the families I have and I value them.

What type of training or education did you receive?

I have a Kindermusik license from Kindermusik International, Simply Music Piano License, Multiple Subject Credential from the State of California, Mastership Level 1 in Early Child Music from The Gordon Institute of Music Learning (GIML), a Bachelor's degree from UC San Diego, a Master's degree in TESOL, and a love of music through dance and years of singing in various choirs, both church and community-based.

Do you have any "aha" moments or insights to share about your work?

I think for me the biggest "aha" moment is the realization that you can't control everything and in fact when you let go, things work out better than what you had planned for. Often times the best thing is to just go with it.

What advice can you give to anyone that wishes to teach music to young children from birth and up?

Take your cues from the children and let them lead you! Children are born innately musical and they come into this world with very specific ways in which they learn and relate to the world— it's up to us to nurture what's already there and help them along the musical and life journey.

శొ౷

ORGANIZATIONS

Music Together

Music Together classes are based on the recognition that all children are musical. Music Together is founded on the concept of a research-based, developmentally appropriate early childhood music curriculum that strongly emphasizes and facilitates adult involvement.

Music Together
66 Witherspoon Street
Princeton, NJ 08542 USA
http://www.musictogether.com
email: info@musictogether.com
phone: 800-728-2692

Kindermusik International

Kindermusik is built on the teachings of music education pioneers like Orff, Kodaly, and Suzuki and combines the latest research demonstrating the benefits of music at each stage of a child's development.

Kindermusik International
203 South Church St.
Greensboro, NC 27401 USA
http://www.kindermusik.com/Teach
email: teach@kindermusik.com
phone: 336-273-3363

Kids' MusicRound

Kids' MusicRound (KMR) music classes are designed to guide children through the stages of early childhood music development to achieve basic music competence. This music class curriculum sparks the inner musician in everyone - infants and toddlers as well as preschool through elementary aged children.

Kids' MusicRound
PMB #2008
25 Route 31 South, Suite C
Pennington, NJ 08534 USA
http://www.kidsmusicround.com/teacher.asp
phone: 609-333-0100

The Music Class

The Music Class understands that children who grow up in an enriched music environment are better able to understand and enjoy music for the rest of their lives. The most effective way to learn music is by being immersed in the sounds of music, including a broad variety of musical scales, rhythms, and styles, and starting at a very young age. The Music Class provides just that opportunity.

The Music Class
1875 Old Alabama Rd Suite 815
Roswell, GA 30076 USA
http://www.themusicclass.com
phone: 770-645-5578

International Board Certified Lactation Consultant (IBCLC)

An International Board Certified Lactation Consultant (IBCLC) has completed educational requirements and passed an international exam showing competence and expertise in breastfeeding support and lactation management. IBCLC's work in various public and private health care settings, assisting mothers and babies to successfully breastfeed.

Search words: lactation consultant, IBCLC, lactation consultant training, ibclc training, lactation consultant association

Getting Started

Read the most current requirements to become an IBCLC, which can be found at the website of the International Board of Lactation Consultant Examiners. Obtain the necessary educational and clinical practice hours. Become a member of the International Lactation Consultant Association (ILCA). Ask a local IBCLC to serve as your mentor.

Organizations

International Board of Lactation Consultant Examiners

The International Board of Lactation Consultant Examiners (IBLCE) is committed to advancing the health and well-being of mothers and children worldwide by improving the quality and increasing the number of practitioners of lactation and breastfeeding care.

http://www.iblce.org

International Lactation Consultant Association

The International Lactation Consultant Association (ILCA) is the professional association for International Board Certified Lactation Consultants (IBCLCs) and other health care professionals who care for breastfeeding families. They strive to advance the profession of Lactation Consulting worldwide through leadership, advocacy, professional development, and research.

ILCA Office
2501 Aerial Center Pkwy
Suite 103
Morrisville, NC 27560 USA
http://www.ilca.org
email: info@ilca.org
phone: 919-861-5577

Lactation Consultants of Australia and New Zealand

Lactation Consultants of Australia and New Zealand (LCANZ) is the professional organization for International Board Certified Lactation Consultants (IBCLC), health professionals and members of the public who have an interest in lactation and breastfeeding.

LCANZ
PO Box A811
Sydney South NSW 1235
Australia
http://www.lcanz.org
email: info@lcanz.org

New Zealand Lactation Consultants Association

The New Zealand Lactation Consultants Association (NZLCA) is the professional association of Internationally Certified Lactation Consultants in New Zealand.

New Zealand Lactation Consultants Association
P O Box 29-279
Christchurch 8540
New Zealand
http://www.nzlca.org.nz
email: secretary@nzlca.org.nz

United States Lactation Consultant Association

United States Lactation Consultant Association (USLCA) works to build and sustain a national association that advocates for lactation professionals.

USLCA Headquarters
2501 Aerial Center Pkwy
Suite 103
Morrisville, NC 27560 USA
http://www.uslca.org
email: info@uslcaonline.org
phone: 919-861-4543

Academy of Breastfeeding Medicine

The Academy of Breastfeeding Medicine is a worldwide organization of physicians dedicated to the promotion, protection and support of breastfeeding and human lactation.

Academy of Breastfeeding Medicine
140 Huguenot Street, 3rd floor
New Rochelle, NY 10801 USA
http://www.bfmed.org
email: abm@bfmed.org
phone: 914-740-2115

Canadian Lactation Consultant Association

The Canadian Lactation Consultant Association (CLCA) supports and advocates for Canadian Lactation Consultants. CLCA is committed to the promotion, support, and protection of breastfeeding.

http://www.ilca.org/i4a/pages/index.cfm?pageid=3519
email: info@clca-accl.ca

European Lactation Consultants Alliance

European Lactation Consultants Alliance supports and promotes breastfeeding with a collective of International Board Certified Lactation Consultants throughout Europe.

http://www.velb.org
email: office@elacta.org

Association of Lactation Consultants in Ireland

The Association of Lactation Consultants in Ireland (ALCI) promotes the professional development, advancement and recognition of International Board Certified Lactation Consultants for the benefit of breastfeeding infants and children, mothers, families and the wider community.

http://www.alcireland.ie

Word Alliance for Breastfeeding Action

The World Alliance for Breastfeeding Action (WABA) is a global network of individuals and organizations concerned with the protection, promotion and support of breastfeeding worldwide.

World Alliance for Breastfeeding Action
PO Box 1200
10850 Penang, Malaysia
http://www.waba.org.my
email: waba@waba.org.my

Example Education Programs

University of California Davis Human Lactation Center

The UC Davis Human Lactation Center provides a focal point for communication among researchers, clinicians, policy makers and educators to assure that the latest research-based information is available to professionals working with women and their families.

Human Lactation Center
Department of Nutrition
University of California, Davis
One Shields Avenue
Davis, CA 95616 USA
http://lactation.ucdavis.edu
email: lactation@ucdavis.edu
phone: 530-754-5364

University of California San Diego Lactation Education

This university-based program provides clinical training for Lactation Consultants.

http://www.breastfeeding-education.com

Health e-Learning

Health e-Learning provides high quality lactation and breastfeeding courses using evidence-based research as well as responsive tutoring and customer service.

Health e-Learning
PO Box 47, Kilcoy
Queensland, Australia, 4515
http://www.health-e-learning.com

Breastfeeding Outlook

Breastfeeding Outlook provides resources to help professionals deepen their understanding of breastfeeding issues and improve their clinical practice. They offer live seminars and independent study modules that carry CERPs for Lactation Consultants, contact hours for nurses and CPEs for dietitians. They also help prepare professionals to take the IBLCE exam.

Breastfeeding Outlook
PO Box 387
Herndon, VA 20172 USA
http://www.breastfeedingoutlook.com
email: info@breastfeedingoutlook.com
phone: 703-787-9894

Breastfeeding Conferences

Breastfeeding Conferences lists all upcoming educational opportunities.

http://www.breastfeedingconferences.com

Lactation Education Consultants

Lactation Education Consultants provide prospective Lactation Consultants and other health professionals with workshops and trainings related to lactation and breastfeeding with information that is practical, current, and evidence-based.

Lactation Education Consultants
618 North Wheaton Ave
Wheaton, IL 60187 USA
http://www.lactationeducationconsultants.com
email: lecoffice@aol.com
phone: 630-260-4847

Lactation Education Resources

Lactation Education Resources provide lactation management training and educational materials for professionals and for new parents online and onsite.

Lactation Education Resources
5614 Dover Street
Churchton, MD 20733 USA
http://www.leron-line.com
email: leronline@yahoo.com
phone: 443-607-8898

Global Online Lactation Conference

The Global Online Lactation Conference (GOLD) is the largest and most easily accessed conference in human lactation in the whole world. Offered completely online they bring together a truly global representation of speakers and delegates from places all around the world.

http://www.goldconf.com

LactSpeak

LactSpeak is a database of professional speakers that specialize in lactation for conferences and workshops, including leading clinicians, authors, and researchers.

http://lactspeak.com
email: info@lactspeak.com

LACTIVIST

Lactivists support and promote breastfeeding. Many ways exist for individuals to build supportive communities, educate families, and implement health care practices that increase breastfeeding rates. Lactivists believe in and have a passion for breastfeeding.

Search words: lactivist, breastfeeding promotion, breastfeeding support, breastfeeding activist, breastfeeding activism, breastfeeding advocacy, nurse-in event

GETTING STARTED

Learn as much as you can about breastfeeding. Attend breastfeeding conferences, seminars, and workshops. Join organizations focused on breastfeeding advocacy. Be a cheerleader for a breastfeeding mom. Wear a t-shirt that supports breastfeeding or a supportive breastfeeding campaign button. Attend a "nurse-in" event in your community.

BOOKS

The Womanly Art of Breastfeeding, by La Leche League

How Weaning Happens, by Diane Bengson

Mothering Your Nursing Toddler, by Norma Bumgarner

৪০৫৪

Career Journey ...

Lactivist, Lisa Cole

How did you get started as a Lactivist?

It was a reaction to criticism about breastfeeding my small baby, I went home and designed a pro breastfeeding t-shirt. Then people started to ask me where they could get one. I sold a few hand painted ones on eBay then with the proceeds had some professionally screen-printed.

Why do you do this work? What do you enjoy?

I do this because there is a need for it; women work hard to breastfeed and don't need negative comments. Lactivist slogan t-shirts, stop negative comments in their tracks. I enjoy positive feedback from customers about the quality of my t-shirts, which are organic, and fairly traded. I also love hearing that my designs have made a difference, and people have had good experiences when their children wear them.

How do you like running a business? What business advice can you share?

If I won the lottery I wouldn't stop doing this, but at the moment, I work silly hours each week for very little money. I'd advise people to get savvy with Facebook.

What type of training or education did you receive?

I have a design degree in Fashion and Textiles.

Do you have any "aha" moments or insights to share about your work?

I'm a designer, so I'm working out designs in my head 24 hours a day. I often dream about them.

What advice can you give to anyone that wishes to become a Lactivist?

Don't be afraid to stand up for what you believe in.

Anything else you would like to share?

If there came a time when a Lactivist wasn't needed, I'd rejoice. If people's feeding choices were not criticized, and new mums were educated and knew the risks of formula, before their babies were born, I'd be happier than it's possible to get. I would love for Lactivists to be obsolete.

ಐಒಐ

ORGANIZATIONS

Lactivist Network

The Lactivist Network is a website that has breastfeeding news, views and support from Lactation Activists.

http://www.lactivist.net
email: moomum@lactivist.co.uk

Lactivist Store

The Lactivist Store sells products related to the promotion of breastfeeding.

http://www.lactivist.co.uk

World Breastfeeding Week

The World Breastfeeding Week website will keep you informed about the events leading up to the yearly weeklong celebration observed in over 170 countries.

http://worldbreastfeedingweek.org
email: wbw@waba.org.my

International Baby Food Action Network

The International Baby Food Action Network (IBFAN) consists of public interest groups working around the world to reduce infant and young child morbidity and mortality.

http://www.ibfan.org

La Leche League International

La Leche League helps mothers worldwide to breastfeed through mother-to-mother support, encouragement, information, and education. They promote a better understanding of breastfeeding as an important element in the healthy development of the baby and mother.

La Leche League International
957 N. Plum Grove Road
Schaumburg, IL 60173 USA
http://www.llli.org
phone: 800-525-3243

Baby-Friendly Hospital Initiative in the USA

The Baby-Friendly Hospital Initiative (BFHI) is a global program sponsored by the World Health Organization (WHO) and the United Nations Children's Fund (UNICEF) to encourage and recognize hospitals and birthing centers that offer an optimal level of care for infant feeding.

Baby-Friendly USA, Inc.
327 Quaker Meeting House Road
E. Sandwich, MA 02537 USA
http://www.babyfriendlyusa.org
email: info@babyfriendlyusa.org
phone: 508-888-8092

United States Breastfeeding Committee

The United States Breastfeeding Committee (USBC) is a coalition of more than 40 nationally influential professional, educational, and governmental organizations, that share a common mission to improve the Nation's health by working collaboratively to protect, promote, and support breastfeeding.

United States Breastfeeding Committee
2025 M Street, NW, Suite 800
Washington, DC 20036 USA
http://www.usbreastfeeding.org
email: office@usbreastfeeding.org
phone: 202-367-1132

INFACT Canada

INFACT Canada is a national organization that works to protect the health of children as well as maternal well-being through the promotion and support of breastfeeding and optimal infant feeding practices.

http://www.infactcanada.ca
email: info@infactcanada.ca
phone: 416-595-9819

Centers for Disease Control and Prevention

The Centers for Disease Control and Prevention (CDC) is committed to increasing breastfeeding rates throughout the United States and to promoting and supporting optimal breastfeeding practices toward the ultimate goal of improving the public's health.

Centers for Disease Control and Prevention
1600 Clifton Rd
Atlanta, GA 30333 USA
http://www.cdc.gov/breastfeeding
email: cdcinfo@cdc.gov
phone: 800-232-4636

Wellstart International

Wellstart International advances the knowledge, skills and abilities of health care providers regarding the promotion, protection and support of optimal infant and maternal health and nutrition from conception through the completion of weaning.

Wellstart International
P.O. Box 602
Blue Jay, CA 92317 USA
http://wellstart.org
email: info@wellstart.org

MASSAGE DOULA

Massage Doulas are licensed Massage Therapists trained to understand pregnancy, birth, and postpartum. They attend women during labor and birth combining both massage and Doula services.

Search words: massage doula, massage birth, massage labor, massage doula training, massage doula certification

GETTING STARTED

Research and learn about the work of Massage Therapists and Doulas. If you are a licensed Massage Therapist, pursue training and certification as a Doula. If you are a Doula, but not a Massage Therapist, consider training and becoming licensed as a Massage Therapist to offer more services to your clients.

ORGANIZATIONS

Massage Doula

Massage Doula workshops are taught in partnership with the Institute of Somatic Therapy. They are the certifying organization for Prenatal Massage Therapists and Massage Doulas. Massage Doulas are certified Massage Therapists who have completed advanced study in prenatal massage, postpartum massage, labor, delivery support and, optionally, infant massage.

http://massagedoula.com

Bodyworkers Association for the Birthing Year

Bodyworkers Association for the Birthing Year (BABY) offers a Massage Birth Doula Certification program. BABY considers information and resources a vital component towards empowerment. They support women and their companions in their endeavor to make truly informed choices.

http://www.babyinc.org/masbirasdoul.html

Claire Marie Miller Seminars

Claire Marie Miller Seminars offers a Pregnancy Massage Certification course to train professionals in pregnancy massage, labor massage and support techniques, postpartum massage and infant massage.

Claire Marie Miller Seminars
8703 Rollingwood Rd
Chapel Hill, NC 27516 USA
http://www.clairemariemiller.com
phone: 877-319-5772

MASSAGE DOULA EXAMPLES

Houston Pregnancy Massage and Doula Care

Houston Pregnancy Massage and Doula Care provide women with the care, comfort and support they need to make pregnancy and childbirth even more enjoyable.

http://www.doula-training.com

Tranquil Touch

Tranquil Touch provides individualized care so women find the support they need to combat the effects that stress has on their physical and emotional states. Tranquil Touch believes that by providing education and support to women and their families during pregnancy and childbirth, they can help women feel empowered and knowledgeable about their choices for birth.

Tranquil Touch
33425 Grand River Ave. Suite 102
Farmington, MI 48335 USA
http://www.tranquiltouchforwomen.com
email: info@tranquiltouchforwomen.com
phone: 866-384-1734

MATERNITY COACH

Maternity Coaches provide counseling to women and their families easing their transition through pregnancy into parenthood. They also work with employer groups to effectively facilitate work place transitions meeting the needs of families and allowing companies to retain and support talented skilled workers. Maternity Coaches assist professional women to successfully manage their career goals and aspirations, with the challenges of motherhood. They help employees return to the workplace with the communication skills, strategies, and solutions that build success for both families and companies.

Search words: maternity coach, maternity coach certification, maternity coach training, life coach certification, life coach training, life coach workshop

GETTING STARTED

There are no requirements to become a Maternity Coach, but a background in Human Resources is an excellent foundation. Certification and training programs to become a Life Coach can also provide the skills needed to become a Maternity Coach. Find a practicing Maternity Coach to advise you. Discover the process they went through to become a successful Maternity Coach.

ℰᴏᴄᴙ

Career Journey ...

Family Life Coach, Natalie Nevares

How did you get started as a Family Life Coach?

After experiencing multiple challenges as a new mom (difficult breastfeeding, sleeping, postpartum depression, anxiety, career issues, self-esteem, general unhappiness), I felt called to support other families who were struggling. While holding an executive position in the luxury travel industry, between two of my own newborns, I started volunteering my time in 2005, helping families on both the emotional and practical levels of new parenthood. I devoted myself full-time to my company Mommywise, in 2009. I test-marketed different business models and products; I found that coaching families through sleep transitions was where the most support was needed, and how I could serve them best.

Why do you do this work? What do you enjoy?

I do this work ultimately to create a more supportive community for parents in a world where the extended family concept is extinct; where new families are under-supported and over-judged for their parenting choices. My mission is to dispel some myths about parenting being "the biggest joy of your life"; create more awareness about the negative emotions many new parents face; and inspire families to live happier, more balanced lives. I love inspiring families to unlearn all the parenting advice that doesn't serve them, to trust their instincts, and give them courage to change things that aren't working for them.

How do you like running a business? What business advice can you share?

I love running my own business, but it definitely comes with multiple challenges. My advice for budding entrepreneurs? Be passionate, don't be afraid to fail, test-market your business ideas, services and/or products with minimal investment to see what your customers need (and are willing to pay for). Don't try to serve everyone; instead, fine-tune your niche and serve your target market well.

What type of training or education did you receive?

I have no formal business training or clinical expertise. I have taken several inexpensive to free business classes in New York City, as well as attended many free webinars and tele-training seminars. I have read many business and marketing books, and follow a few business thought leaders i.e. Seth Godin, Tim Ferris, Tony Hseih, and Brendon Burchard.

Do you have any "aha" moments or insights to share about your work?

The most important thing I've learned is that just because you think you have a good business idea, it doesn't mean it's going to sell, or that you're going to be comfortable selling the products. My biggest AHA moment was realizing that my original business idea didn't solve any real problems. It took me a year of test-marketing different products until I found who my target market is, what problems they needed help with, and what they were willing to pay. The best advice I got from my business mentor was to put as little time and money into my business as possible before putting it out there.

What advice can you give to anyone that wishes to become a Family Life Coach?

Think about your passion, your skills, your strengths and weaknesses, and how you think you could help serve families to support them in achieving their goals, whether it's about work-family balance, sleep, career dilemmas, etc. Then consider if you have the drive to create and manage your own business, branding, marketing, operational, finances, etc. Partner with someone who balances your strengths and weaknesses. You could also work for an existing company who takes care of all the business aspects, but you just do the fun job of coaching families, supporting them emotionally, and helping them achieve their goals.

Anything else you would like to share?

Part of my original mission with Mommywise was to brand Mommywise, and allow the brand to be the umbrella for a myriad of possibilities. It could be e-commerce, a YouTube channel, concierge services, a brand name for products, or all of the above. It can also be a portal where users can review maternity and/or postpartum care providers in a Yelp-type interface, (revenue could come from business listings and/or advertising sales).

Ultimately, I would like Mommywise to be a vehicle to employ mothers who want part-time, meaningful work that they can do from home on their own time, AND be there to help their kids with homework after school. I don't think parents should have to choose between careers or parenting, and I want Mommywise to help support a new concept of work/family balance.

℘℧

ORGANIZATIONS

International Coach Federation

International Coach Federation (ICF) has the core purpose to advance the art, science, and practice of professional coaching. ICF sets high standards, provides independent certification, and builds a worldwide network of credentialed coaches.

International Coach Federation
2365 Harrodsburg Rd, Suite A325
Lexington, KY 40504 USA
http://www.coachfederation.org
email: icfheadquarters@coachfederation.org
phone: 859-219-3580

International Association of Coaching

International Association of Coaching (IAC) is an independent, global coach certifying organization that works to expand the path to coaching mastery by inspiring the ongoing evolution and application of universal coaching standards. Coaching is a transformative process for personal and professional awareness, discovery and growth.

http://www.certifiedcoach.org
email: membership@certifiedcoach.org
phone: 505-819-5773

HR Coach

The HR Coach Network makes it possible for people to turn coaching into a career.

HR Coach
PO Box 2292
Fortitude Valley
Brisbane
QLD, 4006 Australia
http://www.hrcoach.com.au
email: business@hrcoach.com.au
phone: 1300 550 674

European Mentoring and Coaching Council

The European Mentoring & Coaching Council (EMCC) exists to promote best practices in mentoring and coaching across Europe.

EMCC
PO Box 3154
Marlborough
Wiltshire, SN8 3WD
United Kingdom
http://www.emccouncil.org

MATERNITY COACH BUSINESS EXAMPLES

Mommywise

Mommywise was created to help moms empower each other with education, support and personalized coaching, to help their families thrive with the resources they need.

Mommywise
315 West 39th Street
Suite 700
New York, NY 10018 USA
http://www.mommywise.com
email: info@mommywise.com
phone: 917-660-4365

Maternity Coaching

Maternity Coaching supports high-achieving women to successfully manage the transition of having a child in the context of their professional lives. They provide one-to-one coaching and workshop programs to support businesses and employees before, during and after maternity.

Maternity Coaching
The Executive Coaching Consultancy Ltd
125 Kensington High Street
London
W8 5SF
http://www.maternity-coaching.co.uk
email: info@maternity-coaching.co.uk
phone: 20 7795 6556

The Parent Company

The Parent Company offers coaching solutions to help clients optimize their performance at home and at work, and also balance the interests of employer and employee.

The Parent Company
6 Jacob's Well Mews
London W1U 3DY
http://www.theworkingparentcompany.co.uk

Jessica Chivers

Jessica Chivers is the Thinking Woman's Coach. She inspires professional women to make smooth, successful changes.

http://jessicachivers.com

The Baby Gurus

The Baby Gurus provide consultancy services, which cover subjects relating to fertility, maternity, paternity, HR, parenting, families, retaining women and education programs.

The Baby Gurus
Wynndun
Corsee Road
Banchory
Aberdeenshire
AB31 5RS United Kingdom
http://www.thebabygurus.com
email: info@thebabygurus.com
phone: 0845 468 0840

Talking Talent

Talking Talent is an innovative coaching and consulting firm that helps companies attract, retain and maximize the potential of their talented female employees. Talking Talent partners with organizations that are passionate about creating gender diversity at all levels.

Talking Talent
The Studio, Holcombe Lane
Newington, Oxford
Oxfordshire UK
OX10 7AJ United Kingdom
http://www.talking-talent.com
phone: 1865 400087

MIDWIFE

The practice of midwifery has existed since ancient times, making it the oldest medical profession. Women have always assisted other women during childbirth. Midwives deliver babies. They also provide primary health care services to women. They give physical exams and order laboratory tests. They care for women through puberty, fertility, pregnancy, postpartum, breastfeeding, and menopause. They counsel and educate women about contraception. Midwives attend births in various settings such as home, clinic, hospital, or Birth Center.

Search words: midwife, midwifery, midwives, midwife training, midwifery school, license to practice midwifery, lay midwife, midwifery student, midwifery association

GETTING STARTED

A multitude of paths exist to becoming a trained, knowledgeable, practicing Midwife. Investigate what is required where you wish to practice to become a Midwife. Midwifery education and laws to practice are different based upon location, and some places exist where the practice of midwifery is against the law. Contact midwifery schools, associations, and organizations. Find a school or program to begin your midwifery education and training. Take a midwifery intensive or introduction to midwifery class to learn more and explore if this is the right path. Join a student midwifery group. Contact Midwives in your local area and inquire if you can shadow them. Read books about midwifery.

BOOKS

Baby Catcher: Chronicles of a Modern Midwife by Peggy Vincent

Heart and Hands: A Midwife's Guide to Pregnancy and Birth by Elizabeth Davis

Spiritual Midwifery by Ina May Gaskin

Paths to Becoming a Midwife, find at this link:

http://www.midwiferytoday.com/books/paths.asp

ORGANIZATIONS

The Royal College of Midwives

The Royal College of Midwives is a professional organization and trade union for Midwives and led by Midwives in the United Kingdom.

The Royal College of Midwives
15 Mansfield Street
London United Kingdom
W1G 9NH
http://www.rcm.org.uk
email: info@rcm.org.uk
phone: 20 7312 3535

Midwifery Today

Midwifery Today is an international magazine that covers midwifery related topics and it is also a website filled with news and articles for Midwives and Childbirth Professionals.

Midwifery Today
P.O. Box 2672
Eugene, OR 97402 USA
http://www.midwiferytoday.com
email: inquiries@midwiferytoday.com
phone: 541-344-7438

StudentMidwife.net

StudentMidwife.NET is an education-based community supporting student Midwives and those considering a career in midwifery.

http://www.studentmidwife.net

International Confederation of Midwives

The International Confederation of Midwives (ICM) supports, represents, and works to strengthen professional associations of Midwives throughout the world.

International Confederation of Midwives
Laan van Meerdervoort 70
2517 AN The Hague
The Netherlands
http://www.internationalmidwives.org
email: info@internationalmidwives.org
phone: 70 3060520

Midwives Information and Resource Service

Midwives Information and Resource Service (MIDIRS) offers a range of products and services for student Midwives, practicing Midwives and any health care professional working with pregnant women, new mothers, babies and their families.

http://www.midirs.org

Citizens for Midwifery

Citizens for Midwifery (CfM) is a national consumer-based group that promotes the Midwives Model of Care. CfM works to provide information and resources that promote the services of community Midwives, and midwifery care across the United States.

Citizens for Midwifery
PO Box 82227
Athens, GA 30608 USA
http://cfmidwifery.org/index.aspx
email: info@cfmidwifery.org
phone: 888-236-4880

International Center for Traditional Childbearing

The International Center for Traditional Childbearing (ICTC) is an African centered organization located in Portland, Oregon. ICTC was created to promote the health of women and their families and to train African American women aspiring to become Midwives.

International Center for Traditional Childbearing
3821 NE Martin Luther King Blvd
Portland, OR 97212 USA
http://www.ictcmidwives.org
email: ictc@ictcmidwives.org
phone: 503-460-9324

Midwifery Education Accreditation Council

The Midwifery Education Accreditation Council (MEAC) strives to promote excellence in midwifery education through accreditation. The purpose of MEAC is to establish standards for the education of competent Midwives, and to provide a process for self-evaluation and peer-evaluation for diverse educational programs.

Midwifery Education Accreditation Council
P.O. Box 984
La Conner, WA 98257 USA
http://meacschools.org/index.php
email: info@meacschools.org
phone: 360-466-2080

American Midwifery Certification Board

The American Midwifery Certification Board (AMCB) is the national certifying body for Certified Nurse-Midwives (CNMs). AMCB is committed to using professional, progressive, and comprehensive educational criteria to certify Midwives.

American Midwifery Certification Board
849 International Drive, Suite 205
Linthicum, MD 21090 USA
http://www.amcbmidwife.org
phone: 410-694-9424

Association of Midwifery Educators

The Association of Midwifery Educators (AME) is a group of member schools, educators and administrators who have come together with a common goal of building a robust network of support and resources for direct-entry midwifery education. AME is dedicated to the art and science of midwifery education and ensuring that educators have access to the connections, collaborations and coordinated opportunities they need to succeed in the work of teaching, nurturing and mentoring Midwives for the future.

The Association of Midwifery Educators
24 S. High Street
Bridgton, ME 04009 USA
http://www.associationofmidwiferyeducators.org
email: info@associationofmidwiferyeducators.org
phone: 207-647-5968

North American Registry of Midwives

North American Registry of Midwives (NARM) is dedicated to advancing the profession by supporting advocacy efforts for legal recognition at the state and federal level. NARM sets standards for certification that allow a Midwife to support a woman's right to choose her birth attendants and place of birth and to involve those she identifies as her family in the birth experience.

North American Registry of Midwives
5257 Rosestone Dr
Lilburn, GA 30047 USA
http://narm.org
email: info@narm.org
phone: 770-381-9051

Midwives Association of Turkey

The Midwives Association of Turkey is the professional support organization for Midwives and they work to set standards of midwifery care and education, and improve the health of women and their families.

http://www.turkebelerdernegi.com
(use http://translate.google.com)
email: info@turkebelerdernegi.com

Midwives Alliance of North America

Midwives Alliance of North America (MANA) is the only professional organization uniting and representing all North American Midwives, inclusive of all midwifery educational backgrounds and practice styles.

Midwives Alliance of North America
611 Pennsylvania Ave SE #1700
Washington, DC 20003 USA
http://mana.org
email: info@mana.org
phone: 888-923-6262

The Canadian Association of Midwives

The Canadian Association of Midwives (CAM) is the national organization representing Midwives and the profession of midwifery in Canada. The vision of the Canadian Association of Midwives is that midwifery is fundamental to maternal and newborn health services, and that every woman in Canada will have access to a Midwife's care for herself and her baby.

The Canadian Association of Midwives
59 Riverview
Montréal, Québec
H8R 3R9
Canada
http://www.canadianmidwives.org
email: admin@canadianmidwives.org
phone: 514-807-3668

The American College of Nurse-Midwives

The American College of Nurse-Midwives (ACNM) is the professional association that represents certified nurse-midwives and certified Midwives in the United States. ACNM promotes the health and well-being of women and infants within their families and communities through the development and support of the profession of midwifery as practiced by certified nurse-midwives, and certified Midwives.

American College of Nurse-Midwives
8403 Colesville Rd, Suite 1550
Silver Spring, MD 20910 USA
http://www.midwife.org
phone: 240-485-1800

National Association of Certified Professional Midwives

The National Association of Certified Professional Midwives (NACPM) is a professional association committed to significantly increasing women's access to quality maternity care by supporting the work and practice of Certified Professional Midwives.

NACPM is working to be a catalyst for a new era in maternity care by inspiring and engaging Certified Professional Midwives to be an organized force for change.

NACPM
243 Banning Road
Putney, VT 05346 USA
http://www.nacpm.org
email: admin@nacpm.org

Foundation for the Advancement of Midwifery

The Foundation for the Advancement of Midwifery (FAM) is an organization dedicated to increasing access to midwifery care in North America through education, research and public policy.

http://www.foundationformidwifery.org

Nursing and Midwifery Council

The Nursing and Midwifery Council is the nursing and midwifery regulator for England, Wales, Scotland, Northern Ireland and the Islands.

http://www.nmc-uk.org
email: ukenquiries@nmc-uk.org

New Zealand College of Midwives

The New Zealand College of Midwives is the professional organization and recognized voice for Midwives and student Midwives in New Zealand.

New Zealand College of Midwives
PO Box 21 106
Edgeware
Christchurch, 8143 New Zealand
http://www.midwife.org.nz
email: nzcom@nzcom.org.nz
phone: 3 377 2732

MIDWIFE ASSISTANT

Midwifery Assistants work alongside Midwives providing care. Some assistants are students in the process of training to become Midwives. They have a range of skills and knowledge such as taking a mother's blood pressure and pulse or checking fetal heart tones. Also, they have training in CPR and neonatal resuscitation. Assistants often arrive to a birth ahead of the Midwife to assess labor and provide comfort.

Search words: midwifery assistant, midwifery assistant training, midwife intensive, midwifery intensive

GETTING STARTED

Learn about the field of midwifery. Take a Midwife's Assistant training class. Seek out a Midwife in your community in need of an assistant. Read midwifery textbooks, professional journals, and research articles.

RESOURCES

Birth Joy

Birth Joy offers DVDs to train Midwife Assistants, which lay a foundation helping them to gain practical skills.

Birth Joy
40 Newport Way SW Apt 201
Issaquah, WA 98027 USA
http://birthjoyeducation.com
email: midwife@scapellc.com
phone: 425-961-0971

ORGANIZATIONS

The Farm Midwifery Center

The Farm Midwifery Center offers a Midwifery Assistant workshop teaching the skills and knowledge needed to assist a practicing Midwife at a home or birth center delivery.

The Farm Midwifery Center
P.O. Box 217
Summertown, TN 38483 USA
http://www.midwiferyworkshops.org
email: midwives@midwiferyworkshops.org
phone: 931-964-2472

Birth Arts International

Birth Arts International offers a comprehensive Midwives Assistant training program. Students learn the skills needed to practice and work as an assistant. They also learn how to provide support to women during pregnancy, labor and birth, and postpartum.

Birth Arts International
501 Lindsey St
Reidsville, NC 27320 USA
http://www.birtharts.com/monitrice1.htm
email: demetria@birtharts.com
phone: 866-303-4372

Michigan School of Traditional Midwifery

Michigan School of Traditional Midwifery (MSTM) offers a Midwife Assistant correspondence course.

Michigan School of Traditional Midwifery
P.O. Box 162
Mikado, MI 48745 USA
http://traditionalmidwife.com/dma.html
email: traditionalmidwife@gmail.com
phone: 989-736-6583

MURALIST

Muralists create paintings on walls, ceilings, doors, and other large surfaces. Some expecting families desire to have murals painted in their baby's room, and they hire a Muralist to create one.

Search words: muralist training, muralist nursery, muralist children, muralist kids, muralist group, muralist association

GETTING STARTED

If you have an art background and are familiar with creating murals, then you have simply to set your prices, create a website, and promote your services. A formal art background is not required; however, you could enhance your technique by taking a mural class through an area community college. Read books about mural techniques and begin to practice. Contact a Mural Artist and ask if you can learn from them. Join an artists' organization where some of the members have experience in creating murals.

BOOKS

How to Start a Faux Painting or Mural Business by Rebecca Pitman

How to Open and Operate a Financially Successful Painting, Faux Painting, or Mural Business by Melissa Kay Bishop

Mural Painting Secrets for Success: Expert Advice for Hobbyists and Pros by Gary Lord

ഇ൩ന

Career Journey ...

Muralist, Barbara Legacy

How did you get started as a Muralist?

I've been painting or drawing for as long as I can remember. Luckily, my parents provided me with plenty of art supplies and opportunities including a college education majoring in Art. The first mural I did was on my own baby's wall. I did a cherub sitting in a tree, looking down at him. After enjoying that so much, I decided to offer it to others. I started my own part-time business as an applied artist doing murals and decorative painting. That was over 25 years ago.

Why do you do this work? What do you enjoy?

What I love about doing children's murals is that it's an opportunity to share the creative process and make a child's space unique and personal. It is a way of honoring this special little person. It's a fun and satisfying process and product.

How do you like running a business? What business advice can you share?

Running a business is a lot of work, but also a fun challenge to continually figure out how to make it grow. Each interaction, each job no matter how small, is your resume.

Therefore, make sure that customers are happy after you are gone.

What type of training or education did you receive?

My BA degree is in Painting and Art Education. I worked as a scenic artist, where I learned many tricks to painting on a large scale.

Do you have any "aha" moments or insights to share about your work?

I am a believer in following your gut, and noticing the sense of satisfaction you feel when you've accomplished a goal. Those 'aha' moments come when you know you did the best job you could, you get to enjoy seeing the product of your labor. Also, when you get another phone call because they want more.

What advice can you give to anyone that wishes to become a Muralist?

If it's what you really want, you can do it. Get exposure for your work wherever the opportunity leads you. Do the best job you can and make people happy, including yourself.

ଚର

ORGANIZATIONS

Association of Professional Muralists, UK

The Association of Professional Muralists is a self-regulated group of independent artists with their own unique styles, clients, methods and cost structures. They work to promote the use of murals in both public and private spaces, for both decorative and architectural use. They also advocate a pursuit of excellence in the art of murals and promote standards of good practice.

http://www.mural-design.com/apm.htm

Find a Muralist

Find a Muralist (FAM) is a web referral service whose purpose is to simplify the way clients seeking murals locate artists best qualified to serve their specific needs. FAM is also an on-line community of

Muralists, offering a range of resources and information to Mural Artists.

http://www.findamuralist.com
phone: 888-687-2547

Lincoln Financial Mural Arts Center

Mural Training Program

The Lincoln Financial Mural Arts Center offers the Mural Arts Program each year. This training program is for artists interested in adapting their skills to public mural making.

The program includes step-by-step instruction on mural making techniques, including wall preparation, design enlargement, paint application, the cloth method, and sealing the completed project.

Lincoln Financial Mural Arts Center
Thomas-Eakins House
1727-29 Mt. Vernon Street
Philadelphia, PA 19130 USA
http://muralarts.org/node/609
email: info@muralarts.org
phone: 215-685-0750

MURALISTS BUSINESS EXAMPLES

Austin Mural Art

Leigh Watson of Austin Mural Art creates beautiful mural art for residences and commercial spaces all over Texas. Her artwork can be seen in homes, daycares, hospitals, schools and churches and it ranges from dinosaurs, safari jungle, stadiums, fairy-tale castles, underwater themes, and more.

http://www.leighwatson.com

Mural Max

Edina of Mural Max focuses her mural artistry on the young, having decorated children's rooms and playrooms with her drawings. Her work has also been displayed at day care centers, hospitals and hotels.

http://muralmax.com

NEWBORN CARE SPECIALIST ALSO BABY NURSE OR MATERNITY NURSE

Newborn Care Specialists provide in-home care for newborns. They help parents with a wide range of needs for babies from diapering, bathing, feeding, sleeping, and health concerns. They educate parents on effective methods to soothe babies, decreasing crying and colic. They are flexible being available overnight to care for babies, and they are able to travel to or travel with families to provide care.

Search words: newborn specialist training, newborn care specialist workshop, baby nurse, maternity nurse

GETTING STARTED

Contact a placement agency for Newborn Care Specialists, Baby Nurses or Nannies to find out their requirements. Enroll in a training program for Newborn Care Specialist. Seek out a practicing Newborn Care Specialist to serve as your mentor. Take an infant CPR course. Some Newborn Care Specialists have advanced training as Nurses, Doulas, and Lactation Consultants. If you have a strong background caring for infants, you can set up a website and begin to seek families to serve.

BOOKS

The Baby Nurse Bible by Carole Kramer Arsenault

The Baby Book by William Sears MD, Martha Sears RN, Robert Sears MD, and James Sears MD

ORGANIZATIONS AND TRAINING

Zero to Three

Zero to Three is a national organization that informs, trains, and supports professionals, policymakers, and parents in their efforts to improve the lives of infants and toddlers.

Zero to Three
1255 23rd Street, NW, Suite 350
Washington, DC 20037 USA
http://www.zerotothree.org
email: 0to3@presswarehouse.com
phone: 202-638-1144

Newborn Care Specialist Association

The Newborn Care Specialist Association (NCSA) is an international organization that supports professional Newborn Care Specialists. They promote standards of care and ongoing education among professionals in the field.

http://www.ncsainfo.com
email: contact@ncsainfo.com
phone: 888-691-3011

Newborn Education Services and Training

Newborn Education Services and Training (NEST) have a complete training program with ongoing support, advice and guidance. It has been designed as a learning tool to build confidence and promote education in Newborn Care Professionals.

Newborn Education Services and Training
6 Church Street,
Tewkesbury
GL20 5PA United Kingdom
http://www.newborneducation.co.uk
email: enquiries@newborneducation.co.uk

Infant and Child Training Academy

The Infant and Child Training Academy offers workshops for professionals and teaches the care of newborns through early childhood.

Infant and Child Training Academy
750 Third Avenue
New York, NY 10017 USA
http://www.infantcaretraining.com
phone: 212-203-4169
email: info@infantcaretraining.com

Happy Baby Solutions

Happy Baby Solutions is a Baby Nurse agency and they also offer workshops to provide training for professionals.

http://happybabysolutions.com
email: info@happybabysolutions.com

Alexandria School

The Newborn Care Specialist program at Alexandria School provides the training to assist professionals to begin careers as Baby Nurses.

Alexandria School
28500 Miles Road, Suite P
Solon, OH 44139 USA
http://www.alexandria-school.com
phone: 440-914-0044
email: info@alexandria-school.com

NEWBORN CARE SPECIALISTS EXAMPLES

Maternally Yours

Maternally Yours is a professional maternity nurse agency providing screened and qualified Maternity Nurses to families to care for their newborns.

Maternally Yours
http://www.maternallyyours.co.uk
email: maternally@imperialstaff.com

Boston Baby Nurse

Boston Baby Nurse is an agency providing qualified Sleep Specialists, Baby Nurses, and Registered Nurses to families.

Boston Baby Nurse
http://bostonbabynurse.com
email: info@bostonbabynurse.com
phone: 781-690-6776

Pink Newborn Services

Pink Newborn Services offers specialized services designed to help support families through the transition of having a new child. They help ease families into their new roles as parents

Pink Newborn Services
http://pinknewbornservices.com
email: info@pinknewbornservices.com
phone: 877-456-7465

Caring Baby Nurses

Caring Baby Nurses places trained and experienced Baby Nurses with families. Caring Baby Nurses take complete care of newborns by bathing, diapering, dressing, feeding and more.

Caring Baby Nurses
http://www.caringbabynurses.com
email: info@caringbabynurses.com
phone: 646-373-1200

Babiease

Babiease, Baby Nurse services help parents though the first months with new little ones. Babiease provides families with support to help them transition into parenthood.

Babiease
http://www.babiease.com
email: meredith@babiease.com
phone: 410-274-9329

Not to Worry

Not to Worry offers day and night time support for families with new babies.

Not to Worry
http://www.nottoworryinc.com
email: nottoworry@sbcglobal.net
phone: 619-718-4871

Nannies Incorporated

Nannies Incorporated helps families transition through the first weeks of having new babies by providing experienced Maternity Nurses.

Nannies Incorporated
http://www.nanniesinc.com
email: london@nanniesinc.com

Sleeping Babies

Sleeping Babies is an agency with a team of live-in Maternity Nurses, Night Maternity Nurses and troubleshooters who work throughout the UK and the world.

Sleeping Babies
http://www.sleepingbabies.co.uk
email: sleep@sleepingbabies.co.uk
phone: 020 8420 7117

Nannies and Doulas On Call Inc

Nannies and Doulas On Call Inc specialize in caring for mothers and newborns during the first few months.

Nannies and Doulas On Call Inc
http://www.nanniesanddoulas.ca
email: nanniesanddoulas@live.com
phone: 416-781-1312

NEW DADS BOOT CAMP TRAINER

New Dads Boot Camp Trainers are fatherly role models or peers and help expecting fathers to become confident in their new roles. The trainer provides instruction on newborn care, feeding, diapering, holding, and swaddling baby. More importantly, the trainer facilitates an environment in which men are able to comfortably ask questions and discuss issues freely.

Search words: boot camp for new dads, training for new dads, new dads class, first time father's class, conscious fathering

GETTING STARTED

Take a New Dads Boot Camp Trainer workshop. Observe a New Dads Boot Camp class to learn how it is facilitated. Contact and join organizations that focus on preparing men to become fathers. Interview new fathers to understand their concerns and discover what information would prepare them.

ΕΟΩ

Career Journey ...

New Dads Class Facilitator, Daniel B. Singley, PhD

How did you get started as a New Dads Class Facilitator?

I had approached the founder of a dads' class, Jeff Jones, PhD and he'd suggested that – because I was a new psychologist and new dad at the time – that I start up a class for fathers of newborns.

Why do you do this work? What do you enjoy?

I'm very enthusiastic about fathering my own kiddos, and really enjoy giving expectant dads as well as dads of newborns a clearer understanding of how they can stay very engaged with even very young babies (and mom too, of course!). I most enjoy actually getting into the room with the expectant/new dads and getting them to interact with each other in ways that males typically don't. Parenting can be nerve-wracking work no matter how you slice it, but when I see dads sharing tips, thoughts, questions, and points of concern with other guys who can empathize – that's when I see the light go on for participants that they're not alone and in fact not even atypical.

How do you like running a business? What business advice can you share?

I enjoy it, but am glad that I don't rely on it to pay the rent. My advice is to find a niche that involves work about which you're passionate, and then do as thorough a market analysis as possible to determine the target market, competition, and the likely return on your investment. That said, I did none of that because I'm passionate about men's issues and especially fatherhood.

What type of training or education did you receive?

I have a Ph.D. in Counseling Psychology, and I have a clinical practice in which I specialized in men's issues. Plus, I have a couple of kiddos and I'd count fathering them as key training related to doing this work!

Do you have any "aha" moments or insights to share about your work?

I have a "veteran dad" come to each of the classes for third trimester dads. The vet dad has already taken the class, had his baby, and comes back to the class to share his experiences before, during, and after the birth. The evaluation forms from the class inevitably indicate that it's hearing from the other expectant dads and the veteran dad that are the most meaningful to them.

What advice can you give to anyone that wishes to facilitate classes for New Dads?

Focus on setting up a form that gives the participants grist for thought, and then work to get the dads to interact with each other as much as possible. I'd also encourage her/him to think hard about what biases and "shoulds" are based on past experience and to think about how to make the class as open and approachable as possible. The parent education industry is generally built on a model of anxiety (e.g. "If you don't [use/buy] product X, your child will be left behind and has no chance to get into Yale"), but taking a one-size-fits-all approach greatly downplays the fact that one's background, history, context, biology, etc all play a huge role and vary enormously from person-to-person.

Anything else you would like to share?

You can't baby-sit your own child. That's fathering.

℘ℭ

ORGANIZATIONS

Boot Camp for New Dads

Boot Camp for New Dads is a unique father-to-father, community-based workshop that inspires and equips men of different economic levels, ages and cultures to become confidently engaged with their infants, support their mates and personally navigate their transformation into dads.

Boot Camp for New Dads
15375 Barranca Pkwy
Suite H-104
Irvine, CA 92618 USA
http://www.bootcampfornewdads.org/bcnd-workshop.php
phone: 949-754-9067

DaddyNatal

The vision of Daddy Natal is to create inclusive services, which empower men to be able to access the learning, and support they need to become great birth coaches, great dads and supportive partners.

http://www.daddynatal.co.uk
email: dean@daddynatal.co.uk

Basic Training for New Dads

Basic Training for New Dads (BTND) is a San Diego-based class for expectant and new fathers in which the teachers are fathers with their newborn children. BTND is two separate "guy-friendly" classes, each targeting the different questions that dads-to-be and new dads tend to have. The classes are dads-only.

Basic Training for New Dads
2423 Camino Del Rio South
Suite #205
San Diego, CA 92108 USA
http://www.newdadsclass.com
email: dsingley@newdadsclass.com
phone: 858-380-4636

National Fatherhood Initiative

National Fatherhood Initiative works to improve the well-being of children by increasing the proportion of children growing up with involved, responsible, and committed fathers.They strive to ensure a brighter future for America's youth.

National Fatherhood Initiative
20410 Observation Drive, Suite 107
Germantown, MD 20876 USA
http://www.fatherhood.org
email: info@fatherhood.org
phone: 301-948-0599

Father's Forum

The Father's Forum began with the belief that the lives of dads could be more meaningful, vital, interesting and enjoyable if they were prepared to become parents. Preparation means being actively involved in the birth process and learning about the transition to parenthood. Bringing dads together to explore the challenging and difficult first year of parenthood makes a huge difference in how they experience fatherhood.

The Fathers Forum
1521-A Shattuck Ave Suite 201
Berkeley, CA 94709 USA
http://www.fathersforum.com
phone: 510-644-0300

Conscious Fathering

This program provides men the opportunity to learn about their newborns five basic needs, understand how babies communicate, and how to not only meet their baby's needs, but also anticipate them.

Conscious Fathering
http://www.parenttrust.org/our-programs/start-a-program
email: bdorsey@parenttrust.org
phone: 206-233-0156

NONPROFIT FOUNDER (ALSO SEE BIRTH ACTIVIST)

Nonprofit Founders start organizations that benefit and serve the public. Founders can be individuals or groups in support of an issue, mission, or cause. Birth Centers, Doula associations, midwifery schools, and parental education groups are examples of nonprofit organizations started by Childbirth Professionals that serve pregnant women and their families. A nonprofit organization could also be founded to support the professionals that serve families by providing services such as networking, certification, training, and advocacy. Nonprofit companies are allowed to make profits, however those profits are usually reinvested into the organization.

Search words: organizing nonprofit, start nonprofit workshop, start nonprofit training, nonprofit status, nonprofit requirements

GETTING STARTED

Read a book about how to start a nonprofit organization. Find out the government requirements for nonprofits in your area. Contact your community business association, library, or college to inquire if they have any services to help nonprofits. Attend classes and workshops offered to assist nonprofit organizations. Volunteer for a nonprofit organization.

EXAMPLES OF NONPROFIT ORGANIZATIONS

Museum of Motherhood

The Museum of Motherhood is a place to meet for baby groups, mothers, and caregivers. It is a place for conversations, advice, self-expression, nurturing, healing and more.

Museum of Motherhood
401 East 84th St
New York, NY 10028 USA
http://www.mommuseum.org
email: info@mommuseum.org
phone: 212-452-9816

Healthy Birth Day

Healthy Birth Day is dedicated to preventing stillbirths and infant death through education, advocacy, and parental support.

Healthy Birth Day
http://www.healthybirthday.org
email: info@healthybirthday.org

Centering Healthcare Institute

Centering Healthcare Institute (CHI) is committed to shifting the paradigm of health services to a group care model in order to improve the overall health outcomes of mothers, babies, new families and all individuals across the life cycle.

Centering Healthcare Institute
89 South Street #404
Boston, MA 02111 USA
https://www.centeringhealthcare.org
phone: 857-284-7570

Bay Area Birth Association

Bay Area Birth Association is a multi-disciplinary organization committed to improving the outcomes of birth in the Bay Area, and committed to doing it in a cooperative manner.

Bay Area Birth Association
http://www.bayareabirth.org
email: info@bayareabirth.org

Mother Health International

Mother Health International is dedicated to respond and provide relief to pregnant women and children in areas of disaster and extreme poverty. They are committed to reducing the maternal and infant mortality rates by creating healthy, sustainable and holistic birth clinics by using the midwifery model of care with culturally appropriate education for the health and empowerment of women.

Mother Health International
http://motherhealthinternational.org
email: info@motherhealthinternational.org

LIFE

LIFE exists to save lives and transform the futures of some of the most disadvantaged children and young people in the UK by supporting vulnerable pregnant mothers, and young families through difficult times, offering them the help they need to turn their lives around.

LIFE
1 Mill Street
Leamington Spa
Warwickshire
CV31 1ES United Kingdom
http://www.lifecharity.org.uk
email: jo@lifecharity.org.uk
phone: 01926 421 587

Tommy's

Tommy's funds pregnancy research and provides information on the causes and prevention of miscarriage, still birth, and premature birth. Tommy's believes it is unacceptable that one in four women will lose a baby during pregnancy and birth.

Tommy's
Nicholas House
3 Laurence Pountney Hill
London
EC4R 0BB United Kingdom
http://www.tommys.org
email: mailbox@tommys.org
phone: 0207 398 3400

Childbirth Australia

Childbirth Australia is an organization focused on improving maternity services through research, knowledge-dissemination and advocacy of woman-centred care.

Childbirth Australia
http://childbirth.org.au
email: info@childbirth.org.au

CHOICE

CHOICE is an organization of parents and professionals supporting the right of parents to choose more humane options in their childbirth experiences.

CHOICE
5721 North High Street
Worthington, Ohio 43085 USA
http://www.choicemidwives.org
email: choicemidwives@aol.com
phone: 614-263-2229

Australian Institute for Patient and Family Centred Care

The Australian Institute for Patient and Family Centred Care was established to promote a new model of healthcare that moves beyond the familiar static model of doctor as giver, patient as receiver.

http://www.aipfcc.org.au

RESOURCE EXAMPLES

Center for Nonprofit Success

The Center for Nonprofit Success is an organization working to provide the training, knowledge and resources to help nonprofit organizations succeed.

Center for Nonprofit Success
3307 19th Street NW, Suite A4
Washington, DC 20010 USA
http://www.cfnps.org
phone: 202-469-6773

Center for Nonprofit Strategy and Management

The Center for Nonprofit Strategy and Management strives to improve the nonprofit sector in the New York area through education, research, and management support.

Center for Nonprofit Strategy and Management
One Bernard Baruch Way, D-901
New York, NY 10010 USA
http://www.baruch.cuny.edu/spa/researchcenters
email: nonprofit.workshops@baruch.cuny.edu
phone: 646-660-6743

Canada Business

Canada Business has information regarding the guidelines to start a nonprofit company.

http://www.canadabusiness.ca/eng
phone: 888-576-4444

Philanthropy Australia

Philanthropy Australia is the national peak body for philanthropy whose members are trusts and foundations, families and individuals who want to make a difference through their own philanthropy and to encourage others to become philanthropists. They strive to represent, grow and inspire an effective and robust philanthropic sector for the community.

Philanthropy Australia
Level 2
55 Collins Street
Melbourne VIC 3000 Australia
http://www.philanthropy.org.au
email: info@philanthropy.org.au

Australian Taxation Office

Australian Taxation Offices provide guidelines and assistance for starting a nonprofit company.

http://www.ato.gov.au/nonprofit

Nonprofit Resource Center

The Nonprofit Resource Center offers comprehensive resources, a professionally staffed library, access to a grant funds database, fundraising workshops and management networking. The Center enables new and existing nonprofits to improve management, operations, fund development, marketing, public relations, board development and more.

Nonprofit Resource Center
1331 Garden Highway
Sacramento, CA 95833 USA
http://www.nprcenter.org
email: info@nprcenter.org
phone: 916-285-1840

The Nonprofit Center of Milwaukee

The Nonprofit Center of Milwaukee has served as the area's primary resource to nonprofit agencies. They provide the tools and training needed to successfully fulfill the mission of a nonprofit company, and improve the lives of people in the community.

The Nonprofit Center of Milwaukee
2819 West Highland Boulevard
Milwaukee, WI 53208 USA
http://www.nonprofitcentermilwaukee.org
email: info@nonprofitcentermilwaukee.org
phone: 414-344-3933

PARENT EDUCATOR

Parent Educators assist parents to understand infant and early child behaviors. Educators help parents develop the essential skills necessary to care for and raise their children. They provide guidance to parents navigating their new roles and responsibilities. They also empower parents to make informed decisions for their families.

Search words: parent coach, parent educator, parenting specialist, parent educator workshop, new parent educator

GETTING STARTED

Take a training workshop for parent educators. Observe a new parent class. Research and learn about parenting and child development. Seek mentoring from an experienced Parent Educator.

ORGANIZATIONS

The Parent Coaching Institute

The Parent Coaching Institute sets standards for Parent Coaching Professionals. Through their coaching model, they co-create with parents new levels of family fulfillment.

The Parent Coaching Institute
1400-112th Ave. SE, Suite 100
Bellevue, WA 98004 USA
http://www.parentcoachinginstitute.com
email: info@thepci.org
phone: 888-599-4447

Bringing Baby Home

The Bringing Baby Home project combines scientific research and service product delivery in order to improve the quality of life for babies and children by strengthening their families.

Bringing Baby Home
2030 1st Ave #205
Seattle, WA 98121 USA
http://www.bbhonline.org
email: bbh.ct@bbhonline.org
phone: 206-832-0355

Center for Early Education and Development

Center for Early Education and Development (CEED) promotes ongoing coordination and expansion of academic leaders interested in early education and development. They offer a variety of online courses for family and child development.

Center for Early Education and Development
University of Minnesota
1954 Buford Ave, Suite 425
St. Paul, MN 55108 USA
http://www.cehd.umn.edu/ceed/onlinecourses
email: ceed@umn.edu
phone: 612-625-3058

Baby Calm

Baby Calm aims to understand a baby's needs from a scientific, biological and psychological perspective as well as understanding and balancing these with the needs of the new parent.

Baby Calm
16 Mandeville Road
Saffron Walden
Essex, CB11 4AQ
United Kingdom
http://www.babycalm.co.uk/training/info_14.html
email: training@babycalm.co.uk
phone: 0845 094 0075

NCT

NCT supports parents by giving them accurate, impartial information so that they can decide what's best for their family. Parents can gain practical and emotional support from a network of others.

NCT
Alexandra House
Oldham Terrace
Acton
London W3 6NH United Kingdom
http://www.nct.org.uk/nct-college
email: ceo@nct.org.uk
phone: 0300 330 0017

Ngala Institute of Education and Learning

Ngala is a provider of Early Parenting and Early Childhood services with a passion for supporting and guiding families and young children through the journey of parenting.

Ngala Institute of Education and Learning
9 George St
Kensington WA 6151 Australia
http://www.ngala.com.au
email: education@ngala.com.au

Happiest Baby

The Happiest Baby Certification Program is part of Dr. Harvey Karp's vision to strengthen the bond between parents and their children and to help them create happier, healthier, more loving families.

Happiest Baby
12300 Wilshire Blvd # 320
Los Angeles, CA 90025 USA
http://www.happiestbaby.com
email: info@thehappiestbaby.com
phone: 888-980-8062

Dr. Sears LEAN Programs

Dr. Sears LEAN Programs build a healthier world one family at a time by focusing on Lifestyle, Exercise, Attitude and Nutrition.

Dr. Sears LEAN Programs
7200 S. Alton Way, Suite B 220
Centennial, CO 80112 USA
http://www.drsearslean.com
phone: 866-446-1967

Hug Your Baby

HUG Your Baby (HYB) provides family-friendly information created from evidence-based child development and medical literature. HYB helps parents prevent and solve problems regarding eating, sleeping, crying, and parent-child bonding and provides innovative training and resources to professionals who serve expectant and new parents.

Hug Your Baby
PO Box 3102
Durham, NC 27715 USA
http://www.hugyourbaby.org
email: hugyourbaby@earthlink.net
phone: 919-923-6609

Dunstan Baby Language

The Dunstan Baby Language teaches parents to understand and respond to exactly what their babies need. Every newborn communicates from birth to 3 months using five distinct sounds that signal hunger, tiredness, need to burp, and discomfort.

http://www.dunstanbaby.com

Attachment Parenting International

Attachment Parenting International (API) promotes parenting practices that create lifelong strong and healthy emotional bonds between children and their parents. Through education, support, advocacy and research, API works to heighten global awareness of the profound significance of secure attachment.

http://www.attachmentparenting.org

Active Parenting

Active Parenting is recognized as an innovator in the educational market and is committed to developing human potential through our programs.

Active Parenting
1220 Kennestone Circle, Suite 130
Marietta, GA 30066 USA
http://www.activeparenting.com
email: cservice@activeparenting.com

PERINATAL FITNESS INSTRUCTOR ALSO PRENATAL AND POSTNATAL FITNESS INSTRUCTOR

Perinatal Fitness Instructors are trained to lead exercise classes for pregnant women that are safe and beneficial. They work with moms from pregnancy through postpartum. Instructors are knowledgeable about the changes to a pregnant woman's body and are able to create appropriate exercise plans.

Search words: perinatal fitness certification, perinatal fitness training, perinatal instructor training, postnatal fitness, prenatal fitness educator

GETTING STARTED

Enroll in an instructor certification or diploma course for prenatal and postpartum fitness. Observe exercise classes that are specifically for pregnant women. Read books and watch DVDs about fitness for pregnant women.

ORGANIZATIONS

International Childbirth Education Association

The International Childbirth Education Association (ICEA) offers a Prenatal and Postpartum Fitness Educator course providing current maternal fitness guidelines and strategies for class development for professionals.

International Childbirth Education Association
1500 Sunday Drive, Suite 102
Raleigh, NC 27607 USA
http://www.icea.org
email: info@icea.org
phone: 919-863-9487

American Fitness Professionals and Associates

The American Fitness Professionals and Associates (AFPA) provides students with an affordable education that gives them the knowledge, skills and awareness necessary to enhance their own lives, the lives of others, and the community at large through innovative program design, teaching, research and service focused on the professional practice of fitness, wellness, nutrition, health and physical education.

American Fitness Professionals and Associates
1601 Long Beach Blvd
PO Box 214
Ship Bottom, NJ 08008 USA
http://www.afpafitness.com
email: afpa@afpafitness.com
phone: 800-494-7782

Baby & Me Fitness

Baby & Me Fitness offers a Prenatal and Postnatal Fitness Instructor certification program.

Baby & Me Fitness
208 Bloor St. W. Suite 503
Toronto, ON Canada M5S 3B4
http://www.babyandmefitness.com
email: info@babyandmefitness.com
phone: 416-604-2249

Oh Baby! Fitness

Oh Baby! Fitness has a Prenatal and Postpartum Instructor training for professionals. The training is web-based, self-guided and includes an online training manual with pictures, illustrations and demonstration videos.

Oh Baby! Fitness
116 Drexel Avenue
Decatur, GA 30030 USA
http://ohbabyfitness.com/train
email: contactus@ohbabyfitness.com
phone: 678-528-1390

Childbirth and Postpartum Professional Association

Childbirth and Postpartum Professional Association (CAPPA) offers a distance course for Pregnancy Fitness Educators.

Childbirth and Postpartum Professional Association
PO Box 2406
Buford, GA 30515 USA
http://www.cappa.net
email: info@cappa.net
phone: 888-692-2772

Motherwell Maternity Health and Fitness

The Motherwell Mindful Pregnancy and Parenting Fitness course provides everything needed to offer safe and effective fitness programs, whether working with pregnant women and new mothers in a group exercise class, or one-on-one.

Motherwell Maternity Health and Fitness
1220 Hillside Drive
Carlisle, PA 17013 USA
http://www.momwell.com
email: bonnie@bonnieberk.com
phone: 717-258-4641

Focus Training

Focus Training offers a course to equip instructors with the essential knowledge to manage Ante and Post Natal exercise classes safely and effectively.

Focus Training
5 Canon Court
Institute Street
Bolton
Lancashire
BL1 1PZ United Kingdom
http://www.focus-training.com
email: info@ focus-training.com
phone: 0333 9000 222

Healthy Moms

The Healthy Moms Advanced Perinatal Fitness Instructor training course covers the benefits, risks, and overall effects of exercise in relation to each phase of the perinatal period.

Healthy Moms
505 Arbor Lane
Centerville, GA 31028
http://www.healthymomsfitness.com/training.htm
email: info@healthymomsfitness.com
phone: 866-672-6667

Aviva Institute

Aviva Institute offers a unique and comprehensive program designed to prepare instructors to teach holistic prenatal and postnatal fitness classes. The course includes the latest perinatal fitness research, guidelines and exercise techniques.

Aviva Institute
1660 South Highway 100 Suite 500
St. Louis Park, MN 55416 USA
http://avivainstitute.org
phone: 800-951-4110

Prepared Childbirth Educators, Inc.

Prepared Childbirth Educators, Inc. offers a Prenatal and Postnatal Fitness Instructor Certification (CPFI).

Prepared Childbirth Educators, Inc.
219 Central Avenue
Hatboro, PA 19040 USA
https://www.childbirtheducation.org
phone: 888-344-9972

Fit for Birth

The Fit For Birth Prenatal Certification provides knowledge and tools to teach safe and effective exercise programs to pregnant women.

http://www.getfitforbirth.com
phone: 786-200-8949

Fit 4 Two

The Fit 4 Two Pre and Postnatal Fitness Specialist (PPFS) certification program prepares fitness instructors and personal trainers to work with this specialized population.

Fit 4 Two
2603-1009 Expo Blvd
Vancouver BC V6Z 2V9
Canada
http://www.fit4two.ca
email: info@fit4two.ca
phone: 604-602-1546

PHOTOGRAPHER

Photographers can develop a thriving business by focusing on pregnant women, babies, and family photos. Families are experiencing a happy and transformative period in their lifespan and search for a skilled photographer to capture their joy.

Search words: baby photographer training, baby photographer association, pregnancy photography, baby photography

GETTING STARTED

Join an association for Child Photographers. Take a class or workshop to learn tips and techniques for takings photos of babies and pregnant women. Read books about child and pregnancy photography. Seek advice from photographers that have experience taking pictures of babies, pregnant moms, and families.

BOOKS

The Art of Pregnancy Photography by Jennifer George

Photographing Children Photo Workshop: Develop Your Digital Photography Talent by Ginny Felch

The Art of Children's Portrait Photography by Tamara Lackey

ORGANIZATIONS

National Association of Professional Child Photographers

The National Association of Professional Child Photographers (NAPCP) is an association that promotes and supports the artistry and integrity of Professional Child Photographers. NAPCP provides the most comprehensive resources for its members, bringing together a community of passionate artists committed to growth in their skills, their artistry, and their businesses.

http://www.napcp.com

Aspire Photography Training

The Aspire Photography course Yummy Mummy will teach how to enhance this most natural of subjects, using sympathetic lighting and appropriate composition.

Photographing a mother during pregnancy or the first, tentative steps of motherhood is a privilege, and must be approached with sensitivity and understanding. This beautiful cycle evokes Mother Nature at her most magnificent, and it takes real skill to capture bumps and babies to perfection, resplendent in all their innocence and beauty.

Aspire Photography Training
Dalton Hall
Units One & Two
The Stable Yard
Burton-in-Kendal
Cumbria LA6 1NJ United Kingdom
http://www.aspirephotographytraining.co.uk/courses.php
email: enquiries@aspirecpt.co.uk
phone: 01524 782200

Bossy Baby Photography

Bossy Baby Photography 101 is an online photography course and mentoring program taught by acclaimed Children's Photographer, Lisa Arnel.

http://www.bossybabyphotography.com
email: bossybabyphotography@gmail.com
phone: 843-439-1699

Pennycress Photography

Pennycress Photography offers a newborn posing workshop.

http://www.pennycressphotography.co.uk/html
email: info@pennycressphotography.co.uk
phone: 07866 389004

International Association of Newborn Photographers

The International Association of Newborn Photographers believes all photographers have the right to explore their creativity and benefit from 21st century marketing techniques.

http://members.bestnewbornphotographers.org

LaurieL Photography

LaurieL Photography offers several different mentoring options for aspiring or seasoned photographers who want to start a Maternity and Newborn Photography business, or just sharpen their existing maternity and newborn photography and post-production skills.

http://www.newbornphotoprops.com

Harriette Hartigan

Harriette Hartigan desires everyone to see what she witnesses during birth, the courage, power, dignity, beauty, love, and passion in the awesome effort of labor and the exquisite truth of birth. Her work is devoted to bringing to sight this epic reality that brings each of us to life on earth.

Harriette Hartigan
3337 McComb St.
Ann Arbor, MI 48108 USA
http://harriettehartigan.com
email: insight@harriettehartigan.com
phone: 734-677-0519

PLACENTA ENCAPSULATION SPECIALIST

Placenta Encapsulation Specialists create capsules from the placenta delivered at birth. The placenta capsules help to decrease or prevent postpartum mood disorders and depression. Each woman's placenta has hormones specifically designed for her and are beneficial to increase her milk production, increase iron supply, boost energy, and promote a healthy balanced mother.

Search words: placenta encapsulation specialist, placenta encapsulation training, placenta encapsulation workshop, placenta ingestion, placenta encapsulation research

GETTING STARTED

Take a Placenta Encapsulation Specialists workshop or online training class. Seek out articles and information about the benefits of placenta ingestion to the health of women. Talk to women who have taken placenta capsules to discover the results they received. Ask a Placenta Encapsulation Specialist to mentor you.

ဆၣ

Career Journey ...

Placenta Service Provider, Tamara Morales

How did you get started as a Placenta Service Provider?

After my oldest was born, I developed extremely severe Postpartum Depression. I was on multiple medications and participated in weekly therapy sessions for over a year. So, when we found out I was pregnant again it was a total shock and the first thing both my husband and I feared was that I would develop PPD again. I immediately started doing my own research and found Placenta Encapsulation. I knew in my heart that this would be my answer to a more enjoyable and better-adjusted postpartum period, so after the birth of our second daughter, we took our placenta home with us from the hospital and I encapsulated it myself with the limited know how I had at the time.

Why do you do this work? What do you enjoy?

After experiencing the benefits firsthand, that Placenta Encapsulation has to offer I realized that I wanted to help other new moms experience a more balanced postpartum period too. Having to find the time to prepare my own placenta after having my baby was a challenge. I wanted to rest and relax with my family, not be working in the kitchen over a steaming pot of placenta. So, that is when I knew other moms in our area could benefit greatly from a Placenta Service Provider coming to their home and doing all the work for them while they cuddled their new bundle of joy. It is very fulfilling to meet new moms and their growing families. I am invited into their homes during a special time and it is such a pleasure to be able to make their transition easier. I am honored to work with their placentas and get to know the families, and have remained friends with many of my past clients which is always heartwarming.

How do you like running a business? What business advice can you share?

Running a business, no matter what type, takes time and dedication. Add to that working with families during such a monumental and intimate time in their lives and you really have to be respectful of the needs of each individual family. I also always remember that I am a mom first and I believe the passion for my family shines through in my work with my "placenta moms" and their families as well.

What type of training or education did you receive?

I started my journey getting trained and certified through a Placenta Encapsulation company in early 2009, but shortly after, I began working independently due to business practices that I could not in good faith align myself with. As an independent Placenta Service Provider, I have had the flexibility to gain more knowledge in Traditional Chinese Medicine practices and herbal medicine, which I feel, adds to the services I can provide new moms taking advantage of Placenta Encapsulation. In order to provide a safe service I must follow all EPA and OSHA standards of safe preparation and handling along with adhering to California State and County laws and regulations that govern all aspects of food handling, blood-borne pathogens, and disposal of small laboratory medical waste. However, beyond my formal training nothing could replace the knowledge I have received from mentor Placenta Service Providers that I have the pleasure of networking with.

Do you have any "aha" moments or insights to share about your work?

It has been hugely important for me to respect each placenta's story. Many people view it as medical waste or a piece of meat but it is much more than that. Aside from the medicinal aspects, I treat the placenta as sacred, and focus on honoring the work it has done to nourish the baby, while preparing it to continue its work nourishing the mother. Placenta Encapsulation is not a fad, but a time honored tradition that should be respected.

What advice can you give to anyone that wishes to become a Placenta Encapsulation Specialist?

This is something that should not be jumped into to make fast money, but should be a labor of love. A Placenta Service Provider should only work professionally after a lot of education in all aspects of this practice. And also a lot of mentoring to ensure they can offer a 100% safe service. When I was getting started, I prepared many placentas free of charge or at a greatly reduced rate in order to gain the experience I needed to be competent in my work. There is only one chance at preparing a placenta, so anyone doing this should have invested both time and money in the proper training and professional equipment to ensure they are offering the best service they possibly can. Working with placentas should be an honor and a deep commitment by the preparer, passing on that positive energy into their work. I feel any goal other than wanting to help postpartum moms should not play a role in wanting to offer this service.

Anything else you would like to share?

In June 2011, I celebrated two years of offering my Placenta Encapsulation services and I hope that I can continue to share the benefits of placenta remedies to moms in our area for years to come. I would like to thank everyone who has helped me in my Placenta Encapsulation journey.

$$\infty\heartsuit$$

ORGANIZATIONS

IPEN Placenta Network

IPEN Placenta Network is an International Network of Placenta Encapsulation Specialists who provide Placenta Encapsulation services to women after birth. IPEN offers training and certification of Placenta Encapsulation Specialist in the UK.

http://placentanetwork.com
phone: 07908 748187

Placenta Benefits.info

Placenta Benefits.info (PBi) offers a training course for Placenta Encapsulation Specialists. PBi strives to make the use of placenta for postpartum recovery a normal part of the birthing process. Trained professionals provide quality Placenta Encapsulation services, adhering to the highest safety standards.

Placenta Benefits.info
3053 West Craig Rd Suite E-195
North Las Vegas, NV 89032 USA
http://placentabenefits.info/certification.asp
email: info@placentabenefits.info
phone: 888-956-9724

EXAMPLES OF PLACENTA ENCAPSULATION SPECIALISTS

Heavenly Health Store

The Heavenly Health Store has over 50 years' experience in Traditional Chinese Medicine (TCM) and provide the best care possible. They properly handle the placenta to retain its invaluable properties for the benefit of a postpartum mother.

http://heavenlyhealthstore.com

Placenta Mom

Placenta Mom provides encapsulation services for families.

http://placentamom.weebly.com

DuChene Natural Health Center

Leigh Anne of DuChene Natural Health Center provides a quality, safe, and beneficial Placenta Encapsulation service to postpartum mothers.

http://dallasplacentaencapsulation.com

Placenta Encapsulation San Diego

Placenta Encapsulation San Diego provides encapsulation in-home services.

http://placentaencapsulationsandiego.com

PODCASTER

Podcasters produce audio content about childbirth, parenting, baby care, or other topics and upload it to a website for the public to hear. A podcast can have any format, be a radio show or an informative class. Podcasters are free and flexible to create whatever type of style and content they choose. A podcast that you create can be heard all over the world through the internet. Podcasts that are produced as a series can be uploaded to the iTunes store.

Search words: pregnancy podcast, childbirth podcast, podcast tools, podcast apps, how to podcast

GETTING STARTED

Listen to podcasts through iTunes or website blogs to learn about the format and content used by Podcasters. Read books about how to podcast. Use the learning center or community forum of a podcast website to understand how to get started and the process of podcasting.

ΣΟΩ

Career Journey ...

Podcast Host, Penny Johnston

How did you get started as the host of ABC Babytalk?

I was incredibly lucky to be given this opportunity by my manager after returning to work from maternity leave. He'd identified a gap in our programming for new parents. Australia has been experiencing a small baby boom and the increase in new parents has centred around a group of older parents who possibly don't have the skills or family connections to easily adapt to parenthood! The idea of a weekly podcast to deal with the sort of issues I had experienced as one of these older unskilled parents was mine, and so in choosing topics it was easy to remember my own recent experiences and wonder how I might have been helped by having more information!

Why do you do this work? What do you enjoy?

Well it's a fantastic way to earn a living. I get to ask all the silly questions many parents are afraid to ask. I get to have some real insight into the science of raising children and since becoming a mother I get to spend time talking all day about my new favorite topic, babies! I have which is rather odd for most journalists, a background degree in science (biochemistry and physiology), this science research training means I can pounce on new scientific reports with a bit more understanding. It doesn't mean I ask more intelligent questions, it just means I'm not afraid to! A couple of weeks ago I was a contestant on a big quiz show! I was about to take home a massive prize that would have been about four years' salary... while I didn't win, if I had I'd still be back at work on Monday morning!

Are you employed, independent contractor, or a business owner?

I am employed. I enjoy having the massively supportive back up of my managers and the technical support and expertise that comes with working for the Australian Broadcasting Corporation.

What type of training or education did you receive?

I have a Degree in Biological Sciences. I also have postgraduate degrees in teaching and journalism. I have many years work experience as a radio broadcaster and every element of that experience was completely out the window when I became a mother! It all helps to add to my experience for Babytalk and it helps to have a sense of the absurd and a sense of humor!

Do you have any "aha" moments or insights to share about your work?

I think the biggest thrill to me is connecting with the audience and this happens in a number of ways, people track me down via the traditional routes through ABC Radio but also social media has played a role in that connection. Our Facebook presence gives me instant feedback from our audience. I have received story ideas, suggestions, and comments about aired stories. Just the chance to know how the information from a podcast is helping someone is very rewarding.

What advice can you give to anyone that wishes to host a podcast or work in journalism?

Well working in journalism is a hard feat. Getting a job you're happy with takes a bit of time and an awful lot of effort. It's getting that first break that is the hardest, but working hard at what you love isn't really hard work at all. My best advice is to listen hard and take every opportunity. My advice for podcasting is twofold: first, never be boring, and second, get it right technically. I personally hate listening to waffly, badly produced podcasts. My time is too valuable, and if I hear something that sounds too amateurish, I'm moving on.

Anything else you would like to share?

Never stop having fun, try and always put yourself in someone else's shoes... don't imagine yours is the only opinion that counts!

ℰℭ

PODCAST RESOURCES

BlogTalkRadio

BlogTalkRadio allows anyone, anywhere the ability to host a live talk radio show online, simply by using a telephone and a computer.

http://www.blogtalkradio.com

Cinch

Cinch is a free and easy way to create and share audio, text and photo updates using a phone or computer.

http://cinch.fm

PODCAST EXAMPLES

Pea in the Podcast

Pea in the Podcast provides pregnancy information and advice from experts.

http://www.peainthepodcast.com

PregTASTIC

PregTASTIC is a weekly online radio show celebrating the fantastic journey to motherhood.

http://www.pregtastic.com

ABC Babytalk

ABC Babytalk is a podcast show about babies and their parents.

http://www.abc.net.au/melbourne/babytalk

Mother Love

Mother Love produces a podcast about topics related to pregnancy and breastfeeding.

http://motherloveblog.com/category/podcasts

POLICY MAKER

Policy Makers work through various government agencies, hospital boards, insurance companies, professional associations, university committees, and community groups to implement practices, policies, and laws that often have national and global impact. Policy Makers have a wide range of experience, knowledge, and educational backgrounds. They serve a diverse set of interests. Policy Makers that work in the childbirth field have the ability to improve health care for women and their families.

Search words: maternal health policy, midwifery lobbyist, maternal child health committee, maternal child public health, masters in public health, maternal child health

GETTING STARTED

Learn about Masters in Public Health programs and advanced studies in Maternal Child Health. Join maternal child health associations and groups. Serve on committees that write and implement policies. Research and apply for government and fellowship opportunities in public health. Read and become knowledgeable about beneficial and harmful childbirth health care policies. Work to adopt and spread the practice of evidence-based childbirth health care policies.

EXAMPLE ORGANIZATIONS

Maternal and Child Health Bureau

The Maternal and Child Health Bureau (MCHB) provides leadership, in partnership with key stakeholders, to improve the physical and mental health, safety and well-being of the nation's women, infants, children, adolescents, and their families, including fathers and children with special health care needs.

http://mchb.hrsa.gov/about/index.html

NSW Ministerial Maternal and Perinatal Committee

The purpose of the Maternal and Perinatal Health Priority Taskforce is to provide direction and leadership for (New South Wales) NSW maternal and perinatal services to achieve highly integrated services that reflect best national and international standards.

http://www.health.nsw.gov.au/publichealth/mph/index.asp

Association of Maternal and Child Health Programs

The Association of Maternal and Child Health Programs is a national resource, partner and advocate for state public health leaders and others working to improve the health of women, children, youth and families, including those with special health care needs.

AMCHP's members come from the highest levels of state government and include directors of Maternal and Child Health programs, directors of programs for children with special health care needs, and other public health leaders who work with and support state Maternal and Child Health programs.

Association of Maternal and Child Health Programs
2030 M Street, NW Suite 350
Washington, DC 20036 USA
http://www.amchp.org
email: info@amchp.org
phone: 202-775-0436

Transforming Maternity Care Partnership

The aim of the Transforming Maternity Care Partnership is to accelerate health system change toward the envisioned high quality, high value maternity care system.

Transforming Maternity Care Partnership
260 Madison, 8th Fl
New York, NY 10016 USA
http://transform.childbirthconnection.org
phone: 212-777-5000

United Nations Population Fund

UNFPA, the United Nations Population Fund, is an international development agency that promotes the right of universal access to sexual and reproductive health and reproductive rights and aims to reduce maternal mortality and accelerate progress on the International Conference on Population and Development (ICPD) agenda and MDG 5. UNFPA also supports countries in using population data for policies and programs to reduce poverty and to ensure that every pregnancy is wanted, every birth is safe, every young person is free of HIV and every girl and woman is treated with dignity and respect.

United Nations Population Fund
605 Third Avenue
New York, NY 10158 USA
http://www.unfpa.org
email: hq@unfpa.org
phone: 212-297-5000

Midwives and Mothers in Action

The Midwives and Mothers in Action (MAMA Campaign) is a collaborative effort by the National Association of Certified

Professional Midwives (NACPM), Midwives Alliance of North America (MANA), Citizens for Midwifery (CfM), International Center for Traditional Childbearing (ICTC), North American Registry of Midwives (NARM), and the Midwifery Education Accreditation Council (MEAC). This partnership is working to gain federal recognition of Certified Professional Midwives so that women and families will have increased access to quality, affordable maternity care in the settings of their choice.

Midwives and Mothers in Action
http://www.mamacampaign.org
email: info@mamacampaign

National Perinatal Association

The National Perinatal Association (NPA) promotes the health and well-being of mothers and infants enriching families, communities and our world.

National Perinatal Association
457 State Street
Binghamton, NY 13901 USA
http://www.nationalperinatal.org
email: npa@nationalperinatal.org
phone: 888-971-3295

POSTPARTUM DOULA

The Postpartum Doula provides assistance to new mothers and their families after the birth of a baby. Postpartum Doulas give in home care and support to the mother by answering questions and concerns regarding the baby. They are knowledgeable about breastfeeding and able to offer basic nursing support. They help the family through the first weeks by preparing meals, doing light housekeeping, and running errands.

Search words: postpartum doula certification, postpartum doula training, postpartum doula workshop, postpartum doula association, postnatal doula training

GETTING STARTED

Enroll in a Postpartum Doula workshop or online training class. Join an association or group that supports Postpartum Doulas. Read about postpartum and learn how to help women cope with the emotional and physical transition. Ask an experienced Postpartum Doula to serve as your mentor.

₧₨

Career Journey ...

Postpartum Doula, Molly Rouse

How did you get started as a Postpartum Doula?

Our son, Oscar, was born in January of 2007. After Oscar's birth, I was "doula-ed" in a way that I try to emulate in the services I provide. My mother and sister both attended the birth and then lived with us for the first week of Oscar's life – taking care of everything around the house, and me, so that I could focus on my new baby and the new skills I was learning.

My journey to becoming a Postpartum Doula has been a delightful one. When I became pregnant, I started reading everything I could about parenting, particularly how other cultures raise their children. I developed and taught an Anthropology course at UNCA called "Cultures of Childrearing." Through the research I did for this class and my own experience, I have learned that many other societies recognize and support the transition new families go through much more than we do in the United States. I wanted to find a way to fill the void in my community, and while looking for jobs that fit my interests and skills, I found out about Postpartum Doulas. I trained and completed DONA certification in 2009.

Why do you do this work? What do you enjoy?

I enjoy supporting other families as they continue their journey with a new member. It feels very real and very meaningful. I truly believe that if all children started life with calm, confident, and joyous parents, the world would be a more wonderful place. Likewise, if all parents started out in their new roles feeling supported, educated, and excited about their child and their future together, the world would be a more wonderful place.

I enjoy cooking good food - both nutritious and delicious - for families, seeing parents gain confidence with the care of their baby, helping moms succeed with breastfeeding, and processing any questions or fears that may arise.

How do you like running a business? What business advice can you share?

I like being self-employed, but I have to say that it would be much harder in terms of marketing and networking if I wasn't involved in the local Doula association, Doula Association of the Mountain Area (DAMA).

The only advice I have is to network with other people in the birth world - get your name out in the right circles.

What type of training or education did you receive?

I feel like I have been training for this work all my life. From growing up in a small community when we all helped each other out to studying parenting practices around the world.

Do you have any "aha" moments or insights to share about your work?

Each family is another teacher for me. Humans are so complicated and different from each other that I will constantly be learning. It is this element that will keep me involved in this work for the rest of my life.

What advice can you give to anyone that wishes to become a Postpartum Doula?

I think that it is necessary to come into this work from a place of stability and ease. This work can be emotionally hard, and I don't see how you can offer calm nurturing care if you are not calm and nurtured yourself. I think it is good to have a colleague or two you can discuss clients' situations with (maintaining anonymity, of course) as we all need to process and get ideas from each other.

శంలర

ORGANIZATIONS

DONA International

DONA International provides training and certification opportunities for Doulas of varied cultures, educational backgrounds, ethnic backgrounds and socio-economic levels. They strive to educate health care providers, the public and third-party payers about the benefits of a Doulas presence through childbirth and postpartum.

DONA International
1582 S. Parker Rd, Suite 201
Denver, CO 80231 USA
http://www.dona.org
email: dona@dona.org
phone: 888-788- 3662

Childbirth and Postpartum Professional Association

Childbirth and Postpartum Professional Association (CAPPA) certified professionals strive to facilitate empowerment, connection, and self-advocacy in families from pre-conception through early parenthood. CAPPA works to foster and encourage culturally relevant education, support, and training in countries around the world.

Childbirth and Postpartum Professional Association
PO Box 2406
Buford, GA 30515 USA
http://www.cappa.net
email: info@cappa.net
phone: 888-692-2772

Bastyr University

Bastyr University Department of Midwifery offers a four-day training workshop for Postpartum Doulas.

Bastyr University
Department of Midwifery
14500 Juanita Drive NE
Kenmore, WA 98028
http://www.seattlemidwifery.org
email: simkincenter@bastyr.edu
phone: 425-602-3000

CAPPA Canada

CAPPA Canada offers a Postpartum Doula training to examine the role of the Postpartum Doula in society. The training provides an understanding of postpartum and teaches professionals to identify and meet the needs of families and provide appropriate resources.

CAPPA Canada
3445 Trim Road, PO Box 5
Ottawa, Ontario
K4B 1J3 Canada
http://www.cappacanada.ca
email: info@cappacanada.ca
phone: 613-429-0188

Birth Arts International

Birth Arts International trains dynamic wise women Doulas, Postpartum Doulas, Childbirth Educators, Midwife's Assistants and Breastfeeding Educators in flexible education programs.

Birth Arts International
501 Lindsey St
Reidsville, NC 27320 USA
http://www.birtharts.com
email: demetria@birtharts.com
phone: 866-303-4372

Childbirth International

Childbirth International (CBI) provides a unique approach to training and certification for Childbirth Professionals. The Childbirth International programs have all been designed specifically for home-based learning, with different learning styles in mind.

Childbirth International
http://www.childbirthinternational.com

MaternityWise

MaternityWise was founded with the belief that every woman and her family deserve the benefits of positive community with informative, encouraging support during the childbearing years.

MaternityWise
8503 NW Military Hwy, Suite 105-11
San Antonio, TX 78231 USA
http://www.maternitywise.com
email: trainings@maternitywise.com
phone: 952-457-6506

Aviva Institute

Aviva Institute provides comprehensive and accessible education for Midwives and health care providers, based in their own communities, providing the highest standards of academic excellence, which encompasses a holistic model of integrating mind, body, heart, and spirit.

Aviva Institute
1660 South Highway 100 Suite 500
St. Louis Park, MN 55416 USA
https://avivainstitute.org
email: nikkiguerton.aviva@gmail.com
phone: 800-951-4110

Optimum Birth

Optimum Birth is an online Postnatal Doula training course that individuals can take at their own pace.

http://www.optimumbirth.com.au/index.html

PRENATAL MASSAGE THERAPIST

Prenatal Massage Therapists provide massage services to women during pregnancy. Therapists are usually professionally trained and licensed. They understand the physiological changes taking place during pregnancy and know how to safely treat aches and discomforts.

Search words: pregnancy massage certification, prenatal massage certification, prenatal massage diploma, prenatal massage association, prenatal massage course, prenatal massage school

GETTING STARTED

Enroll in a prenatal massage training course. Join a pregnancy massage association. Read books about prenatal massage. Pursue getting licensed as a Massage Therapist, specializing in prenatal massage.

BOOKS

Prenatal Massage: A Textbook of Pregnancy, Labor, and Postpartum Bodywork by Elaine Stillerman, LMT

Pre- and Perinatal Massage Therapy: A Comprehensive Guide to Prenatal, Labor, and Postpartum Practice by Carole Osborne

Nurturing Massage for Pregnancy: A Practical Guide to Bodywork for the Perinatal Cycle by Leslie Stager

ORGANIZATIONS

American Pregnancy Massage Association

American Pregnancy Massage Association (APMA) is a professional organization promoting the benefits of pregnancy massage. They desire to help women feel good during pregnancy, believing pregnancy massage is a valuable component of prenatal care when done by a trained massage therapist. APMA provides public and professional education, sets professional standards for members, and promotes research in the field of prenatal massage.

American Pregnancy Massage Association
11585 Links Drive
Reston, VA 20190 USA
http://americanpregnancymassage.org

Well Mother

Well Mother supports the wisdom of parents and babies through massage, shiatsu, and exercise. They offer training workshops for professionals. Well Mother promotes relaxation as a core part of 21st century maternity care.

Well Mother
24, Dunkerry Road
Windmill Hill
Bristol BS3 4LB United Kingdom
http://wellmother.org
email: web@wellmother.org
phone: 0117 963 2306

Middlesex School of Complementary Medicine

Middlesex School of Complementary Medicine offers a Maternity Massage Practitioner Diploma course providing confidence and training to professionals seeking to become qualified Maternity Massage Practitioners.

Middlesex School of Complementary Medicine
PO Box 639
Pinner
HA5 9JD United Kingdom
http://www.mscm.co.uk
email: info@mscm.biz
phone: 0845 372 9899

Claire Marie Miller Seminars

Claire Marie Miller Seminars offers courses to train professionals in pregnancy massage, labor massage and support techniques, postpartum massage and infant massage.

Claire Marie Miller Seminars
8703 Rollingwood Rd.
Chapel Hill, NC 27516 USA
http://www.clairemariemiller.com
phone: 877-319-5772

Body Therapy Associates

Carole Osborne, of Body Therapy Associates, an expert in prenatal and perinatal massage therapy, has developed a variety of trainings and a professional certification course for Massage Therapists around the world.

Body Therapy Associates
9449 Balboa Ave. Suite 310
San Diego, CA 92123 USA
http://bodytherapyassociates.com
phone: 858-277-8827

Boulder College of Massage Therapy

The Boulder College of Massage Therapy offers a Prenatal, Labor, Postpartum Massage Therapy Certificate Program providing comprehensive training in the theory and hands-on practice of touch therapies for childbearing women, and setting industry standards for training Massage Therapists and other perinatal health care professionals.

Boulder College of Massage Therapy
http://www.bcmt.org/training/prenatal-massage-training.htm
email: info@bcmt.org
phone: 800-442-5131

Bodyworkers Association for the Birthing Year

The Bodyworkers Association for the Birthing Year (BABY) dedicates itself to educating and supporting Massage Therapists and Bodyworkers who believe massage and touch should be a vital component to women in their journey during pregnancy. BABY trains massage professionals to become certified Prenatal Massage Therapists.

http://www.babyinc.org/prenmascer.html

Massage Doula

Massage Doula workshops are taught in partnership with the Institute of Somatic Therapy. They are the certifying organization for prenatal massage and Massage Doulas. Massage Doulas are certified Massage Therapists who have completed advanced study in prenatal massage, postpartum massage, labor and delivery support, and optionally, infant massage.

http://massagedoula.com

Oregon School of Massage

Oregon School of Massage offers extensive training in massage for pregnant and laboring women and new mothers. More than a practicum in massage techniques, this certification allows participants to explore the wisdom of women that has enabled the birth journey for thousands of years.

Oregon School of Massage
9500 SW Barbur Blvd. Suite 100
Portland, OR 97219 USA
http://oregonschoolofmassage.com/maternity.php
email: osm@oregonschoolofmassage.com
phone: 800-844-3420

PRENATAL AND POSTPARTUM YOGA INSTRUCTOR

Prenatal and Postpartum Yoga Instructors are knowledgeable about childbirth and the physiological changes that take place within a woman's body. They are able to teach yoga classes that are safe and beneficial for pregnant women. Instructors also teach yoga classes to women during postpartum as their bodies return to normal.

Search words: prenatal yoga teacher training, prenatal yoga certification, postpartum yoga teacher training

GETTING STARTED

Attend a prenatal and postpartum yoga class. Watch a prenatal or postpartum yoga DVD. Enroll in a teacher training workshop for prenatal and postpartum yoga. Read books about prenatal and postpartum yoga. Find an experienced teacher to serve as your mentor.

ORGANIZATIONS

Whole Birth Resources

Whole Birth Resources is a mindfulness-based educational forum offering innovative classes, teacher training and educational materials that cultivate a deeper understanding and trust in the everyday miracle of pregnancy, birth and family life.

Whole Birth Resources
413 Western Drive #10
Santa Cruz, CA 95060 USA
http://wholebirth.com
email: info@wholebirth.com
phone: 831-425-7731

Mamaste Yoga

In a Mamaste Prenatal Yoga class, the focus is to prepare the body and mind for labor, birth and motherhood. Women can prepare for these events by releasing tension, maintaining good posture, learning to relax on command, keeping a positive outlook and clearing the mind of stresses during pregnancy.

Mamaste Yoga
http://www.mamasteyoga.com
email: karen@n2yoga.net
phone: 405-474-3302

Birthlight

Birthlight focuses on a holistic approach to pregnancy, birth and babyhood using yoga and breathing methods to enhance well-being. Birthlight continually strives to use the latest research findings in the development of simple but effective movements.

Birthlight
PO Box 148
Cambridge
CB4 2GB United Kingdom
http://birthlight.com
phone: 01223 362288

YogaBellies

YogaBellies School offers the opportunity for like-minded individuals who love all things pregnancy, baby and birth to join the YogaBellies community and to train as YogaBellies instructors.

YogaBellies
10 Grosvenor Crescent
Dowanhill
Glasgow
G12 9AF United Kingdom
http://www.yogabellies.co.uk
email: cheryl@yogabellies.co.uk
phone: 0781 786 4336

Yogababy

Yogababy offers in-depth specialized training in prenatal, postnatal and Active Birth Education. The training course covers safe positions for pregnancy yoga and postpartum.

Yogababy
PO Box 617
Toowong QLD 4066 Australia
http://www.yogababy.com.au
email: info@yogababy.com.au
phone: 1300 769 642

Yogacampus

Yogacampus supports and develops an expanding community of yoga teachers and yoga practitioners by offering workshops, intensives, short and long yoga courses and yoga teacher training, with leading UK and international yoga teachers.

Yogacampus
Top Floor
The Westover
304 Westbourne Grove
London, W11 2PS United Kingdom
http://www.yogacampus.com
email: info@yogacampus.com
phone: 20 7042 9900

Jennifer Wolfe Yoga

Jennifer Wolfe Yoga wishes for every woman to have the pregnancy and birth experience that she desires. In that spirit, she created yoga DVDs to offer women a safe and active option for their prenatal yoga practice. Having personally attended over 400 births and trained thousands of students in Prenatal Vinyasa Yoga, she has seen firsthand the amazing benefits that yoga provides.

http://www.jenniferwolfeyoga.com
email: info@prenatalvinyasa.com

Blooma

Blooma's Prenatal Yoga Teacher Trainings are all about finding the goddess inside. They train professionals in a sequence that is specifically designed to empower and prepare women for birth.

Blooma
3919 44th Street
Edina, MN 55424 USA
http://www.blooma.com
email: info@blooma.com
phone: 952-848-1111

PUBLISHER

Publishers oversee the creation of childbirth education books, pamphlets, magazines, and other related materials. Some Publishers write and distribute publications enabling them to increase their profits. Publishers serve hospitals, health clinics, childbirth education centers, and others needing preprinted booklets and handouts to educate pregnant women and their families.

Search words: childbirth education materials, prepared childbirth books, childbirth class books, childbirth education publisher, breastfeeding education booklets, parenting education booklets, parenting publisher, breastfeeding publisher

GETTING STARTED

Read booklets and educational materials from existing Publishers. Find out what needs exist in the publishing market. Research and explore successful publishing models. Attempt a trial run at publishing, by creating a booklet or pamphlet for a doctor's office or birth class in your community.

ℰℭ

Business Journey ...

The Family Way Publications, Jeanne Green and Debby Amis

We started as a group of four Childbirth Educators who taught for our own community-based group named, The Family Way. We complained about working hard to keep copies of our handouts looking neat, and then finding that many were left under chairs in class. Why not put those handouts into a little booklet? We thought it would be easy. It was not.

Writing is really hard work. It is even harder to share your work with colleagues and have them criticize it. For over a year, we sat around a kitchen table and labored over our "booklet." We argued, we cried, we compromised. Thank goodness we had one person in our group who was adept at soothing hurt feelings and making each of us feel that our work was important and contributing to the whole. In 1981, we worked on typewriters (yes, typewriters!). *Prepared Childbirth – The Family Way* would never have gotten off the ground if we hadn't had a printer in one of our classes who volunteered to typeset our book. We drove him crazy with revision after revision after revision. When it finally came time to print our book, we each put in $500 to cover costs. Five hundred dollars was a lot of money for each of our young families. We got books back in return to use in our classes.

We proudly showed off our book to friends and to other Childbirth Educators. We were surprised when they asked if they could buy our books for their own classes. We used our profits to buy films and teaching aids for our classes. Two members of our group moved away, leaving Jeanne and Debby to continue the book, or not. We decided to break off our book business from our non-profit childbirth group. With the help of a lawyer-husband, we incorporated the book business as The Family Way Publications.

The home computer was a big breakthrough for us. We bought Apple 2E computers (we still use Apple computers to this day). We sent our book off in the mail to be scanned so that we could put it on our computers. It took weeks. We became desktop publishers.

We were members of both ICEA and Lamaze International and took the big step (for us) of exhibiting at their conferences. We designed a brochure and mailed it to every hospital in the U.S. offering a free preview copy of our book. Gradually sales increased. We are grateful that our husbands have become involved in our business. One does our layout and serves as our IT department, while the other is our medical consultant and editor.

As requests for more products came in, we added a Spanish version of our book, a handbook for families expecting multiples, a comprehensive teaching strategy guide for Childbirth Educators, and a PowerPoint CD with illustrations from our books.

One of the biggest strengths of our books is that we update them each time we print them. It is still really hard work. Occasionally one of us still gets her feelings hurt when the other rewrites a section *again.* But we have learned that we are a perfect team. Our interests and strengths complement one another.

We feel very lucky that our book publishing business has evolved into careers that allow us to focus on birth and childbirth education. We have spent our careers teaching childbirth classes, attending births, going to childbirth conferences, reading, writing, and talking about birth and evidence-based maternity care. We became certified as Doulas. We have trained new Doulas and Childbirth Educators and have spoken at national and international childbirth conferences. Our favorite moments are when we hear back from students who have had empowering births, or when we hear from a nurse, educator, or Doula whom we taught, who shares her impact in helping women to have life-changing births.

As educators and writers, it has been challenging to learn about the nuts and bolts of running a business. We are mostly self-taught, but we are grateful for the advice and help of our accountant and our printer. When we go to a movie, we can often name the font used in the credits. We almost never read a book without finding a typo. We can tell you all about paper quality and brightness, strength of packing cartons, how to mail a book to Japan, and SUTA, FUTA, 1099s, and W-9s. The internet has opened up a whole new world of customers for us, but we have also had to learn more than we ever wanted to know about internet security.

If you write a book, you can send it to a publishing company in hopes that they will decide to publish it. If they do, they will help you with editing, choosing a cover, and other publishing details. They will pay you royalties, a small percentage of the sales of the book.

Or you can do what we have done and self-publish. Self-publishing is not for the faint of heart. It requires a financial investment, knowledge and skills, and the day-to-day commitment of running a business. It has enabled us to have careers devoted to helping women develop confidence in their ability to give birth and to helping families have positive birth experiences. We wouldn't have it any other way.

ℰↃℭℜ

EXAMPLES OF PUBLISHERS

Plumtree Baby

Plumtree Baby creates relevant, appealing, and interactive educational resources for Childbirth Professionals and expectant parents.

Plumtree Baby
P.O. Box 462680
Centennial, CO 80046 USA
http://www.plumtreebaby.com
email: info@plumtreebaby.com
phone: 800-939-0134

The Family Way

The Family Way provides evidence-based, up-to-date, and comprehensive information in booklets for childbirth classes.

The Family Way
5407 Ashby Street
Houston, TX 77005 USA
http://thefamilyway.com
email: info@thefamilyway.com
phone: 713-528-0277

Customized Communications

Customized Communications is a medical publishing company passionate about educating patients with printed publications and e-Learning programs. They are on the cutting edge of innovative, evidence-based materials to meet the ever-changing needs of women's healthcare and childbirth education.

Customized Communications
P.O. Box 5566
Arlington, TX 76005 USA
http://www.customizedinc.com
email: cci@customizedinc.com
phone: 800-476-2253

Birthwares

Birthwares is a one-stop resource to find curriculum, resources, and tools for childbirth education.

Birthwares
8062 Newcastle Cres
Prince George, BC, Canada, V2N 3X6
http://www.birthwares.com
email: customerservice@birthwares.com
phone: 250-981-7885

Noodle Soup

Noodle Soup of Weingart Design specializes in developing low-literacy, low cost, well-illustrated, easy-to-read materials that inspire pregnant women, new moms, and parents to take care of themselves and their children.

Noodle Soup
4614 Prospect Ave Suite 328
Cleveland, OH 44103 USA
http://www.noodlesoup.com
email: Cydney@noodlesoup.com
phone: 800-795-9295

REPRODUCTIVE JUSTICE ADVOCATE

Reproductive Justice Advocates work to bring change and equality to all phases of women's reproductive health care. Reproductive justice addresses the lack of economic, social, and political power women possess to make decisions and/or receive care regarding their bodies, sexuality, and reproductive health. Advocates assist women in many ways helping change laws, providing legal assistance, lobbying government officials, and bringing awareness to inequality in women's healthcare.

Search words: reproductive justice, reproductive justice activist, reproductive justice lawyer

GETTING STARTED

Join a reproductive justice organization. Read books about reproductive justice. Enroll in a training program or course about reproductive justice. Volunteer your time to work on reproductive justice issues.

BOOKS

Reproductive Justice: A Global Concern by Joan Chrisler

Undivided Rights: Women of Color Organizing for Reproductive Justice by Jael Silliman, Marlene Gerber Fried, Loretta Ross, and Elena Gutierrez

RESOURCES

Read, *Reproductive Justice is Every Woman's Right* by Zenaida Mendez at this link http://tiny.cc/reproductivejustice

ORGANIZATIONS

SisterSong

SisterSong offers comprehensive and in-depth Reproductive Justice trainings for organizations and individual activists who want to: 1) Understand the Reproductive Justice framework 2) Apply the Reproductive Justice framework and 3) Expand the Reproductive Justice framework.

Sister Song
1237 Ralph David Abernathy Blvd SW
Atlanta, GA 30310 USA
http://www.sistersong.net
email: info@sistersong.net
phone: 404-756-2680

Reproductive Health Matters

Reproductive Health Matters (RHM) is an independent charity, producing in-depth publications on reproductive and sexual health and rights for an international, multi-disciplinary audience. RHM promotes laws, policies, research and services that meet the sexual and reproductive health needs of women and men.

Reproductive Health Matters
444 Highgate Studios
53-79 Highgate Road
London NW5 1TL
United Kingdom
http://www.rhmjournal.org.uk

Law Students for Reproductive Justice

Law Students for Reproductive Justice trains and mobilizes law students and new lawyers across the country to foster legal expertise and support for the realization of reproductive justice.

Reproductive justice will exist when all people can exercise the rights and access the resources they need to thrive and to decide whether, when, and how to have and parent children with dignity, free from discrimination, coercion, or violence.

Law Students for Reproductive Justice
1730 Franklin Street Suite 212
Oakland, CA 94612 USA
http://lsrj.org
email: info@lsrj.org
phone: 510-622-8134

Asian Communities for Reproductive Justice

Asian Communities for Reproductive Justice (ACRJ) promotes and protects reproductive justice through organizing, building leadership capacity, developing alliances and education to achieve community and systemic change.

http://reproductivejustice.org

Center for Reproductive Rights

The Center for Reproductive Rights has used the law to advance reproductive freedom as a fundamental human right that all governments are legally obligated to protect, respect, and fulfill. The Center for Reproductive Rights believes that reproductive freedom lies at the heart of the promise of human dignity, self-determination and equality embodied in both the U.S. Constitution and the Universal Declaration of Human Rights.

Center for Reproductive Rights
120 Wall Street
New York, NY 10005 USA
http://reproductiverights.org
email: info@reprorights.org
phone: 917-637-3600

National Latina Institute for Reproductive Health

The National Latina Institute for Reproductive Health (NLIRH) works to ensure the fundamental human right to reproductive health and justice for Latinas, their families and their communities through public education, community mobilization and policy advocacy. NLIRH believes that in order to substantially improve the reproductive health of Latinas and protect their rights to exercise reproductive freedom, NLIRH must locate reproductive health and rights issues within a broader social justice framework that seeks to bring an end to poverty and discrimination and affirms human dignity and the right to self-determination.

NLIRH
50 Broad Street, Suite 1937
New York, NY 10004 USA
http://latinainstitute.org
phone: 212-422-2553

Access Women's Health Justice

Access Women's Health Justice provides information and practical support on all aspects of reproductive health, and builds a community actively working to meet the real needs of women. They combine direct services, community education, and policy advocacy to promote real reproductive options and access to quality health care for California women.

Access Women's Health Justice
P.O. Box 3609
Oakland, CA 94609 USA
http://accesswhj.org
email: info@accesswhj.org
phone: 510-923-0739

California Latinas for Reproductive Justice

California Latinas for Reproductive Justice (CLRJ) is a statewide policy and advocacy organization whose mission is to advance California Latinas' reproductive health and rights within a social justice and human rights framework. CLRJ works to ensure that policy developments reflect Latinas' priority needs, as well as those of their families and their communities.

California Latinas for Reproductive Justice
Post Office Box 412225
Los Angeles, CA 90041 USA
http://www.californialatinas.org
email: info@clrj.org
phone: 213-270-5258

Black Women for Reproductive Justice

Black Women for Reproductive Justice helps Black women and girls realize reproductive justice. They seek to build a grassroots constituency organized to collectively affect change in public and private institutions transforming policies that prevent Black women from obtaining optimum reproductive and sexual health.

An important part of the work at Black Women for Reproductive Justice is communicating to policymakers the impact of policies upon the lives of women, especially Black women.

Black Women for Reproductive Justice
1424-28 East 53rd Street, #306
Chicago, IL 60615 USA
http://bwrj.org/welcome.html
phone: 773-955-2709

SPARK Reproductive Justice NOW

SPARK Reproductive Justice NOW collaborates with individuals, communities, and organizations to grow and sustain a powerful reproductive justice movement in Georgia and the South. They achieve this by developing and sharing a radical analysis in order to change culture, mobilizing in response to immediate threats, and organizing for long-term systemic change.

SPARK Reproductive Justice
2048 Hosea L Williams Dr Unit B
Atlanta, GA 30317 USA
http://sparkrj.org
email: info@sparkrj.org
phone: 404-343-6506

RESEARCHER

Researchers conduct studies, analyze data, and write papers providing information to the childbirth health care community. The work done by Researchers can change medical policies and practices. Researchers help validate and bring understanding to traditional childbirth practices. Their work is also a useful tool in implementing evidence-based medical care.

Search words: childbirth researcher, childbirth research conference, childbirth research studies, maternity care research, normal birth research

GETTING STARTED

Researchers usually have advanced skills and education; consider pursing a Master's degree or PhD. Read research articles and texts on various childbirth health care issues. Create a list of health issues where more research is needed. Seek out fellowships and research opportunities through universities, hospitals, and government agencies. Seek advice from current Researchers in the childbirth health care field.

RESOURCES

iresearch4birth

The main objective of the work at iresearch4birth is to advance scientific knowledge about ways of improving maternity care outcomes for mothers, babies and families across Europe by understanding what works, for who, in what circumstances, and by identifying and learning from the best.

http://www.iresearch4birth.eu

Campaign for Normal Birth

Campaign for Normal Birth believes that integral to making Normal Birth a reality is building an evidence and experience base for normal midwifery practice through the creation, evaluation and dissemination of research. Nationally and globally, Midwives are engaged in research within topics relevant to Normal Birth. Through this campaign, there is an opportunity for all to engage in bringing the research and evidence available to a larger audience.

http://www.rcmnormalbirth.org.uk/research

The Cochrane Library

The Cochrane Library is a collection of six databases that contain different types of high-quality, independent evidence to use in making informed healthcare decisions.

http://www.thecochranelibrary.com

BMJ

The BMJ (British Medical Journal) is an international peer reviewed medical journal and a fully "online first" publication. Their "continuous publication" model means that all articles appear on bmj.com before being included in an issue of the print journal. The website is updated daily with the BMJ's latest original research, education, news and comment articles, as well as podcasts, videos, and blogs.

http://www.bmj.com

PubMed Central

PubMed Central (PMC) is a free archive of biomedical and life sciences journal literature at the U.S. National Institutes of Health's National Library of Medicine (NIH/NLM). In keeping with NLM's legislative mandate to collect and preserve the biomedical literature, PMC serves as a digital counterpart to NLM's extensive print journal collection.

http://www.ncbi.nlm.nih.gov/pmc

Maternal and Child Health Library at Georgetown University

The goal at Maternal and Child Health Library is to serve the Maternal and Child Health (MCH) community, health professionals, and the public with accurate, reliable, and timely information and resources.

http://www.mchlibrary.info

EXAMPLES OF RESEARCHERS

Hélène Vadeboncoeur

Hélène Vadeboncoeur is a Childbirth Researcher who wrote the book *Birthing Normally After a Caesarean or Two*, to provide women with evidence-based information supporting Vaginal Birth After Cesarean (VBAC).

http://www.helenevadeboncoeur.com
(use http://translate.google.com)

Robbie Davis-Floyd PhD

Robbie Davis-Floyd PhD is an anthropologist who strives to make her work relevant not only to students and other anthropologists, but also to the people she studies and to the general public. She is a passionate believer in reaching out across disciplinary boundaries.

http://davis-floyd.com

Motherhood Initiative for Research and Community Involvement

The Motherhood Initiative for Research and Community Involvement (MIRCI) is a feminist scholarly and activist organization on mothering-motherhood.

http://www.motherhoodinitiative.org

Australian Motherhood Initiative for Research and Community Involvement

Australian Motherhood Initiative for Research and Community Involvement (AMIRCI) is a feminist organization interested in promoting research into mothering, motherhood, motherwork, and related areas, including maternal subjectivities and identities, cultural representations and differences. This valuable field of research seeks to raise critical awareness of the particularities and complexities of mothering embedded in Australian society.

http://www.mothering.org.au

Association for Prenatal and Perinatal Psychology and Health

Association for Prenatal and Perinatal Psychology and Health (APPPAH) is an educational and scientific organization offering information, inspiration, and support to medical professionals, expecting parents and all persons interested in expanding horizons of birth psychology.

http://birthpsychology.com

Womb Ecology

Womb Ecology provides a website focusing on the life period with the highest adaptability and vulnerability to environmental factors - the period inside the womb.

http://www.wombecology.com
email: wombecology@aol.com

RETAILER

Retailers sell pregnancy, birth, and baby related goods. Some Retailers focus on selling a specific category of products such as breastfeeding supplies, cloth diapers, or childbirth educational materials. Retailers can sell products through brick and mortar stores, through the internet, or both. Many Retailers attend trade conferences and baby fairs to market their products.

Search words: childbirth retailer, childbirth books, childbirth education materials, birth kits, cloth diapers, natural baby products, baby products

GETTING STARTED

Research and learn about the retail business. Contact existing Retailers for advice on getting started. Take business or marketing courses at your local community college. Sketch out a business plan. Decide on what type of goods you wish to sell, and if you will have an online store, or a brick and mortar store. Join associations and trade organizations for your retail specialty.

ORGANIZATIONS

Juvenile Products Manufacturers Association

Juvenile Products Manufacturers Association (JPMA) is a national trade organization representing companies in the United States, Canada, and Mexico who manufacture, import and/or distribute infant products such as cribs, car seats, strollers, bedding, and a wide range of accessories and decorative items. JPMA has been recognized as an organization dedicated to enhancing children's product safety. JPMA works with government officials, consumer groups, and industry leaders on programs to educate consumers on the safe selection and use of juvenile products.

Juvenile Products Manufacturers Association
15000 Commerce Parkway, Suite C
Mt. Laurel, NJ 08054 USA
http://www.jpma.org
email: jpma@jpma.org
phone: 856-638-0420

Baby Products Association

The Baby Products Association (BPA) was established to promote the baby and nursery products sector in both the UK and Europe. They play an active role in the development of product standards and provide an umbrella of support and specialist services to their membership. The BPA Technical Committee is constructed of industry experts and specialists covering a wide range of baby and nursery products including wheeled goods, nursery furniture, baby walkers, soft goods, child restraints, toys and early learning.

Baby Products Association
2 Carrera House
Merlin Court
Gatehouse Close
Aylesbury HP19 8DP
United Kingdom
http://www.thebpa.eu
email: info@b-p-a.org
phone: 0845 456 9570

EXAMPLES OF RETAILERS

Global Birth Fair

Global Birth Fair is a fair trade company dedicated to providing livable wages directly to artisans worldwide. They donate a portion of profits to organizations that focus on providing optimal MotherBaby care. Global Birth Fair strives to buy in a fair trade model to support small-scale vendors and artisans who demonstrate fair treatment of workers and eco-friendly manufacturing of products related to maternal health.

http://www.globalbirthfair.com

Maya Wrap

Maya Wrap sells beautifully patterned slings to carry babies and young children.

http://www.mayawrap.com

Birth International

Birth International sells a variety of childbirth education books, supplies and products.

https://www.birthinternational.com

Childbirth Graphics

Childbirth Graphics provides educational materials and teaching products for Childbirth Professionals.

http://www.childbirthgraphics.com

Cascade Healthcare Products

Cascade HealthCare Products provide high quality midwifery supplies, medical equipment and natural health care products.

http://www.1cascade.com

In His Hands Birth Supply

In His Hands Birth Supply is a provider of birth supplies to medical professionals and expecting parents.

http://inhishands.com

Your Doula Bag

Amy of Your Doula Bag believes that having a stocked and ready supply bag can enhance the work Doulas provide. Your Doula Bag provides items that are useful for Doulas in a ready to go pack.

http://yourdoulabag.com

Everything Birth

Everything Birth carries birth supplies, cloth diapers, and organic baby products. Everything Birth is committed to supporting women, birth, and the midwifery model of care.

http://www.everythingbirth.com

Cutie Bootie

Cutie Booties offers a Cloth Diaper BootieCamp where parents get to see and touch an assortment of modern cloth diapers. They learn the forms and functions of different diaper styles, and all about fibers and brands. Parents also learn how to use and care for cloth diapers, including washing details, and tips to make cloth diapering easy.

http://cutiebooties.com/bootiecamp.html

Cutting Edge Press

Cutting Edge Press, is owned by Eric and Polly Perez, and they provide Childbirth and Doula products, and are a resource for Childbirth Professionals and expectant parents.

http://cuttingedgepress.net

Birthsource

Birthsource provides evidence-based childbirth and breastfeeding education materials for professionals. They also carry a wide range of tools to use during the birth process.

http://birthsource.com/Scripts/default.asp

Birthcare

Birthcare offers a complete line of breast pumps, nursing bras, and other breastfeeding products. In addition, they offer personalized childbirth classes and insightful forums moderated by a registered labor and delivery nurse.

http://www.mybirthcare.com

Sew Crafty Baby

Sew Crafty Baby started with the vision of a work at home mom who created baby warmers to sell on eBay. She went on to build an online store to sell baby products.

http://www.sewcraftybaby.com

SCHOOL FOUNDER

School Founders see an educational need in their profession and work to bring together the faculty and curriculum to fulfill those educational needs. Founders are often visionary leaders striving to invest in future generations; passing down knowledge, wisdom, and technical skills.

Search words: childbirth education, doula school, lactation school, midwifery school

GETTING STARTED

Research and learn about different schools and their curricula. Contact existing School Founders and ask for advice about what steps to take to begin a school. Try organizing one class as a test of your ideas. Offer the class face-to-face and through the internet to discover if distant or class learning would be a better model for your school, perhaps a combination of both would work. Find out if there are any government or credentialing requirements in your locality for opening a school. Get in touch with a college in your community to see if they will partner with you and offer academic credits.

ORGANIZATIONS

Midwifery Education Accreditation Council

Midwifery Education Accreditation Council (MEAC) accreditation is designed to strengthen educational programs and to preserve the many innovative programs designed by and for Midwives. To mention only a few areas that are scrutinized for MEAC accreditation and continued accreditation status, a program/institution must meet rigorous requirements for demonstrated student success; being fiscally sound; sufficient faculty, staff, and facility resources; and curriculum.

Midwifery Education Accreditation Council
P.O. Box 984
La Conner, WA 98257 USA
http://www.meacschools.org
email: info@meacschools.org
phone: 360-466-2080

EXAMPLES OF SCHOOLS

Birthingway College

Birthingway started in March 1993 as a six-month structured study group in the home of founder Holly Scholles. Soon, the group transformed into a private business, Birthingway Midwifery School, offering a two-year program of classroom and independent study. Holly taught all of the courses with the occasional help of guest speakers. In 1996, to meet MEAC accreditation requirements, the program expanded to three years and increased the clinical requirements for graduation.

Birthingway College
12113 SE Foster Road
Portland, OR 97266 USA
http://www.birthingway.edu
email: info@birthingway.edu
phone: 503-760-3131

Birthwise Midwifery School

Birthwise Midwifery School is a small private institution founded in 1994 in Bridgton, Maine. They offer a comprehensive three-year education program for Certified Professional Midwives (CPMs), accredited by the Midwifery Education Accreditation Council and licensed by the State of Maine Department of Education.

Birthwise Midwifery School
24 South High Street
Bridgton, ME 04009 USA
http://www.birthwisemidwifery.edu
email: info@birthwisemidwifery.edu
phone: 207-647-5968

Newlife International School of Midwifery

Newlife International School of Midwifery is a Christian school for direct-entry midwifery students. The school is based on a United States midwifery curriculum and standards outlined by the National College of Midwifery; however, training is completed in the Philippines. The students are primarily from the United States and Canada, but there are also students from South Africa, England, Denmark, Jamaica, Ireland, China and Switzerland.

http://www.midwifeschool.org
email: director@midwifeschool.org

Australian Doula College

The Australian Doula College (ADC) is an independent childbirth and parenting education center that provides support, education, and continuity of care for women and their families during pregnancy, childbirth and beyond. They operate a fully integrated health care center with practitioners who have a passion for natural fertility management, pregnancy, birth and postnatal care.

Australian Doula College
422 Marrickville Road
Marrickville NSW 2204 Australia
http://www.australiandoulacollege.com.au
phone: 02 9569 8020

Michigan School of Traditional Midwifery

The Michigan School of Traditional Midwifery (MSTM) was developed in the late 1980's by experienced practicing Midwives who collaborated together to create a school that would encourage and foster the development of more practicing Midwives and also provide midwifery education from the holistic, vocational and traditional perspective of natural, non-medical birth.

MSTM
P.O. Box 162
Mikado, MI 48745 USA
http://traditionalmidwife.com
email: traditionalmidwife@gmail.com

STROLLER EXERCISE INSTRUCTOR

Stroller Exercise Instructors lead mothers in exercise classes that include their babes in strollers. The classes are usually held outdoors or inside malls depending upon weather conditions. Stroller exercise classes give mothers the opportunity to workout in a community, build relationships, and be among peers while mothering.

Search words: stroller exercise, stroller fitness, stroller exercise class

GETTING STARTED

Take a stroller fitness class to learn about the techniques and process. Contact a Stroller Exercise Instructor to ask advice and questions about the business. Find out about franchise opportunities to begin a stroller exercise business.

ORGANIZATIONS

Stroller Strides

Stroller Strides is a stroller-based workout that offers moms a great way to get in shape, meet other new moms and have fun with their baby. Stroller Strides instructors weave songs and activities into the routine designed to entertain baby, while mom is led through a series of exercises incorporating stretch tubing, the stroller, the baby and the environment for a total body workout.

Stroller Strides
1850 Diamond Street, Suite 102
San Marcos, CA 92078 USA
http://www.strollerstrides.com
email: info@strollerstrides.com
phone: 866-348-4666

Baby Boot Camp

Baby Boot Camp is an innovative stroller fitness program that helps women regain or enhance pre-pregnancy fitness levels.

Baby Boot Camp
665 S. Orange Avenue Suite 7
Sarasota, FL 34236 USA
http://www.babybootcamp.com
phone: 941-953-5000

STROLLER EXERCISE CLASS EXAMPLES

Stroller Fit

Stroller Fit classes are a low impact workout consisting of walking or power walking with a stroller in the park, interspersed with exercises to help strengthen and tone for an all-body workout.

http://strollerfit.co.uk

Strollers and Toners

Strollers and Toners is an exercise program for adults with babies or young children in buggies or on bikes.

http://www.strollersandtoners.co.uk

The Mommy Movement

The Mommy Movement classes begin with warm-up, stretching, power strolling through the park or mall singing fun songs and stopping for short circuit-style stations filled with cardiovascular and strength training exercises and then ending with a powerful abdominal workout.

http://www.themommymovement.com

My Fit Mommy

My Fit Mommy offers a Stroller Fitness Baby Bootcamp workout that uses the child, stroller, and environment to help moms get fit and have fun in the process.

http://www.my-fit-mommy.com

Bay City Strollers

Bay City Strollers is Australia's most innovative postnatal exercise program for new mothers. Women exercise with their children in an invigorating environment under professional guidance, restoring body and mind, and transitioning their bodies from childbirth.

http://www.baycitystrollers.com.au

TEACHING CENTER

Teaching Centers are a place where parents take classes and receive help, such as breastfeeding assistance. They are a place where families find support and professionals network. Teaching Centers serve their communities often promoting a shared mission, values, and interests. They are a gathering place offering affirmation, advocacy, and empowerment for pregnant women and their families.

Search words: childbirth education center, pregnancy childbirth classes, yoga baby care class, mother center, breastfeeding class, birth classes, childbirth class

GETTING STARTED

Contact the director of a Teaching Center and if possible visit to learn how the center is organized and managed. Write a plan of what you would need to open a Teaching Center. Build a team of professionals that can provide services or teach classes to families at your center.

EXAMPLE TEACHING CENTERS

A Mother's Touch

A Mother's Touch offers a whole range of pregnancy and childbirth services under the umbrella of Bump, Birth and Beyond.

A Mother's Touch
202/2 Ivy House
18-20 Wyndham Street, Central Hong Kong
http://www.amotherstouch.com.hk
email: info@amotherstouch.com.hk
phone: 852 9521 2347

The Tulip Grove

The Tulip Grove provides families with educational classes and resources, including: on the spot lactation support, pregnancy and postpartum nutrition classes, infant and child CPR, infant massage and baby sign language classes. They also provide newborn care workshops and new mom support groups.

The Tulip Grove
2078 Antioch Court
Montclair Village
Oakland, CA 94611 USA
http://www.thetulipgrove.com
email: info@thetulipgrove.com
phone: 510-339-2225

Happy Bambino

Happy Bambino works to create happier families through parental empowerment and community support.

Happy Bambino
4116 Monona Drive
Madison, WI 53716 USA
http://www.happybambino.com
email: hello@happybambino.com
phone: 800-513-0789

Pregnancy and Parents Centre

The Pregnancy and Parents Centre began in a living room as a yoga group for pregnancy offering friendly, caring support. From that small beginning the Centre grew into what it is today: a charity that supports over 150 families per week by offering friendship, information, and activities through pregnancy and early parenthood.

Pregnancy and Parents Centre
10 Lower Gilmore Place
Edinburgh
EH3 9NY United Kingdom
http://pregnancyandparents.org.uk
email: info@pregnancyandparents.org.uk
phone: 0131 229 3667

The Motherhood Center

The Motherhood Center provides the support all mothers need. As the premier resource for women in the Houston area, The Motherhood Center has the unique privilege of helping expecting moms, dads, and grandparents enjoy the precious experience of pregnancy into the adventure of parenthood. They have served hundreds of couples awaiting their babies through childbirth and newborn care classes, as well as breastfeeding and infant CPR classes.

The Motherhood Center
3701 W. Alabama, Suite 230
Houston, TX 77027 USA
http://www.motherhoodcenter.com
email: info@motherhoodcenter.com
phone: 713-963-8880

Rebirth Wellness Centre

Rebirth Wellness Centre is all about making meaningful connections, sharing experiences, and being healthy and well in the process. They offer a wide range of specialized health and wellness services to nurture the mind, body, and heart for pregnant women and their families.

Rebirth Wellness Centre
256 Central Ave
London, ON
N6A 1M8 Canada
http://rebirthwellness.ca
email: info@rebirthwellness.ca
phone: 226-663-3243

Birthing Rites Australia

Birthing Rites Australia is a leading provider of the highest quality education, counseling and support in the field of childbirth and parenting education. They offer prenatal classes, parenting groups, and Doula services

Birthing Rites Australia
10 Denison Street
Bondi Junction NSW 2022 Australia
http://www.birthingrites.com
email: birthingrites@zip.com.au
phone: 02 9387 3615

Center for the Childbearing Year

The Center for the Childbearing Year offers a comprehensive selection of classes and resources designed to help expecting families have the best possible birth experience and transition through the early weeks and months of caring for their babies.

Center for the Childbearing Year
722 Brooks Street
Ann Arbor, MI 48103 USA
http://center4cby.com
email: patty@center4cby.com
phone: 734-663-1523

THERAPIST

Therapists provide counseling and mental health services to families through pregnancy and postpartum. They help families with a wide range of needs from coping with relationship changes to treating postpartum depression. Therapists help families gain skills to manage and overcome challenges and build thriving, healthy homes.

Search words: birth trauma, pregnancy therapist, postpartum depression counseling, birth loss counseling, birth trauma counseling, postpartum therapy, postnatal therapy, postnatal counseling, postnatal depression, postnatal depression support

GETTING STARTED

Therapists usually have advanced education, training, and licensing to offer professional services to assist women and their families. Research what the requirements are for the type of treatment and counseling you would like to provide. Consider pursuing higher education and licensing in the area you wish to practice if it is required. Contact Therapists that work with pregnant women to learn about their training and services. Read books and articles about issues that concern women and their families during the childbearing years. Join associations and volunteer for groups that provide counseling and treatment to families.

BOOKS

Survivor Moms: Women's Stories of Birthing, Mothering and Healing after Sexual Abuse by Mickey Sperlich, MA, CPM and Julia Seng, PhD, CNM

When Survivors Give Birth: Understanding and Healing the Effects of Early Sexual Abuse on Childbearing Women by Penny Simkin, PT and Phyllis Klaus, MFT

ORGANIZATIONS

Birth Trauma Association

The Birth Trauma Association (BTA) supports all women who have had a traumatic birth experience. The BTA wants women to know that they are not alone.

Birth Trauma Association
PO Box 671
Ipswich, Suffolk
IP1 9AT United Kingdom
http://www.birthtraumaassociation.org.uk
email: enquiries@birthtraumaassociation.org.uk

PostpartumMen

PostpartumMen is a place for men with concerns about depression, anxiety or other mood shifts after the birth of a child. They promote self-help, and provide important information for fathers – including a self-assessment for postpartum depression. They host an online forum for dads to talk to each other, and offer support so fathers can be aware of and overcome the baby blues.

PostpartumMen
5835 College Avenue, Suite D3
Oakland, CA 94618 USA
http://www.postpartummen.com
phone: 415-346-6719

Solace for Mothers

Solace for Mothers is an organization designed for the sole purpose of providing and creating support for women who have experienced childbirth as traumatic. The resources available through the Solace for Mothers website offer immediate, personal support to those struggling with birth trauma and anxiety after birth.

Solace for Mothers
http://www.solaceformothers.org
email: info@solaceformothers.org
phone: 408-370-7311

Birth Trauma Counselling

Birth Trauma Counselling works to reach women who have had a difficult or traumatic birth and who feel the need to tell their stories or receive counseling.

Birth Trauma Counselling
http://www.birthtraumacounselling.org
email: info@birthtraumacounselling.org

Birth Trauma Canada

Birth Trauma Canada (BT Canada) is an organization of mothers who have had negative childbirth experiences. They work to give women a voice and to support women traumatized by negative childbirth experiences.

BTCanada
North Hill RPO
P.O. Box 65136
Calgary, Alberta T2N 4T6 Canada
http://birthtraumacanada.org
email: mail@birthtraumacanada.org

Vancouver Birth Trauma

Vancouver Birth Trauma is a resource and support for women who have gone through birth trauma from Vancouver and the surrounding areas.

Vancouver Birth Trauma
http://www.vancouverbirthtrauma.ca
email: vancouverbirthtrauma@gmail.com
phone: 888-886-5016

Postpartum Support International

Postpartum Support International is dedicated to helping women suffering from perinatal mood and anxiety disorders, including postpartum depression, the most common complication of childbirth. They also work to educate family, friends and healthcare providers so that women can receive the support they need to recover and heal.

Postpartum Support International
6706 SW 54th Avenue
Portland, OR 97219 USA
http://www.postpartum.net
email: psioffice@postpartum.net
phone: 503-894-9453

University of Michigan Depression Center

The University of Michigan Depression Center (UMDC) is the first center of its kind devoted entirely to bringing depression into the mainstream of medical research, care, education, and public policy. It is at the forefront in changing the paradigm of how depression is understood and treated.

University of Michigan Comprehensive Depression Center
Rachel Upjohn Building
4250 Plymouth Road, SPC 5763
Ann Arbor, MI 48109 USA
http://www.depressioncenter.org
email: depresswebmaster@umich.edu
phone: 734-936-4400

Postpartum Progress

Postpartum Progress is a blog on postpartum depression and all other mental illnesses related to pregnancy and childbirth. Postpartum Progress offers comprehensive information on the latest research, events and resources, as well as an unflinching look at what it is truly like to experience postpartum depression.

Postpartum Progress
http://postpartumprogress.com
email: postpartumprogress@gmail.com
phone: 678-764-2141

The MGH Center for Women's Mental Health

The Massachusetts General Hospital Center for Women's Mental Health is a perinatal and reproductive psychiatry information center. Their website provides a range of current information including discussion of new research findings in women's mental health and the impact of this research on day-to-day clinical practice.

The MGH Center for Women's Mental Health
Perinatal and Reproductive Psychiatry Program
Simches Research Builiding
185 Cambridge St Suite 2200
Boston, MA 02114 USA
http://www.womensmentalhealth.org
phone: 617-724-7792

Share Pregnancy and Infant Loss Support

Share Pregnancy and Infant Loss Support serves those whose lives are touched by the tragic death of a baby through early pregnancy loss, stillbirth, or in the first few months of life.

Share Pregnancy and Infant Loss Support
402 Jackson Street
St. Charles, MO 63301 USA
http://www.nationalshare.org
phone: 636-947-6164

Post and Antenatal Depression Association

Post and Antenatal Depression Association (PANDA) provides telephone support and information services for women and their families with postnatal depression.

Post and Antenatal Depression Association
810 Nicholson Street, North Fitzroy
Victoria, 3068 Australia
http://www.panda.org.au
email: info@panda.org.au
phone: 9481 3377

Pacific Post Partum Support Society

The Pacific Post Partum Support Society offers telephone support calls, weekly support groups, information in print, and a renowned guide for postpartum depression.

Pacific Post Partum Support Society
http://www.postpartum.org
200 - 7342 Winston Street
Burnaby, BC V5A 2H1 Canada
email: admin@postpartum.org
phone: 604-255-7999

Perinatal Illness UK

Perinatal Illness UK supports women and their families who have, or think they have any type of antenatal or postnatal depression or illness.

Perinatal Illness UK
PO BOX 49769
London WC1H 9WH United Kingdom
http://www.pni-uk.com
email: deb@pni-uk.com

The Postpartum Stress Center

The Postpartum Stress Center (PPSC) specializes in the diagnosis and treatment of prenatal and postpartum depression and anxiety disorders. In addition to this specialty, the PPSC offers a full range of general counseling services to individuals or couples seeking support.

The Postpartum Stress Center
1062 Lancaster Avenue
Rosemont Plaza, Suite 2
Rosemont, PA 19010 USA
http://www.postpartumstress.com
email: kkleiman@postpartumstress.com
phone: 610-525-7527

Association for Postnatal Illness

The Association for Postnatal Illness provides support, education, and information to women and families affected by postpartum depression and related mood disorders.

Association for Postnatal Illness
145 Dawes Road, Fulham
London, United Kingdom, SW6 7EB
http://apni.org
phone: 020 7386 0868

The Miscarriage Association

The Miscarriage Association acknowledges the distress associated with pregnancy loss and strives to make a positive difference to those it affects.

The Miscarriage Association
c/o Clayton Hospital, Northgate
Wakefield, West Yorkshire WF1 3JS
United Kingdom
http://www.miscarriageassociation.org.uk
phone: 01924 200795

EXAMPLES OF THERAPISTS

Integrated Therapy Services NW

Integrated Therapy Services NW (ITSNW) is dedicated to supporting parents and children in their lifelong journey of emotional growth. They equip parents and children to face the challenges of life and strengthen family relationships through the use of state-of-the-art mental health services.

Integrated Therapy Services NW
6004 N Westgate Blvd., Suite 180
Tacoma, WA 98406 USA
http://childtherapynow.com
email: admin@childtherapynow.com
phone: 253-460-7248

Perinatal Pro

Perinatal Pro is a website to help educate and inform women, families and health care providers about the often unexpected challenges of mood change during and after pregnancy. They also provide therapy services for families and workshops to train professionals.

Perinatal Pro
560 Sylvan Avenue NE
Englewood Cliffs, NJ 07632 USA
http://perinatalpro.com
email: susanstonelcsw@aol.com
phone: 201-567-5596

TRAINER

Trainers lead workshops and classes that teach individuals the skills and knowledge they need to grow and advance their careers. Trainers lead various workshops such as Birth Doula, Childbirth Educator, Infant Massage Instructor, Prenatal Yoga Teacher, and many more. Trainers have usually been working in their field for many years and they have a wealth of wisdom and experience to share. Most often, they are passionate, talented, and inspiring professionals, the best of the best.

Search words: childbirth educator trainer, doula trainer, infant massage trainer, prenatal yoga teacher training, doula workshop trainer application

GETTING STARTED

If you belong to a professional organization, contact them to see if any training opportunities are available. Write an outline for a training workshop that you would like to teach. Advertise and promote your workshop. Seek advice from existing Trainers that teach subjects that interest you.

EXAMPLES OF TRAINER OPPORTUNITIES

DONA International Birth Doula Trainer

http://www.dona.org/develop/trainer_birth.php

CAPPA Faculty Member

http://www.cappa.net/trainings.php?become-a-faculty-member

International Association of Infant Massage Trainer

http://www.iaim.ws/TrainerWorkshops.html

Maternity Wise Doula/Postpartum Doula Trainer

http://www.maternitywise.com/doula_leadership.html

Birthworks Childbirth Educator/Doula Trainer

http://www.birthworks.org/site/doula-certificatin.html

WATER EXERCISE PRENATAL INSTRUCTOR

Prenatal Water Exercise Instructors teach fitness classes to pregnant moms in swimming pools. The classes can involve dance, yoga, aerobic exercises, breathing, visualizations, and childbirth information. The water makes for a therapeutic and comfortable environment for pregnant women to move in.

Search words: aquatic prenatal class, prenatal water aerobics, prenatal water aerobics training, water exercise instructor, water fitness instructor, prenatal water class, pregnancy water class

GETTING STARTED

Enroll in a training course or workshop for Water Exercise Instructors. Participate in a prenatal water exercise class to learn more about the techniques taught. Seek advice and mentoring from an experienced Prenatal Water Exercise Instructor. Join an association or related group for instructors.

ෂාඥ

Career Journey ...

Pregnancy Water Exercise Instructor, Joy McDonald

How did you get started teaching Water Exercise classes to pregnant women?

Back in 1980, after the birth of my first child, and when I left full-time work as a physiotherapist, I became involved in teaching early pregnancy classes and antenatal classes with the Childbirth Education Association (CEA) in South Australia. During that time, I attended a workshop on exercise in pregnancy run by JuJu

Sundin, who is a highly regarded Childbirth Educator and author from Sydney. This inspired me to start some of the first exercise classes specifically designed for pregnant women here in Adelaide. These were land-based exercise classes, but led me to later on design and run similar classes at the indoor heated pool where my children were learning to swim. Over the years, I have come to believe strongly in the benefits of aquatic exercise and gradually began to offer more water, and less land classes, until now, all of my classes are in the water.

Why do you do this work? What do you enjoy?

I love the water! It's fun. I love working with pregnant women and new mothers. They are generally a happy, healthy, and positive group of clients. I enjoy helping them to stay more comfortable and active throughout their pregnancies. In addition to the physical benefits of the exercise, the classes provide a relaxed, enjoyable forum for discussion, information sharing, advice, support, and the opportunity for making friends! Many of my clients make lasting friendships and often form their own new mothers' groups amongst themselves. This is of great benefit.

How do you like running a business? What business advice can you share?

Mine is a very small part-time business, which I am happy running myself from my home. So I do all my own class bookings, accounting, advertising etc. This is the least enjoyable, but essential part of providing the service to the women who come to my classes.

The best form of advertising in any business is *positive word of mouth.* If you make every contact with your client a positive experience, they will spread the word!

What type of training or education did you receive?

I am a physiotherapist, so I have a physiotherapy qualification from the University of Adelaide. At the time of starting up pregnancy and postnatal exercise classes, I did a TAFE (Adult Further Education) fitness instructors certificate, which included an aquatic elective. Through the Australian Physiotherapy Association I have attended many relevant professional development courses over the years. These include a Level 1 Aquatic Physiotherapy course, a Level 2 Aquatic Physiotherapy in the Childbearing Year course, a Pelvic Floor Physiotherapy course, and a Fitball training course.

I also keep an up to date certificate in first aid, resuscitation and pool rescue, (which I have so far never needed to use!).

Do you have any "aha" moments or insights to share about your work?

There's a lot more to it then just "instructing an exercise class".

I conduct all of my classes personally, in the pool, as part of an informal group with my clients, not standing on the poolside. I think this is essential for encouraging relaxed interaction and communication, for getting to know my clients and for keeping my eye on their well-being.

I also facilitate coffee get-togethers for my classes, encouraging new mums to bring their babies back for some "show & tell".

What advice can you give to anyone that wishes to become a Water Prenatal Exercise Instructor?

Make sure you have a sound background in the anatomy and physiology of pregnancy, in exercise and the effect of immersion on these things. Take care when selecting pools to use. There are lots of things to consider.

୫୦୯୫

ORGANIZATIONS

American AquaNatal

The purpose of the American AquaNatal method is to provide a holistic fitness and educational program in water that facilitates women's health during pregnancy, birthing and mothering.

American AquaNatal
PO Box 3957
Santa Barbara, CA 93130 USA
http://www.aquanatal.com
phone: 305-923-0382

Birthlight

Birthlight offers Aqua Yoga for Pregnancy, which is a unique series of exercises combining the therapeutic and buoyant nature of water with the energizing and harmonizing effect of yoga.

Birthlight
PO Box 148
Cambridge
CB4 2GB United Kingdom
http://birthlight.com/public/yoga/aquayoga.aspx
phone: 01223 362288

Professional Fitness & Education

Professional Fitness & Education offers Aquafusion Training courses, which provide the knowledge, ability and motivation to enable professionals to deliver safe, effective community based exercise classes during and after pregnancy.

Professional Fitness & Education
9a Cleasby Road
Menston
Nr Ilkley
West Yorkshire LS29 6JE United Kingdom
http://www.pfetraining.co.uk
phone: 01943 879816

Lifestyle Swim School

Lifestyle Swim School offers workshops to teach swimming to infants and toddlers through a gentle, gradual, child-paced and baby-friendly curriculum.

Lifestyle Swim School
http://www.babyswimming.com/workshops.htm
email: mckayswim@aol.com
phone: 561-393-6386

Amnion Aquatics

Amnion Aquatics as a modality blends aquatic and prenatal therapy.

Amnion Aquatics
14000 NE 371 St
La Center, WA 98629 USA
http://amnionaquatics.com/amnion
email: maryseamster@earthlink.net
phone: 360-263-2119

American Fitness Professionals and Associates

The American Fitness Professionals and Associates (AFPA) provides students with an affordable education that gives them the knowledge, skills and awareness necessary to enhance their own lives, the lives of others, and the community at large through innovative program design, teaching, research and service focused on the professional practice of fitness, wellness, nutrition, health and physical education.

American Fitness Professionals and Associates
1601 Long Beach Blvd.
P.O. Box 214
Ship Bottom, NJ 08008 USA
http://www.afpafitness.com
email: afpa@afpafitness.com
phone: 800-494-7782

United States Water Fitness Association

The United States Water Fitness Association is an educational organization committed to excellence in educating and promoting aquatics, including water exercise.

United States Water Fitness Association
P.O. Box 243279
Boynton Beach, FL 33424 USA
http://www.uswfa.com
email: info@uswfa.org
phone: 561-732-9908

Aquatic Exercise Association

The Aquatic Exercise Association (AEA) is an international organization specializing in Aquatic Fitness Education. AEA offers intermediate level Aquatic Fitness Instructor certification and numerous continuing education programs throughout the world. The Aquatic Fitness Professional (AFP) certification is offered in the United States and an international version, the Aquatic Fitness Instructor certification, is currently offered abroad.

Aquatic Exercise Association
PO Box 1609
Nokomis, FL 34274 USA
http://www.aeawave.com
email: info@aeawave.com
phone: 941-486-8600

EXAMPLES OF WATER AEROBIC CLASSES

Physiotherapy Pregnancy & Post-natal Water Exercise

Joy McDonald, a physiotherapist and owner of Physiotherapy Pregnancy & Post-natal Water Exercise believes in the benefits of gentle exercise throughout pregnancy, and finds a heated pool environment helpful. The warm water is relaxing and provides buoyancy and support for the changing body. Backache and pelvic joint problems are common in pregnancy and women with painful joints are able to exercise comfortably and safely in the pool.

Physiotherapy Pregnancy & Post-natal Water Exercise
http://www.joysclasses.com.au
email: joy@joysclasses.com.au
phone: 8364 1323

Aquamums

Aquamums provides aqua aerobics classes especially designed by physiotherapists for pre- and post-natal women.

http://www.aquamums.com.au
email: mandy@aquamums.com.au
phone: 9826 6346

WEB DESIGNER

Web Designers are trained or have the skills and knowledge to create websites. They work with Childbirth Professionals to design their websites and build their internet presence. Some designers are also Doulas or Childbirth Educators with experience in the childbirth field, and have an understanding about what fellow professionals need to successfully market their services to families. They offer a variety of services from building a website to creating a company logo.

Search words: web designers doulas, web designer childbirth professionals, web page design midwives

GETTING STARTED

Read books and take classes about web design. Design a website for yourself as part of your portfolio; network with other Web Designers to learn about the web design business.

EXAMPLE WEB DESIGNERS

Desjean Design

Desjean Design work with Doulas, Midwives, Baby Nurses and other Childbirth Professionals, and are familiar with what it takes to get these businesses to the top of search engines. They help Childbirth Professionals create websites that are appealing to families helping them reach new clients.

http://www.desjeandesign.com

Vibrant Life Web Solutions

Vibrant Life Web Solutions offers websites designed specifically for Doulas, Midwives, and Childbirth Educators. They help professionals easily establish their web presence to connect with and better serve clients.

http://www.birthpros.com

Sprinkle Sparkle

Sprinkle Sparkle offers traditional website design, and mobile and blog design services. They provide hosting, domain registration, social media integration and email marketing.

http://sprinklesparkle.com

Anne Campbell Design

Anne Campbell Design helps businesses jump into the Web for the first time—or redesign an existing website to show their business in the best light.

http://www.annecampbelldesign.com

Mile High Doula Web Design

Mile High Doula provides web design services for Childbirth Professionals.

http://www.milehighdoula.com/webdesign.html

WEBSITE FOUNDER AND WEBSITE CONTRIBUTOR

Website Founders create websites to provide information and resources to pregnant women and Childbirth Professionals. Their websites often fill an information gap and provide news and articles not found elsewhere.

Website Contributors create content and keep websites updated with articles, photos, videos, news and information.

Search words: website founder, website contributor, childbirth website, pregnancy website, free website

GETTING STARTED

Write a plan for the type of website you would like to create. Research the internet for websites that have similar goals. Consider if you can incorporate elements of other websites into building your website. Use free webpage creation tools or hire a web designer to assist you in beginning your website. Read books about website creation or enroll in a class.

৪০০৪

Career Journey ...

Website Manager, Jennifer VanderLaan

What made you decide to start your website?

I actually started it as a way for my childbirth education students to access answers to common questions. It grew slowly as I began to see needs outside my community.

Why do you do this work? What do you enjoy?

I continue to build the website because I still see broad needs for information. For example, I would get many emails asking for a referral to a Childbirth Educator or Doula in a particular location; it was not very easy for me to locate them. I realized if it was that hard for me -- someone "in the business" who knew what keywords to search for -- how much more difficult it must be for a first time expectant mother. I solved the problem by building a directory and finding every website I could.

I actually enjoy the programming aspects of the website. I like designing a page and figuring out how to make it do what I want it to do. I like learning about how people access the website and navigate through it. It teaches me about the way women think about their upcoming birth and the questions they have. It helps me to rethink the way I communicate information to women. I want to communicate so they can understand. It isn't always easy, and the website will never be "done."

How do you like running a business? What business advice can you share?

The business aspects are my least favorite, but if I don't take care of them, then the website will disappear. I would recommend starting at square one when planning any business. Maybe you want to have a website and expect it to be a part-time business. First, you need to figure out how much it will cost you for start-up costs, monthly fees, and don't forget to think about the time you will invest. Then, you need to figure out how you will make enough money to pay back the "loan" you take from your family to pay for the start-up? How will you ensure you have enough income to invest in your continuing education, marketing, and the other things it takes to stay current?

I remember some advice I was given a long time ago …

"If you make money, it is a business. If you spend money it is a hobby. Hobbies are fine, but you better decide how much money you can spend on a hobby before you spend that first dollar."

What type of training or education did you receive?

I was trained as a Childbirth Educator and used self-instruction with books to learn how to program a website. In fact I am still using books to learn how to do more with the website. After starting the website, I became a Doula, which gave me another perspective on the information women needed. Then I became a nurse, which taught me even more about how to help families educate themselves. Now I am in a Midwifery and Public Health program, which is giving me another perspective on how to present the information, and what else can be included.

Do you have any "aha" moments or insights to share about your work?

About a year ago my website suddenly lost half its traffic. I had not made any changes; instead, it was a search engine that had changed its search scoring. I am currently in school, and had thought I had the website set up to practically run itself. I did not have the time to make the changes necessary to regain the lost traffic. Less traffic meant less advertising revenue. I was still making enough money to cover the monthly costs, but will need to do a lot of work before I make enough to invest in serious improvements again.

I needed to accept that there is only so much control I have over whether or not people will see my website. This also reminded me that maintaining a website is a real job, and there is work I need to do at least weekly. It isn't something I can maintain well with the full-time work of school, and I have not been able to add any new information since beginning my latest educational pursuits. At this point, I am doing the minimum updating hoping the website still has traffic in a year when I will be done with school and can begin to give it proper attention again.

What advice can you give to anyone that wishes to start a website or contribute to a website?

I see lots of start-up websites that are the same basic information with a cute logo and promises for more information to come. A year later the website still has very minimal traffic, and the webmaster lets the site go. If you want to start a website, you need to have a reason. Identify what is missing in the available information, don't copy what is already there. Find a niche and stick to it. Become the expert on one small thing.

Make sure you understand the commitment you are making. Creating content (the actual information you are presenting) takes time. You need to write, rewrite, edit and rewrite again. Even to write one blog post a week will take about an hour -- longer if you have less writing experience. Find someone willing to read your content before you make it public. Spelling and grammar errors damage your credibility no matter what your subject.

Anything else you would like to share?

I see a trend for new social media web pages that post information about their page all over social networks. The well-meaning webmaster is hoping to get some traffic through posting comments and links. What the webmaster doesn't seem to understand is that this is a form of spamming and is frowned upon by most websites. It will get you a very bad reputation, and I have had to make changes in the permissions of my social media web pages because it is so common. Don't consider doing that for your marketing plan. Instead create a product other people want to share, and pay for your advertising like a "real" business.

80CR

WEBPAGE CREATION TOOLS

Wordpress

Wordpress is an easy to use blogging tool that doubles as a website design tool.

http://wordpress.com

Yola

Yola has easy-to-use web design tools to help users make a website that has a professional look.

http://www.yola.com

Wix

Wix is a free online website-creation tool. Wix gives users total control over web design without having to know anything about fancy coding or programming.

http://www.wix.com

WEBSITE EXAMPLES

One World Birth

One World Birth is a free online video resource for Childbirth Professionals, Activists and parents who want to keep their finger on the pulse of birth around the globe.

http://www.oneworldbirth.net

Birthing Naturally

Birthing Naturally exists to be a free source of information about pregnancy and birth because the knowledge of how to stay healthy during pregnancy and give birth naturally should be shared freely with every woman.

http://www.birthingnaturally.net

Blissfully Domestic

Blissfully Domestic is for women who want to be true to themselves while choosing to create bliss in their homes and families. They believe in the amazing power and strength in the voices of women. Blissfully Domestic strives to encourage, connect, empower and bless all the writers and readers of Blissfully Domestic. Blissfully Domestic is written by women, and for women, as the smart girl's guide to life.

http://blissfullydomestic.com

Kelly Mom

The Kelly Mom website was created to provided evidence-based information about breastfeeding, child sleep development and parenting.

Kelly Mom
2031 4th St N #9
St Petersburg, FL 33704 USA
http://www.kellymom.com
email: kelly@kellymom.com

Mum Street

Mum Street is a parenting website. They offer fun, friendship, support, and advice regarding the parenting journey.

Mum Street
Unit 15D Tiger Hangar,
Sywell Aerodrome, Sywell,
Northamptonshire, NN6 0BN
United Kingdom
http://mumstreet.co.uk
phone: 1604 495477

Childbirth.org

Childbirth.org is a pregnancy resource website.

http://www.childbirth.org

NaturalBabyPros.com

NaturalBabyPros.com is directory where families can find natural family related businesses and resources about natural, holistic life options.

http://www.naturalbabypros.com

Home Birth Guide

Home Birth Guide is a website that shares the creator's passion and knowledge about homebirth and natural birth.

http://www.home-birth-guide.com

Pregnancy.about.com

The Pregnancy.about.com website answers questions and delivers information about all things related to pregnancy.

http://pregnancy.about.com

Giving Birth With Confidence

Giving Birth with Confidence is an online community, created by Lamaze International, that shares a variety of trustworthy, timely and appealing stories, articles and tips related to pregnancy, birth and parenting.

http://givingbirthwithconfidence.org

WRITER

Writers use their skill to write books and articles that inform and teach pregnant women and Childbirth Professionals. Some Writers offer entertaining reflections about the birth process. They share their knowledge, wisdom, and personal philosophies.

Search words: childbirth author, childbirth writer, pregnancy author, childbirth playwright, writer's workshop

GETTING STARTED

Begin by purchasing a journal and writing down your thoughts each day without judgment. Read articles and books on topics of interest and summarize them. Write about your life, the birth of your children, and your parenting experiences. Take writing classes. Attend a Writer's Workshop for Childbirth Professionals.

EXAMPLES

Birth, a play

Karen Brody is a mother of two boys, born in 1999 and 2001. In 2005 she wrote a documentary-style play called *Birth*, offering a portrait of how low-risk mothers are giving birth in America. As a consequence of *Birth*, Brody founded BOLD, a global movement inspiring communities to use theater and storytelling circles to raise awareness and money to improve childbirth choices for mothers.

http://www.birthonlaborday.com/theplay

Claudia Spahr

Claudia Spahr is a writer, journalist and speaker, who turned her love of story telling into a career.

http://www.claudiaspahr.com

Robin Elsie Weiss

Robin Elsie Weiss is a busy mother of eight and author of numerous pregnancy and parenting books. She describes pregnancy as her life. She shares her passion for normal birth with others, both in the classroom and through the internet.

http://www.robineliseweiss.com

CAREER JOURNEY

As you think about your career, know that it is a journey. That means you don't have to rigidly plan out each step. Your career plan should be flexible. On a journey, you may or may not have a set destination. What is important on a journey is that you enjoy it, take excursions, and have fun.

When people think of work they don't always think of fun and enjoyment. Why not? You must absolutely discover a career that you love and work that you enjoy. Bon voyage! Or, may I offer congratulations to you, if you've already found a career that you love. Where are you headed next in your journey? Keep traveling.

Just when I am content and have mastered a skill in my career, a new opportunity comes my way to challenge me. I have been a Childbirth Professional for over 15 years, and I still have more to learn, and I am constantly growing. I am pleased to be part of a profession in which the work never gets old.

A CASE STUDY

I now want to offer my career journey as a case study. My path holds some universal lessons that I would like to share. In sharing these lessons, my hope is that you will believe in your dreams. I hope that you will pay attention to your calling. You should write a career plan and pursue your plan. All things are possible, no matter what the obstacles are. You must always believe in yourself and in your abilities.

Perhaps most important, you must know what your strengths are and what you are capable of achieving. Never limit yourself. Always try. Take reasonable risks. You will accomplish amazing things.

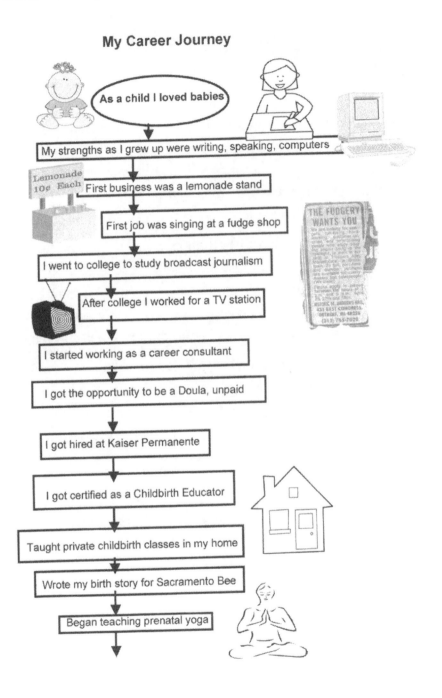

My Career Journey

As a child I loved babies

My strengths as I grew up were writing, speaking, computers

First business was a lemonade stand

First job was singing at a fudge shop

I went to college to study broadcast journalism

After college I worked for a TV station

I started working as a career consultant

I got the opportunity to be a Doula, unpaid

I got hired at Kaiser Permanente

I got certified as a Childbirth Educator

Taught private childbirth classes in my home

Wrote my birth story for Sacramento Bee

Began teaching prenatal yoga

continued, My Career Journey

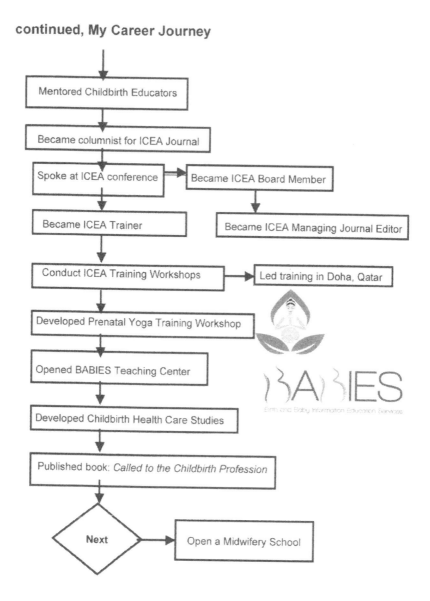

```
Mentored Childbirth Educators
            │
            ▼
Became columnist for ICEA Journal
            │
            ▼
Spoke at ICEA conference ──────► Became ICEA Board Member
            │                              │
            ▼                              ▼
Became ICEA Trainer            Became ICEA Managing Journal Editor
            │
            ▼
Conduct ICEA Training Workshops ──────► Led training in Doha, Qatar
            │
            ▼
Developed Prenatal Yoga Training Workshop
            │
            ▼
Opened BABIES Teaching Center
            │
            ▼
Developed Childbirth Health Care Studies
            │
            ▼
Published book: Called to the Childbirth Profession
            │
            ▼
          Next ──────► Open a Midwifery School
```

FLOW CHART

This flow chart outlines my career. When I see my career visually, I realize at which point a decision or a meeting changed my career. A chart like this may allow you to see a different perspective of your career.

Write a flow chart that outlines your career journey so far. The chart is not a resume, so you are not writing your work history. Don't list every job you've ever held, only what is relevant.

When you create it, include what tells your story, the beginning of your career, where you are, and where you are going.

If you have photos or images that represent stages of your career include them. Your flowchart could be all photos, without any words. Take your time with the process. Write down what you learn.

What I learned from my chart is that:

1. I can do way more than I ever realized.

2. To be more confident about my skills.

3. Don't wait for approval.

4. Reach higher.

Next, I plan to open a midwifery school.

CAREER GUIDANCE WORKSHEET

The following career guidance worksheet is another way to reflect upon your career journey. Take the time to think about and write down your interests, highest skills, passions, dreams, and your purpose.

CAREER GUIDANCE WORKSHEET

My Interests

Work that I have loved...

Adjectives describing this work...

My Highest Skills are

My Passions are

My Dreams are

My Purpose is

INTERESTS

It is essential to consider your interests as you create a career plan.

What are your interests?

_____

_____

To get started, write down the work that you have done so far in your life that you have loved, paid or unpaid. List as many adjectives as possible to describe this work. Refer to the following list of adjectives for assistance.

_____

_____

abundant	early	inspiring	smooth
adventurous	easy	interesting	social
agreeable	eager	joyous	splendid
alive	elated	late	strange
amused	elegant	light	strong
beautiful	encouraging	lively	successful
brainy	energetic	long	super
brave	enthusiastic	lucky	swift
brief	excited	magnificent	sweet
bright	expensive	meaningful	talented
busy	exuberant	modern	tender
calm	faithful	old-fashioned	thankful
careful	famous	open	thoughtful

cautious	fancy	outstanding	tough
cheerful	fantastic	perfect	unusual
challenging	fast	plain	vast
colorful	fresh	pleasant	victorious
comfortable	friendly	poised	vivacious
concerned	funny	powerful	wild
cooperative	gentle	precious	witty
courageous	gifted	proud	wonderful
cute	glamorous	puzzled	young
curious	gleaming	quaint	zany
dangerous	glorious	real	zealous
delicious	graceful	reliable	
delightful	happy	rich	
detailed	healthy	shy	
determined	helpful	silly	
different	hilarious	sleepy	
difficult	important	slow	
distinct	independent	smiling	

HIGHEST SKILL SET

What are your highest skills?

_____

_____

These are skills that you use superbly with little effort and you receive enjoyment when using these skills.

Write them down, and include details describing why you are amazing using that particular skill.

Example

> Writing is one of my highest skills.
>
> I like writing because it calms me. It clears my mind. People respond positively to my writing.

These skills are important to identify, because they will translate throughout your career journey. That means if your highest skill is *writing*, then focus upon using your writing skills in the work that you choose.

Be confident about that skill. Confidence is key. My career journey has sometimes lacked confidence. When you lack confidence, it is difficult to move forward in your career. Lack of confidence may lead to a lack of vision, and without vision, you won't dream about what comes next in your life, and when you don't dream, nothing happens. Your career will not move forward. So, if *writing* is your higher skill, as you create your career plan, a key component must be finding ways to use that skill.

PASSIONS

What are your passions?

_____

_____

_____

_____

Passions wake you up in the morning. They bring you peace. They give you joy. They fulfill you. Don't think too much. Just jot them down.

As you create your career plan, you want to include your passions. Passion allows you to do something without compensation or acknowledgement. That is an important concept to be aware of as you consider how to devote your time and energy.

DREAMS

Write down your dream career. What do you really desire in the depth of your heart?

_____

_____

_____

You can accomplish more than you know. You just have to plan it out.

I never realized I would serve on a board, or teach women about birth around the world. I thought that was for extraordinary people, not me.

You are extraordinary. You can have a dream career.

My advice is to stay focused. Don't compromise on your dream. Work towards it.

PURPOSE

What is your purpose?

_____

_____

_____

If you are not sure then leave this space blank, until the answer comes to you. You do have purpose.

My purpose is to empower women everywhere.

One way I do this is through teaching women to understand their bodies. The prenatal yoga class that I lead helps women gain a greater connection to their body through breathing techniques and movement.

Ahead of my career, my number one purpose in life is to nurture and support the two daughters I have been given, so they become who and all they're meant to be.

Purpose is clear. Purpose is loud. Purpose feels good. You will not miss your purpose. It calls to you.

THE PLAN

Take the time to think about your career journey and the steps you should take next. You should only focus upon what you have written on this worksheet. Whatever job, school, training, or business opportunity you decide upon should integrate your interests, highest skills, passions, and dreams, to align with your purpose.

You only get one chance to live your life. Time is limited. Do what you love. What you are called to do. Live life with no regrets.

This worksheet is your plan. Use it to remind yourself that your education, employment, and professional opportunities should:

Fit your interests
Use your highest skills
Stir your passions
Ignite your dreams
Serve your purpose

INTERNSHIPS AND GAINING EXPERIENCE

I lead workshops for Childbirth Professionals, and as I teach, a common question asked is, "How do I gain experience?"

My advice is to ask other professionals to help you. Mentorships, internships and apprenticeships are a mainstay of the Childbirth Profession. They are the way most people in the field got started and how they continue to grow – by learning at someone else's side, and observing their work.

Professionals in this field are extremely giving and helpful. I know that you will find someone to assist you along your journey. Keep in mind that it may take time and effort before you find the right mentor, internship, or learning opportunity. Don't be discouraged, if it takes awhile. If you are persistent and positive, then doors will open. The following are some practical steps to take towards gaining experience.

USE THE INTERNET

A great place to begin is with an internet search. You want to search for a professional located in your area that is already experienced in the role you desire to learn.

For example if you want to become a Doula apprentice, and you live in Davis, California, then your Google search words would be, "doulas davis california".

This search would provide websites of Doulas practicing in the area. You would need to sift through the search results, click to websites that you think are helpful, and then bookmark them, or write down the information in order to contact those you discovered through your search.

ASSOCIATIONS

Contact a related professional association and ask them if they can suggest anyone to mentor you or offer you an internship. Professional groups and associations have a vested interest in wanting to assist those that are new. You may become a member of their organization, and, they often have a mission and commitment to help professionals grow. Another place to look to for help is a group of similar professionals; they are sometimes called a collective. In the case of Doulas, it may be referred to as the Doula collective of your particular city, i.e. Sacramento Doula Collective.

NETWORK

Use your network. If you have been taking classes and workshops reach out to your classmates, even those online, and ask them for ideas. Social media is a very useful tool. You can post an update to your social media account and ask for leads or opportunities where you can gain experience.

HOSPITALS

Your local hospital is a very good resource. They very often welcome volunteers. If they are not accepting volunteers, then ask if you can observe a Childbirth Educator, Lactation Consultant, Midwife, or other professional as they carry out their work in the hospital setting. Try contacting the childbirth education department at your local hospital to ask any questions you may have.

RESUME

Don't forget to update your resume. I suggest that you print 10 copies and place a single copy in 10 individual folders. As you go out meeting professionals and discussing your goals, you can hand someone that you feel might assist you, a prepared folder that has your resume in it. That type of preparation will reflect well upon you. Also, in this digital age, you should always have your resume ready to email to appropriate professionals. Remember never to email your resume as spam. When you attach your resume to an email, include a well-written and grammatically correct introduction.

Another great resource is LinkedIn and other similar websites, where your profile acts as an online resume. When posting information about yourself through the internet and even in emails, be wise and professional, as you are building a digital image and reputation that cannot be deleted, and is accessible to the world.

OBSERVATION

An easy way to get going is to ask anyone with experience if you can observe the work they do. The following are a few tips to gain the most from your observation experience.

Arrive early – Promptness shows that you are considerate and serious.

Be respectful – This means not interrupting a class you observe or offering unsolicited advice or information to clients and patients. Wait until you and the professional whom you are observing are alone to share.

Ask where to sit or stand – In this way, you will make sure that you are not in the way of any work that is being done.

Ask if you can help – This shows that you have a great attitude, and you might get the chance to learn something right away, by being put to work.

Have an attitude to learn – You want to ask questions when appropriate and show that you are interested and passionate.

Take notes – This shows that you are serious, and you also don't want to forget anything important that you observe.

Say thank you – Don't forget to thank the professional that you observe for the opportunity.

Follow up – It is a good idea to email or phone between 3-7 days after your observation to follow-up and ask questions, and also to express your appreciation once again. This is a great way to show that you are a serious student and an excellent candidate for training.

ASSESSMENT

After your observation, assess what you think about the work you saw. Do you need to observe more? Are you still interested in this work?

Also, assess if you and the individual that you observed are compatible. Did that person inspire you? Did you learn something from their work? Do you feel like you can have a beneficial working relationship?

If your answers point you towards continuing in your training, then I recommend asking the person that you observed to officially be your mentor or teacher.

If it is appropriate, offer to pay them a fee for their time in training you. Consider the cost part of your educational expense.

THE MENTOR RELATIONSHIP

Once you officially begin your mentorship, internship, or apprenticeship, the following tips will help you be successful.

Outline a timeline and goals – In this way it is clear what the expectations are and when they should be completed. For example, after one month, I will be ready to teach a breastfeeding class.

Learn all you can – It is important that you leave the experience with an increased skill level than when you began.

Be professional – Treat the experience better than you would a job. You should go over and beyond the norm i.e. dress well, bring cupcakes, be positive.

Ask for feedback – Don't forget to ask for a formal evaluation. You want constructive advice from your mentor on how you can improve and grow.

Next stage – Plan to move on from your training experience. It is always a good idea to give a nominal gift to your mentor, such as a thoughtful note, a gift card for ice cream, movie tickets, flowers, etc. You want to end the experience and move on to your own professional work, and transition the relationship from teacher to colleague.

LIST OF POSSIBLE MENTORS

NAME	CONTACT INFORMATION
1.	
2.	
3.	
4.	
5.	

TELEPHONE SCRIPT FOR SEEKING A MENTOR

Hello, may I speak to _____

My name is _____

I am in the process of training to become a _____

I learned about you and the services you offer through your website _____, and I was wondering if I could observe your work?

OR

I learned about the work that you do through your website

_____, and I was wondering if I could attend one of your classes?

I want you to know that I belong to the following associations/organizations: _____

I have taken the following classes: _____

I have read the following books: _____

Continue the conversation sharing your enthusiasm for the role you are seeking and share your desire to learn. Ask for the opportunity to meet.

Close the conversation by saying thank-you.

If that individual cannot help you, ask for a phone number, website, or email for someone else they think might be able to assist you.

EXAMPLE EMAIL TO REQUEST OBSERVATION

Dear Best Baby Planner,

My name is Mary Morgan. I am training to become a Baby Planner.

I would like to ask if I could observe your work?

I am a member of the Baby Planner Association and just completed a training workshop for professional Baby Planners. I have been reading the Best Baby Planner Book and feel that my next step is to observe an experienced professional.

I look forward to hearing from you.

Sincerely,

Mary Morgan

999-999-999

MENTORING AND SHARING KNOWLEDGE

I hope that you will become a mentor.

When you share of your time, energy, knowledge, and give of yourself to help another person succeed, then you will receive much in return. First of all, you will gain insight into the skills that you possess, and the work that you do. The job you perform will appear different in your eyes when you have to train someone else to understand it. You will have a greater awareness of everything that you do, big and small, and why you do those things.

If you have done the same job, for a while, you get stuck, often without realizing it. Being stuck does not mean that you're not doing a fantastic job; it just means that you are not doing anything new. When you don't do anything new, then your potential to grow is limited. So I encourage you to mentor someone else as part of your own growth process.

Mentoring is fun. You get a chance to share your knowledge with someone that is positive and receptive. And something else to keep in mind, when you train someone to do your work, then you will have a backup person to call upon when you are in need.

Are you reluctant? If mentoring does not sound like something you are interested in, then don't do it. If you are hesitant because you think your student may compete with you in the future, then you shouldn't be a mentor. Students need to have someone that will give 100% to their training. They need to be filled with positive, well-intentioned energy.

Mentoring is a skill. So, if patience and an upbeat attitude are not your strengths, then mentoring might not be right for you.

Understanding the level a mentor candidate is at may help you decide whether you can commit. Students will usually fall into the following levels of needing assistance.

Teacher – This person is 90% ready to assume a professional role. They don't need much help. They need someone to check over their ideas, and make sure they are going in the right direction. After a short time of mentoring, they will be ready.

In-training – This person is 60% ready to assume a professional role. They will require support and direction. They need to gain confidence. Supervised practice will be important to their success. Your advice and direction will be key.

Basic – This individual is a beginner, and not ready to assume a professional role. They will primarily observe the work that you do. They won't be ready to do tasks on their own for a while. They need structured, assigned tasks in order to build up their confidence. They learn best when they can do team activities.

When you decide to mentor, assess the time you can invest, along with your strengths and weaknesses. Then, based upon your assessment, select the correct type of candidate to mentor.

For example, if you really want to mentor, but have a busy schedule, then select a candidate at the teacher level to mentor. This type of candidate will not require much of your time. And the opposite works too. A basic level candidate would give you the opportunity to teach core principles.

Take the time to interview a mentor candidate, by phone, or in-person to assess which level they are at: teacher, in-training, or basic.

MENTORING PROGRAM

Depending upon your Childbirth Professional role, it might be appropriate to create a mentoring program, and charge a fee for your time and expertise.

As a Childbirth Educator, I have assisted others to become certified by providing the following mentor program. For nominal costs, students would receive the following:

- Opportunity to observe a childbirth class series

- Assistance developing class curriculum

- Evaluation of teaching skills

- Administration of certification test

OUTLINE EXPECTATIONS

Before you begin to mentor someone, it is a good idea to have a written agreement about what is expected of each party. Ask your student what they would like to receive from the mentoring experience. This could be a simple email that mentions what day and time you will meet, and what subjects you will discuss. Also, include the length of time the mentoring process will last, perhaps two months. When expectations are clear, there is less chance for misunderstandings. Also, expectations allow you to see the growth and development of your student. For example, an expectation could be in three weeks the student will be ready to give a pregnancy massage.

THE CONNECTION

Not every mentoring relationship will be right, and that's okay. If once you begin mentoring someone, you feel it's not working out for whatever reason, then try to bring it to a close as soon as possible. It is important that mentoring is beneficial and positive for both parties.

PROFESSIONALISM

Always be professional when mentoring someone. This means that it is not necessary to be a part of your student's personal life. There should be boundaries, although, in some instances a natural bond may develop and you become friends.

RECOMMENDATION

When the mentoring expectations have been fulfilled, then the experience should be brought to a close, and the student will move into their professional role. Set aside time to express to the student your evaluation of their skills, including practical advice. If the student has proficiently completed their experience and has grown in their abilities, then write a recommendation for them. Provide employment assistance or business support if you are able.

SERENDIPITY

Allow for time and circumstance to work in your life. People will connect with you for unexplainable reasons. And you will connect with them. Many people you mentor without even knowing.

EXPECTATIONS OF MENTOR EXPERIENCE
1.
2.
3.
4.
5.

STEPS TO FINDING EMPLOYMENT

Many employment opportunities await you in the Childbirth Profession. The specialized skills and services of Childbirth Professionals are increasingly needed by hospitals, public health clinics, doctor's offices, birthing centers, and many other agencies and institutions. The following tips will help you as you search for employment.

INTERNET

The internet is a useful tool to search for job opportunities. Through using the internet you can make connections with potential employers. There are websites online that keep up to the minute data of current job openings. Search the internet for the websites of hospitals in your area, and check the "career" or "job posting" sections to find out if they are hiring. Government and Health agency websites are also a good place to check for positions.

NETWORK

Tell everyone that you know about your job search and describe the type of position that you are seeking. You will be surprised at how many job leads can come from random conversations.

Attend events that are related to the job you're seeking. For example, a baby fair, although aimed at new parents, may have vendors and speakers that you can connect with, and they may lead you to a job. Use social media tools to network, such as Twitter, Facebook, and LinkedIn. Be sure that you have a professional photo posted and that your profile includes relevant information that would be of interest to a potential employer.

REACH OUT

If you know of a possible job opportunity, it is sometimes advantageous to reach out and make contact, instead of waiting for a phone call. In order to do this, find out the name of the person that will be making a hiring decision. Give them a phone call, and let them know that you are qualified for the job, and would like to meet with them to discuss the opportunity.

This is a simple technique that has worked for me on several occasions.

You may have to do some detective work in order to find the right person to speak to. I have discovered that whoever is usually in charge of answering the phones is very knowledgeable about current job openings and the overseeing staff involved. This person is usually great at offering you assistance. Just be professional, polite, and direct. Ask for the name, title, and phone number of the person in charge of hiring for the job you're seeking.

VOLUNTEER

If you know of a place that you would like to work for, but they do not have any current positions, ask them if you can volunteer. In this way they become familiar with your skills, and you will already be in place when an opening comes up.

COMMUTE

Many people that work in the Childbirth Profession simply love it, and will stay in the same position for 10, 15, or 20 years. This means that the turn over rate is not very high. Keep this in mind during your job search. If you are not able to find a job in your local community, you might consider commuting to a nearby town in order to find a position.

Who You Know

The Childbirth Profession is small when it comes to knowing the people that work within it. Who you know is an important factor. If you build a relationship with the right person, then you will have access to more opportunities. Many job positions are not posted for the general public. They are filled by referrals from within the profession. So it is important to build relationships through the work that you do, through volunteering, and through attendance at community or networking events. Also, become an active member of a professional association or group.

Interview

Be ready for formal and informal interviews as you seek employment. An interview is a meeting that assesses your experience, skills, education, training, personality, temperament, and potential. An informal interview may take place over a cup of coffee with a person you met through your networking efforts. You may not even be aware that an interview has taken place. This person may be discreetly screening you in order to recommend you for a position.

Know that every interaction within the Childbirth Professional community could lead to advancing your career. Always put forth your best.

A formal interview usually takes place at your potential employer's place of business. You should prepare for a formal interview. Learn as much as possible about the company, the person interviewing you, and the responsibilities of the job. Make sure that you wear appropriate clothes to the interview. You want to impress the person or people that you meet. You want to leave an interview with the confident feeling that you will be offered employment.

Be sure to interview for positions where you meet most of the qualifications and already have the necessary skills or training to perform the job. Then an interview is more of a conversation explaining your abilities and talents. The purpose of the interview is also to learn about your personality and if it will blend with those you will work for.

You should have objectives as well when you go to be interviewed. You are also conducting an assessment. You should prepare questions to ask the interviewer. You are trying to learn if the company or employer will meet your career needs. You want to leave the interview without any doubt that you would fit in with the culture and work ethic of the company, and that it would be a place where you would grow. Think about what else would be important for you to find out when you go to interview for a job.

Write down what you need to find out from an employment interview.

_____

_____

_____

_____

_____

RESOURCES

So many good employment resources are available on the internet, in your community, through colleges, and at the library. Seek them out. Many of them are for your use, free of charge. If you have never written a resume or cover letter, and don't have much interview experience, then seek professional help through these resources.

PRACTICE INTERVIEW QUESTIONS

Tell me something about yourself.

This question requires you to say one fluffy thing, and then discuss your training, education, and why you are qualified for the position. For example, you could say, "I love to write," and then share about your writing experience, "For two years I wrote articles for..."

Why are you leaving your current job? or Why did you leave your last job?

Explain your accomplishments and discuss your future career goals.

What are your strengths?

Name specific skills and give examples of how you have used them in your career.

What are your weaknesses?

Don't really share a weakness. You want to share a strength as a weakness, for example, "I am a perfectionist to a fault and work extra hard to satisfy customers."

What is your five-year plan?

Briefly share long-term goals that are related to the job you are interviewing for. An example, "I plan to get CPR certified in the next year."

Anything else you would like to share or ask?

This is your opening to summarize 2-3 reasons why you are qualified for this job. It is always a good idea if you can explain how you currently use or recently performed the same job duties required. As you close, ask for the job. You can state, "I am qualified, your company is a good fit, I want to work for you. How soon can I expect to hear from you?"

BASIC STEPS TO START YOUR BUSINESS

Starting a business is an empowering act. I recommend it. I love working for myself. My first business as a Childbirth Professional was to teach childbirth classes in my home. I borrowed the idea from the educator whose class I attended at her home when I was pregnant. The idea to teach classes in my home had not occurred to me before I took her class. At that time, I was employed at a hospital teaching classes. Seeing her success motivated me to try. She was my example that it was possible to have a business in the Childbirth Profession.

I believe that everyone can start a business and be successful. I encourage you to try, because you have so much to gain. Don't let the thought of starting a business overwhelm you. If I can start a business, then you can too.

Starting a business can be very simple. I dislike when a process appears complex. If a task seems difficult, then that discourages me from trying. I feel as though I will not be able to succeed. I don't want you to feel that way, so I will share some basic steps you can take to begin your business today.

These basic steps will explain how to start a business that has a single owner, and is unincorporated. This type of business is straightforward. You conduct an activity for which you receive payment, and the money you earn is included as part of your income when you file taxes.

BUSINESS IDEAS

You should start by thinking of business ideas. There are many successful businesses centered around the Childbirth Profession, such as teaching childbirth classes, supporting women at birth, helping women breastfeed, providing massages, and the list goes on. Any possible need that a pregnant woman and her family may have can easily be turned into a business opportunity.

Your business could provide services, sell products, or combine both.

Write a list of business ideas.

_____

_____

_____

_____

_____

_____

TIME

Think about how much time you want to invest in your business. No rule exists that states you have to put all your energy and time into your business. The following are all options:

- Work part-time to supplement your income as you begin, then switch to running your business full-time as it becomes profitable.

- Operate and manage your business full-time.

- Maintain a regular job, and a business.

The wonderful part about deciding to go into business for yourself is that you get to make all the decisions, and you define what works. You can have a successful business no matter which option you choose.

ORGANIZATION

Think about how you will organize and run your business.

Will you need employees? Will you need office space or can you operate your business out of your home? Very successful individuals that are self-employed in the Childbirth Profession teach classes, offer massages, provide lactation counseling, or midwifery services in their client's homes, so the need for office space is not a part of their business plan. What would work best for your business?

_____

_____

_____

BUSINESS ADVICE

As you get started planning your business, you should seek out advice and assistance regarding what licenses or permits you need to obtain in order to conduct business in your area, and also, what government regulations you are required to fulfill. The following resources can provide the information you need:

BUSINESS GROUPS

Ask for assistance through your local Chamber of Commerce or Business Association, for example "Middletown Chamber of Commerce."

GOVERNMENT AGENCIES

United States
Small Business Association
http://www.sba.gov

Canada
Canada Business Network
http://www.canadabusiness.ca/eng

United Kingdom
Federation of Small Business
http://www.fsb.org.uk

Australia
Australian Government's Business Resource
http://www.business.gov.au

WEBSITES

SCORE

SCORE is a nonprofit association dedicated to educating entrepreneurs and helping small businesses start, grow, and succeed. They offer free and low cost workshops. They also have a mentorship program.

http://www.score.org

Inc.com

Inc. is a magazine and website resource where entrepreneurs and business owners can find useful information, advice, insights, and inspiration for running and growing their businesses.

http://www.inc.com/start-up

BOOKS

The Small Business Start-Up Kit: A Step-by-Step Legal Guide by Peri Pakroo

The Women's Small Business Start-Up Kit by Peri Pakroo

ATTORNEY

Hire a business attorney for legal advice, or for assistance writing contracts, etc.

BUSINESS NAME

Think of a name for your business. You can use your own full name, or a fictitious name, often referred to as DBA or *doing business as*. When you have an officially registered DBA name, you can open a bank account and receive checks made in your DBA name.

Example: A business is named **Sweet Doulas**, and is registered as [Your Legal Name] DBA Sweet Doulas.

So the business name when registered is:

Abigail Hagar DBA Sweet Doulas

Once you open a bank account in the name of your business, then all checks can be made payable to **Sweet Doulas**, and deposited.

To register your business name contact the government agency where your business is located that administers registering fictitious names. They will check to make sure that the name you choose is not being used by someone else. It is also a good idea to conduct your own web search to make sure the name you select is not already being used by a business.

If you want to keep the process very simple, the name of your business can be your legal name. If your name is Jane Doe, then the name of your business is Jane Doe.

Write down your ideas for a business name.

_____

_____

_____

_____

REVENUE

Summarize how your business will make money.

_____

_____

- What will your fees be for services?
- What prices will you charge for products?
- What do other businesses charge?

_____

_____

Keep in mind as you set your fees or prices, to charge appropriately. Do not short change yourself. Add an additional 10-20% over the initial prices you set. If you are not sure what to charge, then find out what similar businesses charge for their products or services. A quick internet search should give you an idea. You can also call or email businesses to inquire about their fees.

START-UP COSTS WORKSHEET	
What do I need to start my business?	**$ Cost**
Office Space	
Website	
Logo	
License, Permit fees	
Equipment, Supplies	
Add Total Start-up Costs	$
Divide by 12	
= Total Monthly Start-up Costs	$

START-UP COSTS

Write down what your start-up costs will be. These include supplies, licensing fees, equipment, business books, and so forth, anything that you need to spend money upon in order to get your business going. These are a one-time expense. (*See Start-up Costs Worksheet*)

EXAMPLE OF START-UP COSTS	
Type of Business: In-Home Childbirth Classes	
Birth Movies	$ 300
Anatomy Posters	$ 100
Class Booklets	$ 200
iPad2	$ 500
Business License	$ 100
Total startup costs	**$ 1200**
Start-up costs divided by 12 months = monthly expense for first year	
$1200/12 = $100 Total monthly start-up expense first year	

MONTHLY EXPENSES

What will your monthly business expenses be? These include things like leasing office space, gas, mileage, utilities, internet service, cell phone service, and so forth. These are recurring expenses you will need to pay to operate your business.

Start-up costs and monthly expenses are usually tax write-offs and are deducted from your total business profit. Consult a tax advisor for advice regarding tax write-offs.

EXAMPLE OF MONTHLY EXPENSES
Business: In-Home Childbirth Classes
Website Hosting Fee = $10
Photocopies = $10
Internet Service = $30
Total Monthly Expenses = $50

MONTHLY REVENUE EXAMPLE

Business: In-Home Childbirth Classes

Fees:

$100 for a four week childbirth class series, 10 slots available

$200 for a two day weekend childbirth class, 5 slots available

Schedule:

Four-week class meets consecutive Mondays, Wednesdays, or Fridays, each month, 6:00 to 8:00 p.m.

Two day weekend class meets on Saturdays, 2 sessions offered each month, 9:00 am to 5:00 pm

Revenue for four week class:

10 slots x $100 fee = $1000 per series

3 series per month is 3 x $1000 = $3000

Revenue for two day class:

5 slots x $200 fee = $1000

2 series per month = 2 x $1000 = $2000

Four week class total + Two day class total = Total Monthly Revenue

$3000 + $2000 = $5000

Projected Total Monthly Revenue = $5000

PROJECTED MONTHLY PROFIT WORKSHEET	
Projected Monthly Start-up Costs	$
+ Projected Monthly Expenses	
= Total Monthly Expenses	$
Total Projected Monthly Revenue	$
- Total Monthly Expenses	
= Projected Monthly Profit	$
Total Projected Profit	$

BUSINESS PROFITABILITY

Project what your profit will be by the month for an entire year. (Use *Projected Monthly Profit Worksheet*) To calculate this amount:

1. Determine the amount of your monthly revenue. (See *Monthly Revenue Example*)

2. Add up your total start-up costs and divide the amount by 12, this will determine your start-up costs spread over the first year.

3. Add up your total monthly expenses. (See *Example of Monthly Expenses*)

4. Add the monthly start-up costs to the monthly expenses to get a total amount of your monthly expenses.

5. Subtract your total monthly expenses from your total projected monthly revenue. This is your projected monthly profit for the first year. (See *Example of Projected Monthly Profit*)

This should give you an idea of the total profit you can expect each month for the first year. When you start the next year your profit should increase, since you will not have start-up costs.

EXAMPLE OF PROJECTED MONTHLY PROFIT

Business: In-home Childbirth Classes

Projected Monthly Revenue = $5000

Monthly Start-up Expenses = $100

Monthly Expenses = $50

$100 + $50 = $150 Total Monthly Expenses First Year

$5000 - $150 = $4850 Monthly Profit First Year

FUNDING YOUR BUSINESS

Consider if you have enough money on hand to pay for your start-up costs. If you do not have enough money, then you will have to find a way to fund your business. The following may be options to obtain start-up funds:

- Obtain a bank loan

- Ask for a loan from family members or friends

- Use credit cards

- Seek a government loan or grant

- Find an investor

- Delay the purchase of some start-up expenses

CREATE A WEBSITE

Once you have completed your business plan and have determined that your business will be profitable, you should create a website. Having a website is the number one way to promote your business and increase your revenue. You can hire someone to design your website, or you can do it yourself.

It is not necessary to spend a lot of money on your website. There are many low cost options to choose from when creating a website.

- Use a free website domain name and free design tools (although, you will have a prefix after your domain name, such as bestdoula.yola.com.)

- Purchase your own website domain name and design your website with the creation tools provided. This way you can have a domain name without the prefix, such as bestdoula.com. You can buy a domain name from many online sources. Search the internet for a good deal.

- Use a Facebook page as your website. Simply go to Facebook and look for the "create a page" link. Once you have enough fans for your page, you can personalize your Facebook web address, so it would be facebook.com/bestdoula.

- Create an internet business profile and use the listing as your website.

RESOURCES

Yola.com

Webs.com

Weebly.com

Yellow Pages

Google Places

MerchantCircle.com

Local Newspaper websites

Yelp.com

Thumbtack.com

BUSINESS LOGO

A digital business logo is a low cost easy way to promote your business. You can insert your logo into your email signature; include it on your website, and in your Facebook profile. You can design your own logo or have someone design it for you. There are many very good logo design providers on the internet such as http://www.logonerds.com. Conduct a web search for business logo designers to find companies to help you with your logo.

What ideas or images do you think would make a great logo?

MARKETING IDEAS

Marketing is a key component to the success of your business. To market your business is to let others know about the services or products that you offer. Marketing can be done in a variety of ways. As mentioned, it is important that you have a presence on the internet through a webpage or a business profile. This is a very important way to market your business.

When I began my business to teach childbirth classes in my home, I had no idea if I would be successful. I started by creating a free website to promote my classes, list my fees, and class schedule. I was amazed after a short amount of time, an expecting couple registered through my website to attend a class. In my experience, a business website is an extremely useful marketing tool.

ADVERTISING

Try advertising your business in many different ways.

- Google AdWords
- Facebook Ads
- Craigslist.org
- Print Newspapers
- Online Newspapers
- Local Parenting Magazines

As you start off, set a firm advertising budget, and wait to see the results your ads bring. Do not overspend your money on ineffective advertisements.

EMAIL NEWSLETTER

A newsletter is a purposeful marketing tool. People that are interested in your company will give you their email address so they may stay up to date on your services and products. Each month, every two weeks, or even weekly, you can send an interesting newsletter filled with stories, photos, videos, coupons, news, polls, and whatever information you think would interest customers and clients. This is a way to continue to subtly market your business.

You can use your regular email account to send an email that you write as a newsletter to a list of subscribers. Another option is to use an email newsletter service through the internet. They often include professionally designed templates and multiple tools to create an effective newsletter campaign. Here are some example websites:

MailChimp
http://mailchimp.com
Tiny Letter
http://tinyletter.com

PARTNERSHIPS

Building partnerships with other businesses is another way to market your business. For example, if your business is teaching childbirth classes to families then you may refer parents to a store that sells baby products. In return, the store hands out fliers telling expecting families about the classes you offer.

Think about what partnerships would be mutually beneficial to your business.

WORD OF MOUTH

Tell everyone you know about your business. Hand out business cards. Ask customers or clients to recommend you to others. Many amazing businesses have been built, simply through word of mouth.

Summary

There is much to learn about running a business. However, don't let a lack of knowledge prevent you from getting started. You will learn what you need to know and more, just by starting. If you get stuck, feel overwhelmed, have questions, or need assistance do the following:

- Conduct an internet search
- Ask for help
- Take a class
- Read a book
- Hire someone

BUSINESS START-UP WORKSHEET

My ideas for a business are:

How much time can I devote?

Will I need employees?

Will I need office space?

Will I need space in my home?

Ideas for my business name:

How will I fund my business?

What is my website plan?

BUSINESS START-UP WORKSHEET

What are ways I can market my business?

Diversity and Inclusion

Our profession should reflect the world.

A need for diversity and inclusion exists in the field of Childbirth Health Care and among Childbirth Professionals. Perhaps less than 8% of all Childbirth Professionals in the United States are non-Caucasian, disabled, homosexual, non-Christian, lower class, nonreligious, or speak a second language. The numbers are not tracked and published. However, attend any workshop, training, or conference and the lack of diversity is obvious.

Among leadership boards, among those that set policies, and within childbirth groups and professional organizations the need for diversity and inclusion is even greater.

Diversity is the representation of all the members of a community and society. Inclusion is preparing, building, organizing and creating so everyone is included and none left out, even if not everyone participates. When someone who is different chooses to participate, they are expected, and preparations have been made, in this way language, technology, meeting space, meeting dates and times, and so much more, are accessible to all without modifications, because inclusiveness prepares for all possibilities and all peoples.

Diversity and inclusion are both challenging and important topics that need to be addressed by the Childbirth Professional community for the following reasons:

- So opportunities are available for all professionals
- So different perspectives are included in decision making

- So service is provided for all women and their families

Let's discuss these reasons and conclude with an action plan, steps that can be taken to increase diversity and inclusion among Childbirth Professionals and within organizations.

OPPORTUNITY

The Childbirth Profession is so vast that everyone can find their personal niche and be successful. However, it is important to make sure that opportunities to enter the field are available to all. It is also crucial that each individual grows as a professional reaching their full potential and making contributions. Some of the barriers that prevent diversity are:

- Socioeconomic

- Education

- Accessibility

- Mentorship

- X-factor

SOCIOECONOMIC FACTORS

Lack of money to attend a training workshop or to buy books, or a plane ticket are reasons that prevent entry into the field. Individuals that lack access to the internet or smart phones can also be at a disadvantage as certification information, research, and professional networking are often done through the worldwide web.

EDUCATION

To be a well-trained Childbirth Professional requires basic skills, but not necessarily a high school or college degree. Although, a diploma or degree because of the skills they bring are beneficial. Childbirth

Professionals must usually read books written at a college reading level and analyze the material, interpret the information, and draw conclusions. In order to complete some certification programs a passing score on a test is often required. For those lacking in reading, analytical, and test taking skills it can be difficult to obtain certification.

ACCESSIBILITY

Currently there are not enough colleges, schools, programs, or workshops to train and certify Childbirth Professionals in the communities where they live. Often times an individual interested in the field must travel to receive training or take an online course. It is essential that education and training be accessible to everyone.

MENTORSHIP

Experienced and seasoned Childbirth Professionals are needed to mentor those entering the field, and those working to achieve additional skills. Strategic and appropriately targeted mentoring programs should be established to recruit the underrepresented. Childbirth Professional associations and organizations can develop peer groups so that individuals in training have others that can relate to their struggles and successes. Individuals are more likely to complete their training when they have peers and can offer each other mutual encouragement, and can problem solve together on common issues.

X-FACTOR

The work Childbirth Professionals carry out is important and benefits their community. Does the community recognize and understand the expertise and skill of the Childbirth Professional? In underrepresented communities, the work done by Doulas, Midwives, Lactation Consultants, and other Childbirth Professionals might not be as widely known. Our profession should be promoted like any other industry. To become a Childbirth Educator can be the same as joining the NBA. It is all about image and advertising. It is crucial that communities know about the work we do and how rewarding it is. You can make a living as a Childbirth Professional and love the work that you do. Those in the field know it has the X-factor, a special quality. Somehow, that must be more widely communicated and understood.

DIFFERENT PERSPECTIVES

Giving birth is a rite of passage for women. Childbirth has distinct cultural customs practiced in the past and present day. The professionals that assist pregnant women are part of a community. Within the birthing community, important work is being carried out at the political level within government agencies, and at the policy level within hospitals, health insurance companies, and within related organizations. When debate is being carried out – when laws and policies are being set regarding healthcare for women and rules for the professionals that serve them, then it is necessary that many voices are included in the process.

In the United States, when midwifery was outlawed, how many women were involved in the debate? Still, today in places where direct entry Midwives cannot practice legally, consider if those who hold the power to implement change are a diverse group.

Outcomes in society are often improved for the greater population when we listen to many different types of perspectives and opinions, not just those similar to our own. For this reason, we should seek out the unrepresented within our profession. Otherwise how will their voices be heard, and how will we really know what is in their best interest, unless we ask and include their views.

Most of all, those not represented among leadership, must be. It should not be that an elite, homogenous group makes the decisions for all. We cannot assume that the decisions and policies implemented are in the best interest of all if a diverse collective does not participate in decision-making.

SERVICE

It is well-known that people feel more comfortable around those they share something in common with. This commonality is often gender, ethnicity, religion, culture, language, etc. Diversity in Childbirth Health Care is needed so that families find those commonalities with those providing services. For example, when Lactation Consultants speak Spanish misunderstandings decrease, and when the Lactation Consultant is of the same ethnicity, trust can be instant, and the success of breastfeeding increases.

The more diverse the Childbirth Profession becomes, increases the opportunities for all families to receive care from professionals that are familiar with the traditions, languages, cultures, and rituals of those they serve. This increases the effectiveness of service. Diversity and difference is a topic that is not often directly addressed, even when it is obviously a key element of the service and care that families receive. It is important to discuss ways that we can meet the needs of all, without ignoring differences, and acknowledging the role diversity plays in delivering service and care. Understanding difference and diversity is to recognize, respect, and create institutional room for beliefs, opinions, and practices that we may not have considered, and that we may oppose.

ASSUMPTIONS

In considering diversity and inclusion, it is important to let go of assumptions. This refers to a variety of personal and societal assumptions. For example, there are a few programs in place in the United States to train Doulas to serve non-English speakers, homeless, and incarcerated women. These are excellent programs and they provide valuable training and service to the community. However, there are not enough programs that train individuals that have a prison record, that don't speak English, or that have been homeless, to serve the opposite population. Sometimes it is assumed that the individual from a background labeled as other, should serve their community. An individual who is Native American, should not be expected to only serve the Native American population. It is important that we do not presume to define community for others.

The Childbirth Profession is a vibrant, growing field and individuals given the opportunity for training can experience a transforming life change. When they experience this change, they may become part of a broader community.

ACTION

Consider what steps can be taken to increase diversity and inclusion in the Childbirth Profession. The following are a few suggestions to start an ongoing process:

- Check if the association you belong to has a diverse leadership board, if not institute ways to increase diversity among board members.

- Create a mentorship program for the unrepresented of your Childbirth Professional role i.e. Lactation Consultants.

- Organize a forum where a group of diverse professionals can have an open and honest conversation regarding issues about which they are concerned.

Write down steps you think would increase diversity and inclusion in the Childbirth Profession.

_____

_____

_____

Interview of Claudia Booker from MANA Newsletter December 2010

As a midwifery student of color, what are some of the barriers you have encountered?

Claudia responded without hesitation, the most difficult thing as a midwifery student of color is finding a preceptor. About five percent of Certified Professional Midwives (CPMs) are midwives of color but of those, less than two percent are women of African descent. Therefore, the number of Black CPMs to apprentice with is extremely small. Moreover, European-American CPMs rarely apprentice African-Americans. At a recent MANA conference in Clearwater Florida, Makeda Kamara asked the European-American midwives who apprentice women of color to stand—none stood. Claudia spoke of her local midwifery community, the group of white student midwives who have apprenticeships around her and her four-year search to find a local preceptor. Claudia contends that some European-American CPMs are concerned with their clients' comfort in having a woman of color participate in their prenatals and birth. Another factor is the "Old Girl Network"—there is always a long line of women who either birthed with the midwife, were a doula with the midwife, or who refer clients to the midwife, who are ahead of you in line waiting for an apprenticeship. Not to mention the cultural and interpersonal challenges of women (preceptor-apprentice) from different cultures navigating their relationship. Within a 200 mile radius of Washington DC there are at least 50 home birth midwives and only two African-American apprentices. Because there are homebirth midwives within driving distance, there should be no need for midwifery students of color to uproot their families, give up their jobs and move half way across the country to apprentice. She expressed the desire to be an apprentice close to her home, in her own community just like the white midwifery students around her. Claudia now works with two home birth midwives, both with very welcoming clients.

The expectation that apprentices should have the ability to set aside their personal lives and be available for their preceptor with little notice, is a hurdle not many potential apprentices of color can meet. She enlightened me that a large percentage of African-American women over the age of twenty-five have at least one child and are single heads of household. And since most African-American women are single heads of households, it is necessary for them to have a paying full time or part time job while pursuing midwifery in order for their families to thrive. This makes it extremely difficult for them (and their family) to pursue midwifery. There are no loans available for those pursuing the PEP apprentice process. For those few apprenticeship opportunities, relocation may be the only option. "The prospect of uprooting your entire family, giving up your job, moving to another part of the country, resettling your children and finding child care, finding employment that will allow you time to go to births so you can apprentice is a sacrifice most cannot afford to make. African American women who are birth workers have children to raise; we do not have partners to support us and our children through this; we are not able to move and start over— we have children to care for." To find a preceptor who is supportive of these challenges is another challenge. For those who are interested in the MEAC process, the challenge of funding the program is a huge one since financial aid is not often available, and the necessity for full-time employment in order to support the family is real. In addition, finding a program that is culturally sensitive to women of color is also a challenge. Plus, you still have the challenge of finding a local preceptor.

Although many of these obstacles exist also for European-American midwifery students, these obstacles are greater in economically, ethnically, and geographically marginalized communities because there are fewer resources to support their midwifery students.

As a woman of color (WOC), how do you feel you bring something unique to your practice? Why is it important for WOC to serve their communities?

"It is imperative that the broader community of midwifery understand, appreciate, value, and support the unique ability of women of color to serve each other. For us, being with women who look at us as their sisters, aunts, cousins, and/or mothers reinforces a care provider relationship that cannot be duplicated with any cultural sensitivity training," Claudia states. "Every woman of color I come into contact, be she a "round the way girl," soul-sista, earth mother, or up and coming corporate woman, all are viewed through my eyes as a long lost cousin, niece, aunt, sister, and I treat them accordingly. We have an instinctive rapport at a DNA level that puts us at ease with each other. Our clients know, like, and trust us. They can see themselves in us and vice versa." Once again, it is birth political—a community who cannot birth itself cannot survive—if we have to go outside of our own resources to ensure the birth and growth of our children, our future is out of our hands.

Reprinted with permission.
By Janelle Lucido-Conate and Claudia Booker

CALLING YOUNG WOMEN

Attention, young women! The Childbirth Profession needs you. This career is such a great opportunity for young women. Certainly, women of any age may become Childbirth Professionals. But, this chapter is an open letter to call upon the young, because they are the future of the profession.

So hear this call...

Young woman, I am speaking directly to you. I want to share with you the things I wish some one told me.

#1 You are strong!

When you are young and don't have children yet, you have a greater amount of stamina and mental acuity to do the work in the Childbirth Profession that requires one to be on-call and work through the night.

#2 This is great income for a student.

In the Childbirth Profession, there are great paying jobs and wonderful business opportunities. You do not need a college degree, and often, not even a high school diploma. The work is perfect for teens and college students, a great part-time or summer job, providing income while you attend school.

#3 You will be wise and empowered.

Your training to work as a Childbirth Professional will equip you to be extremely knowledgeable about reproductive health, pregnancy, childbirth, breastfeeding, infant development, and so much more. When it comes time for you to make decisions about your own health and that of your children, you will already be prepared and informed.

I trained to become a Childbirth Educator before I ever experienced a pregnancy. I feel privileged that I had this knowledge ahead of time. When years later I had children, I was fearless and able to make informed decisions, because I was educated and experienced about the childbearing process.

#4 You are a change agent!

When you are young, you absolutely see the world differently then when you get older. You have the capacity to bring change, because of your youth. It is true. Young women have an energy and insight that the Childbirth Profession needs.

#5 Become a Midwife.

The world needs more Midwives. We just don't have enough Midwives to provide care. And, the science of midwifery will astound you! I implore you to take an introductory midwifery class to learn about the priceless work these wise women do.

#6 Teach and train others.

The collective knowledge held by Childbirth Professionals must be passed down to the next generation. In order to do this we need more teachers. I encourage you after you have been trained to teach others. This generation of childbearing women are in danger of losing the core knowledge of how to give birth. Entire communities are void of professionals that possess the skills to teach breastfeeding. Childbirth practices are thousands of years old. It is important that we have teachers to continue to pass on tried and true childbirth practices.

#7 Build schools.

There are not enough schools to educate Childbirth Professionals, especially Midwives in the United States. We need more schools. I encourage you to start a school.

#8 Change laws and policies.

In this age of protest and unrest, we need indignation at how many laws work against supporting pregnant women and their families. Please work to change laws, policies and the health care system, so choice and affordable care exist. So many safe, effective, low cost choices are not available to women when they give birth. Options such as giving birth at a Free-Standing Birth Center, having a VBAC (vaginal birth after cesarean), having Doula services, or using midwifery services for childbirth are not widely available to all women. In some places, these options are banned, not covered by insurance, or outlawed, and these issues are just the highlights. There are also issues concerning increasing maternity leave and supporting breastfeeding and ...

#9 You are needed!

Simply put, you are needed in this profession not only to serve, but also to empower women and bring change.

NURSING AND THE CHILDBIRTH PROFESSION

A nursing career fits perfectly within the Childbirth Profession. Nurses bring additional skills and training that can increase their marketability and income as Childbirth Professionals. So if you are a nurse or considering nursing, obtaining training in the field of childbirth can complement the work that you do.

In the field of childbirth, those that provide care to the mother and her family are all part of one team. Each member of the team has a different role, or multiple roles. So you might be a nurse caring for women in labor, and also a Lactation Consultant, assisting new moms and babies to breastfeed.

Individuals combine nursing and the Childbirth Profession in many different ways. A person might be unsure about pursing a nursing career, so they first decide to train and work as a Doula, in order to gain a better understanding of childbirth. In another scenario, they work as a nurse, and are asked to teach the childbirth classes for their hospital, so they train to become a Childbirth Educator.

There are so many ways that nursing and the childbirth field are complementary. More nursing programs could allow for a minor in the skills and training that Childbirth Professionals provide, so nurses graduate from school already trained to provide breastfeeding support, Doula care, teach childbirth classes, offer postpartum counseling, and so forth.

A component of nursing education could cover in-depth, the full scope of childbirth, including the anthropology, the history, the politics, and the economics of birth.

MALE CHILDBIRTH PROFESSIONALS

The Childbirth Profession is comprised mostly of female professionals; however, there are male Childbirth Professionals that work in this field.

Professionals that are men or women can give care to families; the work is not gender specific. The knowledge, energy, and skill that a professional possesses are the important factors.

The call to the Childbirth Profession is for all, men and women.

Male Childbirth Professionals serve an important role supporting fathers in a way that a female professional cannot. They lead Boot Camp classes for new dads, giving men the opportunity to be in a testosterone-filled environment, and learn about fatherhood from other men.

Some male Childbirth Professionals work in a team with their wives to teach childbirth classes to expecting couples together. Many opportunities are available for men in this field. They provide pregnancy massages, childproof homes, conduct research, train professionals, take photographs, create birth art, advocate for policy changes, and so much more.

Any of the Childbirth Professional roles listed in this book are available for both men and women to pursue.

NURTURE YOUR INTUITION

You possess an inner wisdom that seldom fails, but you may fail to trust yourself.

Effective and successful Childbirth Professionals use their intuition. These individuals touch others leaving a lasting impact. You feel inspired in their presence. They are self-assured and wise. Intuition is a guiding force in their lives.

What is intuition?

Intuition can be referred to as the sixth sense that guides you. It is a perception, a knowingness that you possess when no other evidence is apparent. Intuition is your best advisor.

Unfortunately, because intuition is often equated to a feeling, it is discounted. People don't rely enough upon their intuition to make decisions.

Intuition is always right

Rarely, will your intuition lead you the wrong way. Usually, you experience a bad outcome, and say to yourself I should have trusted by first feeling. That was your intuition. Intuition is usually correct, 99.9% of the time.

We are born knowing the right decisions to make. Children are clear about what they like and do not like. Somehow, as we age we stop trusting our intuition.

To be the best at the work you do, it is important to nurture your intuition, and allow it to grow.

Nurturing Intuition

Your intuition can be best nurtured by simply listening to it. It is that voice that speaks inside your head. Don't trivialize it. Don't discount it. Listen, and do what it tells you to do.

When you see that your intuition led you the right way, the next time it speaks, you listen, again and again. This is how you nurture your intuition.

Astonishing Things Happen

Consider that you really do know the right decisions to make, even if they are risky. Listen to your inner voice. Trust yourself. The right answers are within.

Just wait. Be surprised and in awe of the things that will take place in your life when you allow intuition to be your guide.

THINKING POINTS

Reflect on a time when your first instinct was correct. What lesson can you take away from that situation?

_____

_____

_____

_____

Think about the last time you listened to your inner voice. What was the result?

_____

_____

_____

List the rewards of living by your intuition for yourself and others.

_____

_____

_____

"A woman's intuition is always precise." Linda Smith

"I feel there are two people inside me - me and my intuition. If I go against her, she'll screw me every time, and if I follow her, we get along quite nicely." Kim Basinger

HONOR AND EMPOWER WOMEN

Women both deserve and need to be honored and empowered. This is the duty of the Childbirth Professional. The positive energy and compassion you send to women may be all they receive.

Believe in her body's abilities

Trust her and affirm her decisions

Guide her through education and information

Care about her complete well-being

Appreciate her strength, her accomplishments, her uniqueness, her individuality

Soothe her fears

Comfort her when she is in discomfort

Touch her heart and soul

Listen to what she shares

Teach her what you know

Protect her right to be informed

Implement evidence-based, family-centered, baby-friendly, mother-friendly care

GROW!

Life Long Learning

There is so much to learn in this field. I don't feel like I will ever know it all. I encourage you to keep learning.

Take classes, attend workshops, read books, network, observe the work of other professionals, keep current with new research.

Once you have mastered the work that you do, take on a new role within the Childbirth Profession.

Chart Your Course

Use the information within this book to plan your Career Journey.

The world is filled with unlimited possibilities. What I love best about the work that I do is that I am constantly inspired. I have vision. I have hope. I have dreams. The work I do serves a purpose and makes a difference. That is how I define career.

What is your definition?

_____

_____

_____

I know for sure that you can live out your dreams. That is my experience.

Have a fabulous career!

HOW DO YOU KNOW YOU ARE CALLED?

You know you are called...

BECAUSE you are reading this page.

Because you need a sign and you want affirmation.

You are searching, checking, and need to be sure.

Perhaps, you tell yourself, if I hear a voice...

I will know what to do.

Listen.

This is the voice. These words you are reading.

You are called
You are called
You are called
You are called
You are called
You are called

ACKNOWLEDGEMENTS

Thank you to Elizabeth Vose for your timely review and valuable feedback.

Thank you to the Childbirth Professionals that shared their stories.

INDEX

THE AUTHOR

Donyale Abe is available for interviews, workshops, and conference sessions.

Website: http://thechildbirthprofession.com

Email: childbirthprofessionals@gmail.com

Made in the USA
San Bernardino, CA
07 August 2015